Renewing
America's Soul

HOWARD E. BUTT, JR.

Renewing
America's Soul

*A Spiritual Psychology
for Home, Work, and Nation*

CONTINUUM · NEW YORK

1996
The Continuum Publishing Company
370 Lexington Avenue
New York, NY 10017

Printed in the United States of America

Library of Congress Cataloging-in-Publication Data

Butt, Howard E.
  Renewing America's soul : a spiritual psychology for home, work, and nation / Howard E. Butt, Jr.
      p.   cm.
  Includes bibliographical references.
  ISBN 0-8264-0880-X (alk. paper)
  1. Mental health—Religious aspects—Christianity. 2. Spiritual life—Christianity. 3. Butt, Howard E.   4. United States—History–Religious aspects—Christianity. I. Title.
  BT732.4.B88   1996
  248.8'6—dc20   95-41258
                                                             CIP

Unless otherwise indicated, Scripture quotations in this book are from The Holy Bible, New International Version. Copyright © 1973, 1978, 1984 International Bible Society.
Other quotations are from the following versions:

The King James Version of the Bible *(KJV)*.

The New English Bible *(NEB)*, Copyright © the Delegates of the Oxford University Press and the Syndics of the Cambridge University Press, 1961, 1970.

The New King James Version *(NKJV)*. Copyright © 1979, 1980, 1982, Thomas Nelson, Inc., Publisher.

The New Testament in Modern English (Phillips) by J. B. Phillips, published by The Macmillan Company, © 1958, 1960, 1972 by J. B. Phillips.

The Revised Standard Version of the Bible *(RSV)*, Copyrighted 1946, 1952, © 1971, 1973 by the Division of Christian Education of the National Council of the Churches of Christ in the U.S.A.

The Living Bible (LB), copyright 1971 by Tyndale House Publishers, Wheaton, IL.

The Bible: A New Translation (Moffatt) by James A. R. Moffatt. Copyright 1922, 1924, 1925, 1926, 1935 by Harper & Row, Publishers, Incorporated. Copyright 1950, 1952, 1953, 1954 by James A. R. Moffatt.

For all those who
with me
feel they have been entrusted
with a thorn in the flesh

. . .

And for my children
Howard III, Stephen, and Deborah Dan
each of whom demonstrates
in the language of this book
not only forgiveness toward their father
but also the power of faith, hope, and love

Acknowledgments

*T*he psychiatric professionals without whom these pages would never have happened are Edward E. Landis, M.D., of the University of Louisville School of Medicine, and Lawrence Stone, M.D., of the University of Texas Health Science Center at San Antonio. My dear friend and counselor Dr. Wayne Oates, one of the nation's leading Pastoral Care pioneers, started me toward them and the behavioral sciences.

Two of my all-time favorite professors, at both the undergraduate and graduate level, taught me Greek. My study with Professor Henry Trantham and Dr. Ray Summers years ago enabled me to confirm, in the original language of the biblical texts, what I thought I was seeing in our English translations.

This enterprise began as a series of lectures for a Laity Lodge Study Week in the summer of 1983. My fellow speaker during that time, Dr. David Redding of Liberty Presbyterian Church, Columbus, Ohio, and his wife, Dee, encouraged me to think that in them I might have a worthwhile book. Further encouragement from my friend, Jarrell McCracken, put me in touch with his publishing associate of many years, Floyd Thatcher. Floyd sent me to Anne Christian Buchanan.

Anne greatly improved what I had already written, making it clearer, better transitioned, easier to read. She does superb editing; working together (beyond the inevitable pain) has been inspiring fun. As Anne and I worked, the manuscript grew and grew. She pushed and pushed me, "Howard, make yourself clear!" and I kept adding and adding. Then we decided that you can stand only so much clarity.

Lastly, therefore, two winsome friends and distinguished editors, William Griffin and Maggie Holmes, took the full, fat manuscript and helped me shorten, tighten, and improve it.

Baylor University's Dr. Steven Sadler, out of a scholar's mind and a pastor's heart, strengthened my work through a wide range of advice and research. The noted pastoral psychology writer and teacher, Dr. Samuel Southard, read the text and made helpful suggestions.

My Administrative Assistant and former secretary across more than thirty-five years, Dorothy Parish, supervised the typing and the notes and carried their biggest preparation load. Karen Robinette also gave much help in the earlier stages, and Joanne Bransford in finishing up.

Most importantly, my wife, Barbara Dan, loved, cheered, and suffered with me—across forty-seven years of marriage—as I wrestled to learn the lessons that I share here with you.

My glad thanks to all of these, as well as my wider gratitude to my H. E. Butt Grocery Company and H. E. Butt Foundation associates for their enduring support, both tangible and intangible.

Contents

Part Three: Relationships and Democracy
Flex Thinking: The Citizen as Player-Coach

An Opening Word

*I*f you don't have a problem in the world, then you won't like this book. It's for people who struggle with frustrations, setbacks, failures, or griefs. It's for those who wrestle with themselves and their relationships—in marriages, families, organizations, churches, and society—and who sometimes find it hard to feel positively or think confidently about what's happening to them.

Sound familiar? It ought to. I've just described everyone except Wonder Woman, Superman, Barbie, and Mickey Mouse.

We all carry burdens. But in a way, that's good news, because the raw materials for our inner growth come to us in our troubles. Growth is a positive response to our difficulties. Character is learning to make lemonade out of our lemons, and its recipe depends on the puckered fact that lemons taste sour.

That's what I'm learning, anyway. You might say, in tribute to the facts, that everything you read here comes from my *own* personal problems. Forty years ago, I was a young Baptist lay preacher, working hard in our family's retail grocery business, for which I had been reared, but also frequently on the road to conduct crusades by and for lay people. My life raced along, jam-packed: merchandising meetings, store visits, company expansion, speaking engagements, crowds, attention, publicity.

But I couldn't keep on managing such a complex and pressured schedule; stress and exhaustion combined to trigger the paralyzing anxieties of a serious clinical depression. Planting my feet in extreme resistance, kicking and screaming inside, finally I got dragged to get psychiatric help—my heel marks blackening the long, twisting road to that wise doctor's office. As you know, there are certain circles where to be really "in" you need your own psychiatrist. In case you might not be aware, Baptist evangelism is *not* one of those circles.

What has taken place in these intervening years? My "nervous breakdown," as earlier generations called it, and my ongoing struggles with depression contributed eventually to a profound enrichment of my faith and my marriage. This same enhancement took place in our family, ministries, business—our entire life.

This improved quality, of course, remains the constant possibility inherent in our sufferings. When life forced me to go to a psychiatrist, I thought it was the worst thing that had ever happened to me. Now I know it was one of the best. More and more I'm learning to think positively about my troubles. This book illustrates the method.

Out of my struggles with depression, I wound up bandaged but battling to make sense of the Scriptures and my own life experience.[1] Increasingly I saw that the Bible speaks to us much more psychologically than I had ever realized. Slowly it dawned on me that one inescapable purpose of the often-controversial "new birth" is precisely our psychological health.

Gradually I began to wonder: Do we who think of ourselves as "born-again Christians" realize what those words truly mean? Psychologically? With others? In our day-to-day relationships with ourselves and the people closest to us? None of us, most certainly not I, understands fully. But we only start from where we are now; we cannot start from where we are not.[2]

First off, however, let me admit the obvious about what I call "spiritual psychiatry." Vocationally, I am neither a clergyman nor a behavioral scientist, neither an academic theologian nor a medical practitioner. In the fields of theology and psychology I am only an amateur, a learner, a layman.

However, I'm convinced that my nonprofessional status in both theology and psychology constitutes an asset. In these two fields *every* person remains a journeyman; expertise is always relative, and nobody has all the answers. Sheepskins on the wall may help. But with or without them, we all grapple with the same practical and decisive questions—and these questions are at once theological *and* psychological.

Every day, for example, we make value judgments, either deliberately or "without thinking," which reflect what we prize most highly and where we give our allegiance. We live by habits of the heart.[3] Our ethics reveal our faith; our principles disclose our worldview, our standards of esteem, our ultimate ideals, our deep belief systems. These yardsticks of respect and mirrors of concern, our undergirding perceptions of reality, make up the essence of our everyday theology: We live out what we believe in. For worshiper and atheist alike, the nonstop issues of life remain theological. Whether we call it by that name or not, a value system *is* a theology.

These never-ending issues are also psychiatric. The scientific study of the human mind and of human personality looks recent in comparison with our earth's long, drawn-out history. But what science has done in the last couple of hundred years is simply to discover, confirm, and explain what has all along been true—that our inner attitudes, our thinking, and our emotions influence our decisions and our behavior.

Psychiatry aims at healthy interaction between the inner self and the outer group—between our individual selves and the people around us. So we each practice, constantly, our own brand of first-person psychiatry as we relate to ourselves and to each other. We apply it around the clock in our day-in-and-day-out living.

The presupposition underlying this book, therefore, is that every-one has both spiritual and psychological aspects. Each of us prac-tices amateur theology and amateur psychiatry every day. And this should not surprise us, for ours is a do-it-yourself, self-help genera-tion. We live our lives, from delivery rooms to diapers, from diets to data processing, from drudgeries to distractions, out of kits, courses, books, tapes, and videos. Perhaps this fact alone can help us face our condition honestly: Every person is both a do-it-yourself theologian and a do-it-yourself psychiatrist. The question remains always and only: Is my amateur theology good or bad? Is my ama-teur psychiatry sound or unsound?

My attempt at synthesizing, as I have struggled with these two interrelated searches for wellness, shapes what I write. Nothing in these pages requires technical knowledge in either theology or psychology. Nor do I give you unchecked theories, off-the-wall guesswork, or wild speculation. In both theology and psychiatry, my views represent core, classic, historic orthodoxy. Their posi-tively merged vision may sound a little far-out to you. If so, it is because, sadly, our generation as a whole has not thought deeply or broadly about these two fields' interaction. In both of these sciences, as in all the others, our understandings remain limited and partial. Still, as the British critic and novelist, Charles Williams, said, "It is as difficult to be quite orthodox as to be quite healthy. Yet the need for orthodoxy, like the need for health, is imperative."[4]

My reference to "orthodox psychiatry" demands further definition here. Classic psychiatry in its various contemporary forms stems from the work of Sigmund Freud and his followers. But since, according to many secular and religious interpreters, Freud rejected not only religion per se but also moral guilt as such, obviously I do *not* have in mind those rejections. I am not defending what is known today as "Freudianism," nor do I support Freud's worldview, which is separable, different from, and ultimately unrelated to his scientific insights.

Ernest Jones, Freud's authorized biographer in *The Life and Work of Sigmund Freud*, describes "the two great deeds of Freud's scientific life"[5] as his discoveries of "free association" and the "Oedipus complex."

By "free association" Freud meant something quite simple. Today, we widely, even commonly, accept his underlying concept: All of us *repeat* our childhood experiences—our childhood training (or the lack of it, or the abuse of it) and our responses to it—throughout our adult lives.

This phenomenon is what makes psychoanalysis possible. By a "free association" of thoughts, the patient repeats with the medical doctor the previously existing dynamics of his or her emotional world. He *transfers* his childhood feelings onto the doctor. This transfer enables the doctor to observe, accept, and interpret these phenomena for the patient. Psychoanalysis gets its name from that process; the doctor *analyzes* the "free associations" that the patient "transfers" onto him.

But our free mental associations always—not just with psychiatrists—reveal our transferences. And our transferences—or "displacements" or "projections"—constitute the emotional lens through which we interpret and respond to whatever happens to us. This subjective lens colors and shapes our views of our objective experiences. Early in my own course of therapy, the psychiatrist said to me, "You're looking at life through dark glasses."

Transference, then, refers to the discolorations, dysfunctions, and distortions in our emotional glasses—and our tendency to see life through those glasses and interact with others on the basis of that distorted vision. All the relationships and the occurrences of our emotional histories—their characteristics, strengths, idiosyncrasies, and illnesses—make up our transference lens. Genetically speaking, none of us has 20–20 psychological vision to begin with, but everybody wears these fouled-up emotional glasses too. Sometimes we call their out-of-focus confusions our "blind spots." Inevitably, they affect the way we relate to one another.

The "Oedipus complex," which Freud also discovered, involves the *source* of these blind spots: the pain of our psychological wounds. Freud said these inner wounds—inflicted by ourselves as well as by others—represent favoritisms (and rejections) that children feel toward one of their parents (or caretaking authorities) versus the other one.

This "Oedipus" analytic term deals thoughtfully and seriously with the relationships—both original and ongoing—between the older and the younger generations. Since some of its aspects go beyond this book's limits, we will consider only its broader implications and general applicabilities. In particular, we will consider:

• *Generational conflict* in the tensions between parents and children;

• *Childhood favoritism* for one parent above the other, plus parental preference toward different children;

• *Conscious or unconscious hostility*—on the part of the child toward the unfavored parent—which contains within itself the seeds of father-hate and/or mother-hate;

• *Adult ambivalences* throughout later life—in relating both to organized group structures and to established authorities—transferred from these parent-child conflicts.

The following, then, is a discussion of classic psychiatry's contributions to my own healing and to my continuing efforts toward psychological and spiritual wholeness. Simply and broadly, in nontechnical language, these concepts of "transference," and "generational conflict" have been most helpful to me.* In this book, I hope

---

*For *transference*, I will also use occasionally the parallel terms *displacement* or *projection*. In academic psychiatry, these terms identify different, distinct, but simito show that these two core psychiatric ideas are thoroughly—indeed, inescapably—biblical.

In describing the complexities of human relationships, and in perceiving the realities of our generational denials, Freud took seriously the Scriptures' teaching on our spiritual Fall. Surely he must have meant just that when he "spoke of his having been greatly influenced by his early reading of the Bible." As a scientist, he recognized humanity's defective character.

And those of us who meditate on the Hebrew Scriptures and on the New Testament find something else more than curious in one other detail of history, a detail about Freud's family, his own father, his own generations. Late in his life, Jakob Freud, Sigmund's father, gave his son a Bible with a powerful personal inscription in Hebrew:

> My dear son,
>
> It was in the seventh year of your age that the spirit of God began to move you to learning. I would say the spirit of God speaketh to you: "Read in My Book: there will be opened to thee sources of knowledge and of the intellect." It is the Book of Books; it is the well that wise men have digged and from which lawgivers have drawn the waters of their knowledge.
>
> Thou hast seen in this Book the vision of the Almighty, thou hast heard willingly, thou hast done and hast tried to fly high upon the wings of the Holy Spirit. Since then I have preserved the same Bible. Now, on your thirty-fifth birthday I have brought it out from its retirement and I send it to you as a token of love from your old father.[6]

The date for this inscription? May 6, 1891, just before the decade of Freud's "two great" scientific discoveries.[7]

Reluctantly on both sides, but inexorably for each, behavioral science and biblical theology move toward each other. Whatever

---

lar phenomena. I will use them interchangeably because of their close kinship.

Also, I realize that the child's "favoritism" between his or her parents—expressed here as *generational conflict*—is a big umbrella to describe what Freud stumbled across and named the "Oedipus complex." I believe, however, that this description is accurate relationally, as I hope will become increasingly clear. Freud learned nothing that had not been relationally inherent in the Bible all along.

scientific label suits you—psychiatry, psychology, or family counseling—each originally springs from *interactions between the generations*. For its part, biblical faith—Trinitarian faith based on the relationships between the Father, Son, and Holy Spirit—points to Deity itself as the source and secret of all healthy generational relationships.

· · ·

In form, this book makes up what I call a confessional study-meditation. It derives not just from my own experience—although my experience appears from first to last—but, more basically, from two viewpoints which, progressively, we will see as one.

My *study* rests on the biography and thinking of the apostle Peter as we see him in our faith's original documents, particularly in his startling First Epistle. I track first the famous problems of his immature temperament, and the how-to of his later, increasingly remarkable psychological growth. Then I take a twentieth-century psychiatric look at his unexpectedly futuristic mature psychology. I focus particularly on his astounding viewpoint about our old and historic sex-role stereotypes, and on the wider social strategy dramatically implicit in his argument.

My *meditation* centers on what all this means for the believing laity—for those of us *not* in religious or church-related vocations. We will contemplate these implications for our ordinary secular lives, in our homes, jobs, and governments. Amidst the turbulence of the nations, we will also consider what Trinitarian faith—through its relationships—crucially means for political democracy.

I write from long years of reflecting on how tragically we misunderstand biblical psychology, and of pondering what "the priesthood of all believers" means politically and organizationally now. I write unapologetically as one who has been helped both by the application of professional psychiatry and by the insights of the behavioral sciences. Finally I write as a servant of the churches, confident that our greatest days lie ahead.

Most of all, however, I write as a fellow pilgrim, a kindred traveler who endlessly finds on his road the same lessons you find on yours. In the words of the spiritual writer, Oswald Chambers, the goal is the process.[8] And the process of growing to spiritual and psychological health remains not only long and difficult, but also our great adventure.

•   •   •

During the week after the April 19, 1995, bombing of the Alfred P. Murrah Federal Building in Oklahoma City, CNN's *Crossfire* hosts, Michael Kinsley—from the Left—and John Sununu—from the Right—interviewed Nat Hentoff of *The Washington Post* and Sheriff Richard Mack of Graham County, Safford, Arizona.

Sheriff Mack defended the formation and growth of local and state militias. He was challenged by Michael Kinsley: "Sheriff Mack, you told our staff that you think that the government—the U.S. government—may have sunk the Lusitania and assassinated JFK. Do you really believe that sort of thing?"

Sheriff Mack replied, "Well, I reminded some people about the JFK movie which showed—Oliver Stone clearly showed—governmental corruption. . . . The key issue here is the people of America, the people who have formed these militia groups are afraid of their own government. They do not trust our government."

Oliver Stone on the Left, Sheriff Mack on the Right, each—from opposite ends of the political spectrum—talking about governmental conspiracies.

Scary stuff.

But in a democratic republic like America, the voters themselves form the government. "We the people" *are* the government. That night's CNN *Crossfire* was profoundly revealing. Do "we the people," in America today, conspire against *ourselves?*

Our study answers that question. And proposes the solution. We examine the underlying spiritual and psychological causes, not only for the various conspiracy theories in recent years, but also for the concern all of us face about the quality of our government and the quality of our own lives.

Genuine renewal—which includes our psychology—offers to each of us the vigor of a fresh my-life-for-yours spiritual power.[9] It offers America the trigger for a transforming explosion—of internal ethics, upright morals, common courtesy, and old-fashioned good manners.

PART ONE

❧

Our Core Relationships

The Good Relational Source, Family, and Work

One reason I believe in the Trinity is
that no human could have thought it up.
—*C. S. Lewis*

A little hurt from one of your kin is
worse than a big hurt from a stranger.
—*Jewish Proverb*

When are men most useless, would you say?
When they can't command and can't obey.
—*Goethe*

1

Just Call Me Bar-Jona!

Psychoanalysis and Simon Peter

❧

Matthew 16:13–25

Science increases our power while
it lessens our pride.
—*Claude Bernard*

*L*ooking at the Bible has made many of us feel unavoidably
nervous—out of old-fashioned screaming-preacher stereotypes, or out of more modern holier-than-thou put-downs. Yet I like
what England's famous Charles Haddon Spurgeon said: "Defend
the Bible? I would as soon defend a lion. Unchain it, and it will
defend itself."[1]

Since the Bible for many of us has often been chained, I intend
to unchain it—in the only language the twentieth century seems to
understand—the language of politics and psychology.

In the midst of our despair—about our own situations and our
nation's—only one question on this subject finally matters: Is the
Bible's message true? Is the hope it offers trustworthy? Does its
wisdom still make sense? If looking at it makes you uneasy—as has
often happened for me—I ask you to suspend judgment long enough
to look at some of its psychological realities that life has forced
me—often unwillingly—to think through.

In their ultimate sense, spiritual and psychological healing are
one and the same. In fact, the very Greek word used for "soul" in

the Bible—*psyche*—serves as the root for our word "psychiatry." At its highest and best, psychiatry becomes "soul healing." The renewing of America's soul offers our only real hope for the nation's healing.

You remember, of course, that the church and the discipline of psychology have not had the friendliest of relationships—at least not during most of the twentieth century. Part of the blame lies in psychiatry, in its pride, confusion, and limitations. But fault equally the church's own smug, self-righteous stodginess. As in many cases of scientific breakthrough, the church has typically reacted to psychological discoveries with defensive hostility, fearfully clutching the status quo.

Jesus, however, transcends the shortcomings of both classical psychiatry and the historical church.

The future of authentic psychological healing and truly reliable relationships takes us back to the church—the church in Jesus' mind. Back to a biblical psychology. Back to the church's first-and-future psychoanalytic depth. Back to a new honesty about our own feelings. Back to a bright tomorrow that only starts today.

Multifaceted Circles

This particular study builds itself on the principle that classical psychiatry and orthodox Christianity share the same lasting purposes—the healing of society and relationships through the healing and growth of the individual—and that the Bible gives us the key to our fullest psychological health.

Our study focuses on Simon Peter, one of the New Testament personalities about whom we know most. This chapter looks briefly at the psychological content of his early "Great Confession," which has carried such influence across the centuries. But first, let's consider briefly what it means to be psychologically healthy.

Professional psychiatry has long recognized that psychological wholeness involves several basic levels of relationships. If you visualize our lives as three concentric circles—first, ourselves as individuals, next, our family systems, and then our broader organizations such as vocational groupings, social bodies, and political entities—you can see this more clearly. Psychological health involves vital, invigorating interactions among each of these three circles. Such wholesome interconnections, for which all of us yearn, contribute indispensably to our health and growth.

Let me say this another way: Psychological healing is inescapably relational—it involves the healing of relationships.

Which explains why Simon Peter's story jolts us as being so advanced. As I studied him in the narrative accounts and in his First Epistle, his behavioral-science insights first astonished, then overwhelmed, and finally awed me. Specifically, he stunned and bewildered me by his extraordinary viewpoints on sex-role stereotypes. What caught me off-guard in all these scriptures is an eye-opening, ahead-of-its-time, ultramodern centering on relationships.

In looking at Peter, I propose to look at Christ's own meaning for our diverse levels of psychological need—how, in Him, human beings can grow to full relational health and maturity. For Simon Peter's lifelong story, like yours and mine, portrays the amazing growth potential waiting to be revealed through all our tragedies. And that growth starts with progressively healthy interactions at every level—every circle, ring, or sphere—of our relationships.

This faces us with another shattering truth—still deeper, higher, and bigger—which increasingly I see as crucial to understanding spiritual psychology: the historic Christian declaration that God is a Trinity, that He is Triune.

By this realization, we learn that God's perfect spiritual health, His Oneness, consists in Three perfect persons—Father, Son, and Holy Spirit. His indivisibility is by nature relational—both social and psychological—the harmoniously ordered relationships of Oneness in Threeness. This Trinitarian thinking provides us a model and a dynamic for psychologically healthy relationships that can transform the way we think about our personal lives, our families, our organizations, and our governments.

Years ago, when this "relational" approach to theology kindled lots of controversy in evangelical circles, a very conservative theologian friend of mine approached me. "Howard," he asked, his voice dripping with cynicism, "just what do you *mean*, 'relational theology?'"

"That the Triune God is, within himself, relationships," I replied, "and, therefore, that he changes all our human relationships too."

"Huh!" he grumped. "That's nothing new!"

You might say so.

Or else, as for the Jews of Jesus' day, that it's *so* new we haven't caught up with it yet.

And that's precisely the point. There's nothing really new about spiritual psychology, and yet it remains ever out in front of us, growing us toward a healthy future.

The Core of Our Relationships

Having laid these foundations, let's start looking at Simon Peter, his spiritual psychiatry, and its meaning for us, beginning with the all-important inner circle of our closest relationships.

> Now when Jesus came into the district of Caesarea Philippi, he asked his disciples, "Who do men say that the Son of man is?" And they said, "Some say John the Baptist, others say Elijah, and others Jeremiah or one of the prophets." He said to them, "But who do you say that I am?" Simon Peter replied, "You are the Christ, the Son of the living God." And Jesus answered him, "Blessed are you, Simon Bar-Jona! For flesh and blood has not revealed this to you, but my Father who is in heaven. And I tell you, you are Peter, and on this rock I will build my church, and the powers of death shall not prevail against it. I will give you the keys of the kingdom of heaven and whatever you bind on earth shall be bound in heaven, and whatever you loose on earth shall be loosed in heaven." Then he strictly charged the disciples to tell no one that he was the Christ.
>
> From that time Jesus began to show his disciples that he must go to Jerusalem and suffer many things from the elders and chief priests and scribes, and be killed, and on the third day be raised. And Peter took him and began to rebuke him saying, "God forbid Lord! This shall never happen to you." But he turned and said to Peter, "Get behind me, Satan! You are a hindrance to me; for you are not on the side of God, but of men."
>
> Then Jesus told his disciples, "If any man would come after me, let him deny himself and take up his cross and follow me. For whoever would save his life will lose it, and whoever loses his life for my sake will find it."[2]

Today from these momentous verses—traditionally named the Great Confession—one deadly omission in our church history stands out. We have interpreted this passage ecclesiastically, but not psychologically; institutionally, but not generationally; hierarchically, but not relationally.

From a lay person's point of view, the issue before us is not whether Peter was the first Pope, which is the traditional Roman Catholic viewpoint, or whether he represented all the apostles, which is the traditional Protestant point of view. The deeper issue is in what sense Peter exemplifies all us believers. For if this passage connects with the rest of the Bible, which I believe it does, then what Jesus says here to Simon Peter he says also to you and me.

He talks to us, first, about a relational God—endorsing Peter's insight on His relationship with His Father. Next, immediately after affirming his own relational Identity, Jesus confronts us with our most basic relationships—those involving our family of origin. From these, our human-parent relations, he moves us to the church, his new, broader, therapeutic, worldwide family.

This Great Confession account presents us with three great mysteries—who Jesus is, who Peter was, and who Peter would become—and points us toward one interconnected solution: the essence of spiritual therapy.

I. Who Jesus Is

Our Scripture begins with the question Jesus raises—the question of who Jesus is. In so doing, it raises the question of how any of us understands God.

I first spoke publicly on this topic to an Alcoholics Anonymous group (at our Laity Lodge retreat center in Texas). The enthusiasm of that AA group's feedback both reassured and encouraged me. One basic AA principle is to pray to "God as you understand him." That remarkable insight makes up part of the genius of Alcoholics Anonymous, particularly here in America where so many alcoholics have been damaged in various ways by neurotic forms of religion.

Of course, you probably realize that AA's genius really lies in tapping into a universal reality: The only way *any* of us *ever* prays to God is "as we understand him."

The problem in our amateur theology, reflected in our amateur psychiatry, comes because *we all tend to understand God in terms of our parents.*

The Mantle of Authority

In South Texas, the scope of my father's business and philanthropic accomplishments, as well as his capacity to inspire loyalty in people, looks to me like the stuff of legends. His strengths rested not only in his character and brilliance, but also in his discipline and hard work. Dad died in 1991, at ninety-five, after being severely restricted by a series of strokes. I, as well as he, found it hard to adjust to his incapacities during those last years. His sitting quietly in his wheelchair or lying restfully in his bed was so strikingly out of character.

During his active career, my father worked faster than anyone I ever knew. For many years his company reputation included being able to unload a truck in a shorter time than anybody else. He barreled through grocery stores at thirty miles an hour on slow days. Yet he could see more, analyze more, and come up with more ideas on display, merchandising, fixtures, or operations to jot down in his little black notebook than you could possibly believe. Not for him the "fast track"; by the 1930s he was already in the jet stream. I remember him half-running up the steps two at a time to the second-story grocery company office at the old Corpus Christi headquarters. That was Dad; when he was in a hurry he took steps three at a time—hat cocked jauntily, swinging his big, fat, tan leather briefcase.

As my spiritual life intensified in my later teens, I began to picture God and wonder: What would a more "godly" vision for myself look like? In short order I became a hard-driving lay evangelist, rushing compulsively from place to place and sermon to sermon at breakneck speed. That was my idea of Christian obedience in those days: breathless service, hurry-up holiness; stripped gears, burned-out motors, and shrieking tires.

A compulsive, workaholic parent, in other words, can give you a compulsive, workaholic God.

In the same vein, if your parents were cruel, you will tend to envision a harsh and cruel God. If your original family seemed distant and indifferent, you will find it hard to feel God close to you. But if your folks at home smothered you with closeness, your picture of God may get too heavy to love. If your parents lacked reliability, you will tend to question the trustworthiness of God, and the particular shape of your doubts will reflect your own parent-child relationships. If one of your parents was overbearing, your image of God may be oppressive, too. If, as a child, you lacked your dad's approval, you will struggle to feel God's approval later as an adult.

"God as you understand him" is where the rubber hits the road.

And it's *not* just fathers, of course. Bosses, coaches, mentors, idols, celebrities, teachers, older brothers or sisters, grandparents, religious leaders, political figures—and most surely of all, mothers—all those in our lives who wear the mantle of authority also shape our image of God.

Unconsciously. Involuntarily. Continuously. Inevitably.

Have you ever wondered how people can read the same Bible, yet come up with dramatically different ideas about God? If we understood relationships better, we'd have more clues. One man preaches a hard God of condemnation. Another preaches just the opposite—God as sentimental mush. Still others, I'm glad to report, proclaim a more wholesome, balanced God, perfectly combining both virtue and compassion. These incredible varieties and astounding contrasts all emerge out of not only divine but also human relationships: mothers, fathers, pastors, professors, authors, and heroes.

The important people in our lives exercise vast relational power over us. Even "peer pressure" demonstrates nothing but the authority of others aggregated; herd instinct or group approval becomes the parental replacement. In our adult lives, doctors, lawyers, administrators, bankers, officials, executives, academics, and experts, through their "pecking order" positions, become a kind of parent substitute. Each one of them has the potential, for good or bad, to color our image of God—or even take God's place in our lives—without our being aware of it.

For example, as psychologist Myron Madden points out, the "God is dead" movement, arising from its own philosophical roots, gained in recognition and popularity in the United States shortly after President John F. Kennedy's 1963 murder. The presidential "father" to our country's unconscious had been killed; national attention then projected that death onto God.

That's why Jesus' words grip us not only spiritually but also psychologically: "And call no man your father on earth, for you have one Father, who is in heaven."[3]

The Battle of the Generations

Because parents and parental figures hold so much power over us, we almost inevitably grow up with mixed feelings and ambivalent attitudes toward them.

So all of us fluctuate in our feelings about our fathers (and mothers). This again shows why Christ is essential, the Bible and Church indispensable: to give us objective data about God. We need data that does not waffle according to our temperament, our happenstances, or the insects in our particular family's tree. We need solid information and specific knowledge, not subjective speculation. We need steady, reliable, historic, realistic, trustworthy facts. Therefore, even if none of us understands him completely, we need Jesus. He is God "with a face"; he defines God objectively. Jesus enfleshes God for us, makes Him real. He describes Him through his own human personality. He embodies Him. Christ himself is the Rock on which the church is built.

Who is this Jesus to you? You heard Simon Peter's belief. Listen to the apostle John's: "It is true that no one has ever seen God at any time. Yet the divine and only Son, who lives in closest intimacy with the Father, has made him known."[4]

On the night before he was crucified, Jesus himself said, "I and My Father are one."[5]

Of course, that kind of oneness cannot describe us human fathers and human sons (or mothers and daughters). Not only are we not one; much of the time we're more like belligerent armies sniping at—or assaulting—one another. It's the battle of the generations. We tear each other and society apart, usually not so much physically as psychologically—although sometimes we do end up slugging it out at home or shooting it out in the streets.

Generational conflict ebbs and flows in tides as old as history. No doubt it is universal. Sometimes it seems quiet and subtle, sometimes loud and violent, but it never quite disappears. The power of procreation and parenting, our sexual and then familial creativity, produce not only godlike joy but also hellish pain. From childhood to adulthood, in their *positive transitions*, procreation and parenting prepare sons to become good fathers and daughters to become good mothers. In their *negative breakdowns*, however, they turn into the diametric opposite, MAD: Mutual Assured Destruction.

None of us understands fully our relationships with our parents. In us all, negative, double-minded attitudes toward them make us sick; they poison our souls. These two individuals physically gave us life. Of all people we should love purely, it is these two. Yet when our parents' imperfections tangle with our own imperfections, these primary relationships get twisted, riddled with love-hate ambiguities.

Then, toward this universal tragedy, Christ advances. Through the anguished mystery of parents and children, he takes us into the precincts of the divine, there to give us his body and blood. Out of all the world's agonies, including yours and mine, only his suffering turns out completely positive. So to the awkwardness between fathers and sons, the tensions between mothers and daughters, the estrangements between adults and young people—to this primordial social torture—perfect love has come. *Agape* has appeared.* Resurrection, on "the third day . . . according to the Scriptures,"[6] has arrived.

Scholars agree that Jesus captures his unrepeatable uniqueness, his unparalleled distinctiveness, and his ultimate unity with the Father in the name he used for God—"Abba."[7] To us today, "Abba" would come off something like "Daddy," a term of absolute trust and intimacy. The human Jesus unites, forever one, with the Creator of the cosmos, the Authority over all that is: "the Father . . . from whom all fatherhood—earthly or heavenly—derives its name."[8] The union that holds the universe together and keeps it from flying apart rests in that flawless *agape* love, that faithful loyalty, that indivisibility. That inviolate love forms the open heart of the Trinity.

Agape is Greek for the divine kind of love.

To fouled-up fathers and fouled-up sons, fearful oldsters and wilding youngsters, muddled mothers and muddling daughters, *perfect love* has come. And that's who Jesus is.

Which helps us get real about who we are.

II. Who Peter Was

Review Peter's Confession and look once more at this mountain peak of revelation. Listen again to its immortally sparkling dialogue:

> "Who do you say that I am?" . . .
> "You are the Christ, the Son of the living God." . . .
> "Blessed are you, Simon Bar-Jona, for flesh and blood has not revealed this to you, but My Father who is in heaven."[9]

Bar-Jona. Simon *Bar-Jona.* I think it was the *Bar* that kept me blind for so long to the relational significance of this conversation.

Bar-Jona means *"son of* Jona." The precise word form calls us to think child-parent, daughter-mother, son-father, to think generations, just as we would consider Tom Smith "Tom, son of the Smith family." In this historically pivotal conversation, was it just a coincidence that Jesus used the prefix *Bar* to focus so explicitly onto Peter's family of origin?

Yes, it was a coincidence—in the same sense that all the other circumstances of Jesus' ministry were. When disciples' names are given in the Gospels, they usually don't include the "Bar" usage. Jesus chose it strategically here and one time later, after Peter's rooster-crow defection. His use of "Bar-Jona," deliberately picked up from common speech, reflects a coincidence just like the other circumstances that combined to speed the message worldwide in that unique "fullness of time" moment in the human story: the Roman roads, the *Pax Romana,* and the universal language, Greek.[10]

Coincidence? I think not.

Look closely at what is happening in this encounter between Jesus and Peter. No sooner has Peter spoken his words of faith, no sooner has he publicly acknowledged Jesus' divine parentage, no sooner has he said out loud this truth that "flesh and blood" had *not* revealed to him—no sooner has he done this than, instantly, Jesus takes Simon back to his childhood's name, back to his earthly parentage, back to his own flesh and blood, back to his original family.

"Blessed are you, Simon Bar-Jona."

In this one sentence Jesus points Simon not only to his future—his heavenly home—but also to his past—his parents' house. He starts Simon's growth by not rushing past his intimate personal history, by not ignoring his initial primary experiences, by not speeding through the relationships where he had learned to talk and think and feel and react and work.

And Jesus does the same with us. As soon as I identify who he is, he says to me, too, "Blessed are you, Howard Butt, Jr., son of Howard Butt, Sr." Immediately I am called to confront the basic psychological realities of my life, to look as I have never looked before at the family system from which I came. My name—and yours—is also Bar-Jona.

Parents and Children

What we face here, then and now, is dialogue pivoting on parents and children: two fathers and two sons, Jesus the son of God and Simon the son of Jona; the perfect father and the perfect son, the imperfect father and the imperfect son. Holy Father—Holy Son; sinful father—sinful son: You can't acknowledge the first without confronting the second.

What was Simon Peter's mother's name? We don't know. We were given the last name, the male name (for cultural reasons, no doubt, but also to call us fathers, through the societal fabric and language of that day, to face up to our family responsibilities). For alliteration's sake, let's call Simon's mother Jane.

And so we have Jona and Jane, the two human beings who gave Simon birth, the ones from whom he learned to speak, dress, behave, work, and play. But, of course, Simon had absorbed from his parents a great deal more than these external things. He had absorbed ideas and feelings about God, about structures and organizations, about citizenship and government, about leading and following, about the universe and humanity, about brothers and sisters. Most specifically, in a million ways, he had gleaned from Jona and Jane their sexual stereotypes—their assumptions that certain traits, patterns, attitudes, and actions are masculine, while others are feminine.

The day Simon began to learn who Jesus is, however, he began to unlearn and relearn everything he had picked up from Jona and Jane—everything he had ever known before about anything at all, and especially everything he had ever learned about himself. And now, two thousand years later, you and I can also acknowledge who Jesus is. With Peter we can say, "Jesus, you are the Christ, the son of the living God." And like Simon, we, too, will begin the process of rethinking all the things we ever thought we knew.

What kind of people were Jona and Jane? We don't possess much data; we have limited information even about their son. We do have records that show Peter was Jewish and from Galilee, that he left his family of origin to get married, that he worked in the commercial fishing industry out of Bethsaida, which was probably the fishing district of Capernaum. We recollect he had a brother named Andrew, to whom he was close. Tradition says he was physically large.

We recall, much more specifically, that whatever family system Jona, Jane, Simon, Andrew and their other kinfolk had produced, and however Simon had responded to it, his genetics, environment, and individual will had combined to produce an unreliable, loud, impulsive, extreme, driven, and moody man. If you've read the Gospels, you remember the stories. Simon Peter seemed excruciatingly insecure, horrifically vulnerable to peer pressure, agonizingly desperate for public applause. He appeared so hungry for acceptance in the group that he would unwittingly turn hypocrite to get it. He couldn't stand up alone. He couldn't say a trustworthy "No"; he couldn't say a trustworthy "Yes."

You've heard of "an accident waiting to happen"? Well, describe Simon Bar-Jona as a calamity waiting to occur!

So why do I especially love this man? Well, you can call it our common humanity, our fellowship of weakness, our bond of shared sinfulness. You can call it "our little problem." You can call us Pharisees Anonymous.

I love Simon Bar-Jona because he was a little like I am a lot. Which makes the good news of what Peter would become very good indeed.

III. Who Peter Would Become

If it had been someone like me in Jesus' shoes for this momentous conversation, I certainly wouldn't have named Simon as he did. Jesus renamed Simon the rock, not I. I'd have called him as I saw him: Wishy or Washy or Soupy or Mushy, certainly not Rocky. Or perhaps, as he turned out when the rooster crowed, The Spineless One. Old Jelly Legs never deserved to be called The Rock.

Of course he never deserved it. That's the point. Peter's new identity was a gift—it was grace; it was love. Jesus saw his disaster's potential. Call Jesus the original Man of La Mancha, looking at Aldonza the Whore and renaming her Dulcinea, My Lady. He gazed at us all, dreamed The Impossible Dream, and made it possible. The prototypical positive thinker, Jesus looked beyond his predestined cross. Anticipating his Resurrection, past his own chosen, inescapable anguish, he imagined our transformed capacities unleashed. Therefore he gave Simon a new name, a new power, a new character, a new birth.

Jesus gave Wishy-Washy a new father, a new mother, a new family. He gave the rock-solid strength of his own identity to dwell and grow inside Simon. And gradually, on a perfectly timed schedule, "Old Jelly Legs" changed into Gibraltar.

It didn't happen overnight. To be truthful (and those of us in the "born-again" camp sometimes forget this) it happened with excruciating slowness. Years following, far past the "rock" dialogue, far past Jesus' final week, far past Pentecost, many long years and many slow miles later, Peter still sometimes acted like Jelly Legs. You can read about it in Galatians 2, where, on the circumcision controversy, Peter's two-faced craving to be popular with the "in crowd" surfaced again. Dear old mushy Bar-Jona: You don't turn into a rock in a hurry.

How did it happen? We don't know the details. But I'm convinced that during that time Simon was able to work through, as the psychiatrists say, his Bar-Jona family history. He faced up to his own feelings, problems, and sins. He freely forgave each one in his original family as well as his married one; he sought their forgiveness toward him, too.

Most likely Peter never completely understood the mystery of his relationships with these up-close people in his life. Who of us ever completely understands these things? But the day he believed who Jesus is, he started an entire lifetime of reconciliation and psychological healing. His relationships both within his own marriage and among his Early Church friends became deeper and more real. These people around him would "speak the truth in love." They would get "angry yet not sin." They accepted him but called him to shape up.[11] For Peter, the early church turned out to be a Christ-centered therapy group.

Now, almost two thousand years later, those of us who have believed in this very same Jesus have begun a similar journey toward psychological maturity. And for me the trip has included professional therapy—psychoanalysis.

The fact that I am able to tell you this represents a personal victory. For years I couldn't tell anyone past the tiny circle who "had to know"—not even close members of my own family.

I remember the furtive embarrassment, the humiliated shame, the sense of spiritual failure when I first went to see the psychiatrist just a few blocks from the city auditorium where I had once conducted a big evangelistic crusade. Then later, the first time I spoke about this publicly, I was ashamed again.

I told you I went for help reluctantly. Why? My pride. Pride in my Christian leadership, in my reputation, and, maybe above all, in my own intelligence. For me, the fear we all have of losing our minds had turned intensely personal. None of us ever wants to admit we have a screw loose. Yet we all do.

Don't misunderstand me. I'm certainly not saying that you need a psychiatrist. Each one of us differs. My particular form of screwiness needed the formal treatment that was professional, structured. My genetic predispositions and body chemistry played a part in my specific need; so did my own attitudes, anxieties, situational pressures—and God's inscrutable mercy. Your case may be entirely different; you may not need professional help. Like Simon Peter.

Why Spiritual Psychiatry?

All of us need spiritual psychiatry—the kind of personal growth and relational healing that turned Simon Peter into the Rock. Why? For three reasons:

First, *Our own particular weakness.* Each of us, individually, is a distinctly fouled-up person, badly in need of help. Jesus said, "It is not the fit and flourishing who need the doctor, but those who are ill. I did not come to invite the 'righteous,' but the 'sinners.'"[12] We don't even know how to love *ourselves* wisely, much less others.

Second, *Our current condition in the church.* As a whole, to a deadly extent, we are superficial, mediocre, sickly, appallingly ineffective. Broken relationships characterize the church, just as they do the world. We have left our first love for God, each other, and our healthy selves. We have become "a nation of strangers," so relationally shallow that we are blind to our broader calling to be the church to each other in the secular world every day.

Third, *Our "chutzpah" civilization.* Leo Rosten explains the brassiness, effrontery, and gall involved in this famed Yiddish word for insolence: "Chutzpah" is when you murder your father and your mother and throw yourself on the mercy of the court because you are an orphan![13] But tragically and not comically, chutzpah echoes the very first chapter of the Sermon on the Mount, which warns us about what our contempt for others *really* means. Some psychologists would probably equate chutzpah with what they think of as the character disorder of our time, arrogant and insensitive narcissism—our unchecked selfishness.

Leo Rosten's Jewish humor gently introduces us here to some terms, for our spiritual psychiatry, that at first sound harsh, shocking, or frightening. But they capture our selfishness-between-the-generations. After being confronted with my own self-centeredness for so many years, I have concluded that these stark terms are not only fully defensible but also precisely accurate—both theologically and psychologically.

Sigmund Freud once observed that the three greatest tragedies in human literature, Sophocles' *Oedipus Rex,* Shakespeare's *Hamlet,* and Dostoevsky's *The Brothers Karamazov,* all concern the same theme. They all pivot on *father-murder.*[14] He was stating the critical point that the Bible had first asserted many centuries before: Unconsciously we tend to war against authority and the structures of authority.

This emotionally loaded word symbol, "father-murder," faces the generational conflict in us head-on—naming it at its most dramatic, at its most extreme. It spotlights the battle between the generations, making it memorable. Of course, there's also "mother-murder," and "parent-hate." I use *father-murder* as shorthand for all this generational resentment.

I admit that this term is a blown-up color graphic for what is usually a much more subtle dynamic. Our father-murder is mental, attitudinal, hidden. Here's what happens. Our love for our parents gets tangled up with jealousies, frictions, antagonisms, grudges, and hostilities. Then our denial, our unacknowledged guilt about these jumbled responses, makes us sick. Snarled-up feelings about the most important relationships in our lives then scramble our other emotions, and this in turn ends up twisting our thinking itself. Our mixed-up feelings thus produce mixed-up anxieties and mixed-up conduct in a thousand personal and organizational ways that are not only undramatic, but are also—usually or often—unnoticed.

Generational realism and the psychology of the Trinity take us one step further. They teach us that *father-murder is also the murder of the son.* Between the generations you cannot split cause and effect; it seeps by osmosis through the thin tissues of our family circles. Rebellious children make tyrannical parents; tyrannical parents produce rebellious children. Untreated infections from our family of origin contaminate our home and our family today—and out from there, spreading the epidemic in wider and wider circles.

In other words, our problem with authority extends to those under us as well as to those over us. Parent-hate, lockstep and rigid, cannot separate itself from child abuse. Neglected children become neglectful parents. We don't want anyone else in charge, but we don't want the responsibility of being in charge ourselves. When it comes to authority, we're all irrational.

What else explains the defiant "death to the parents" pounding in some of our rock music? Or gangsta' rap? Or our neglecting to follow through on our children's schoolwork, therefore hurting their chances to reach their full potential? Or impassioned and brilliant attacks on establishment values, combined with unthinking indifference as to the consequences? What else explains "Kill the Umpire!" rioting in sports? Or tasteless jokes that ridicule struggling presidents, or public fury holding back appropriate congressional perquisites and pay? Or "to hell with the bosses" attitudes that poison the workplace—not to mention overbearing attitudes of bosses toward employees? What else explains our unconscious resistance toward treating our grown-up children as our equals, fully adult?

On a more personal level, why do I sweat doctors, deadlines, policemen, administrators, media, government officials, and editors today? You know the answer as well as I. It's my current carryover of parent-hate, my inner rage against authority. Crying there in my crib, I learned it early. I wanted constant attention from everyone, the universe revolving exclusively around me. So I turned furious when I didn't get what *I* wanted.

But a baby's crying is a natural way of telling us his needs. Of course, that's the point. Parent-hate *is* natural, in the sense that it arises naturally out of our innate human selfishness. But at the same time, it is clearly unnatural—perverse, crazy, and self-destructive. Hating my parents, I hate myself and my children. And so, inside my heart, I kill myself even more surely than I kill them. Because I was born to this specific twosome, my humanity is indissolubly tied to theirs.

Father-Murder and the Cross

The crucifixion of Jesus—for the sins of the world—makes our father-murder unforgettable. And the unknowing ways we so often react to the people around us are what killed him.

If we take at face value Jesus' description of himself, "I and My Father are one,"[15] we acknowledge that he alone among all us humans is worthy to be our ultimate Parent and our final Authority. Then we see his cross, at least in part, as the inescapable consequence of how we unconsciously tend to think, not only about God, but also about each other across the generations within the circles of our own families.

That fouled-up process then—by transference—becomes how we treat one another continuously in structures, organizations, and institutions, every day, unaware. It even becomes our unconscious attack on democracy's basic premise: that the power for change rests underneath, in the "consent of the governed."

This unwitting psychological assault—on the presupposition underlying our democracy—explains the current climate in our nation's public discourse. In nostalgia for a better time, *New York*

Times columnist Anthony Lewis says that it has now become "a national sport to savage the great."[16] We should not be surprised: The cross shows us the end result of our generational resentments, our familial disloyalties, our marital disunities, our organizational alienations. It shows us—our savaging transferred, crystal-clear, onto God, the One True Great—our Father-Murder.

Or still, if you prefer, father-hate; Jesus said it is the same thing. The supreme psychoanalyst cut through to the heart of our emotional intentions, telling us that hatred equals murder: the bitter heart *is* the smoking gun.

Jesus' Sermon on the Mount specifies exactly what our chutzpah and our animosities mean:

> You have learned that our forefathers were told, "Do not commit murder; anyone who commits murder must be brought to judgment." But what I tell you is this: Anyone who nurses anger against his brother must be brought to judgment. If he abuses his brother he must answer for it to the court; if he sneers at his brother he will have to answer for it in the fires of hell.[17]

No doubt Jesus uses *brother* here as a generic term for the human race. According to such an understanding, fathers and mothers would represent brothers of the closest kind, brothers toward which we all nurse anger.

Generationally speaking, this anger we nurse emerges, at least partly, from our varying and fluctuating parent-child and child-parent favoritisms. Preference for mother classically pivots on bias against father. Discrimination in favor of father reflects negative prejudice against mother. Twistedness between the generations continues our universal impairment, father-hate or mother-hate, one or both. And shockingly, but with motivational accuracy, Jesus calls our consequent contempt and estrangements murderous.

St. John made it stark: "Anyone who hates his brother is a murderer."[18] In the most dramatic language conceivable—the language of murder—Jesus says to us, "All have sinned." And elsewhere, with penetrating candor, he tells us, "You have done it unto me."[19]

Not only did God the Father forsake his Son on the cross ("For our sake he made him to be sin who knew no sin"),[20] he also shared fully in that self-sacrifice himself ("God was in Christ reconciling the world to himself").[21] The Father abandoned Christ; the Father was dwelling in Christ. The overwhelming tension—the bewildering enigma—between those two adjoining scriptures captures the crucifixion-resurrection's paradox, which John Donne called "bones to philosophy but milk to faith."[22] The mystery of God as Triune makes the cross the key to generational healing.

The Trinity's sociological and psychological common sense confronts all our generational pathologies with one underlying reality: You can't heal one generation without healing the other.

Bar-Jona and Transference

What does Simon Bar-Jona reveal about himself—and his area for growth—when, immediately after identifying Jesus as God's son, he straight off tells him that his cross-and-resurrection strategy is hopelessly wrong? ("Peter took him and began to rebuke him saying, 'God forbid, Lord! This shall never happen to you.'"[23]) What does he demonstrate but transference? He shows us not only his reflexive desire to control Jesus, but also his prior and unconscious desire to control Jona and Jane.

Bar-Jona, in these words, projects his lifelong response to Jona and Jane's human authority onto Jesus' divine authority. No doubt, in various little ways, he has been crucifying both of his parents relationally his whole life. But here he is blind to that transparent fact. His drive to rule the roost and dominate them has been as murderous psychologically as Jesus' cross later became physically. But he has never faced this obvious relational truth about himself with his most significant others.

In focusing on Simon as Bar-Jona, Jesus hones in on what all of us unconsciously practice every day. We transfer all our own flawed, family-of-origin, authority relationships onto God, the ultimate authority—as well as onto all our other "beyond the home" authority relationships. It works two ways:

First, *positive transference.* Simon transfers—or projects—the *good* in his Jona-Jane relationship onto Jesus, calling him "the Christ, the Son of the Living God."

Second, *negative transference.* Simon transfers—or displaces—onto Jesus the *bad* in his Jona-Jane relationship when, immediately after acknowledging him to be God, he nevertheless tells Jesus that he doesn't know what he's doing! Is his controlling, negative reaction logical, rational, or sane?

Transference's positive, up side is its echo of love's true relationships, like those in the Trinity. Its negative, down side distorts, twists, and perverts those *agape*, self-giving relationships. We see transference's down side, obvious through the pain, in the power of our transferences not only to estrange us, but also to make us sick. Let us never forget that religion itself, for reasons of transference, has perpetrated many of history's greatest crimes.

Jesus' commandment, "Judge not, that you be not judged," warns us against these unrecognized transferences.[24] What did he mean? He meant that our condemnations of others only reveal, in fact, the guilt within our own fractured hearts. He meant that those uncontrollable angers we harbor toward other people each tell us something profound about our own unacknowledged, hidden poisons of rage, fear, or bitterness.

"Judging others" portrays for us, biblically, the exact scientific phenomenon Freud ran into with his patients. They transferred onto their feelings about him their own lifelong inner attitudes, their previously concealed thinking. They projected onto him love, hate, rebellion, dependence, criticism, and denunciation. They became enraged by the objectivity of his analysis. They felt deeply and personally hurt by his imagined slights. They even began suspecting and accusing him of sexual seduction. They judged him. And in the process, when he did not judge them in return, they gained insight into themselves. They found help and healing in Freud's understanding, reassuring, and accepting words.

No doubt more of Jesus operated in Freud than he realized. His medical uncovering of transference gives us modern illumination from Jesus' Sermon on the Mount again, as long ago he described our negative transference:

> Why do you see the speck that is in your brother's eye, but do not notice the log that is in your own eye? Or how can you say to your brother, "Let me take the speck out of your eye," when there is the log in your own eye? You hypocrite, first take the log out of your own eye, and then you will see clearly to take the speck out of your brother's eye.[25]

Both positive and negative transference surround us like the ocean depths where the fish swim. Transference constitutes the mental air we breathe, our ever-present relational climate, our constant emotional atmosphere. While behavioral science humbles our family and religious pride, Christ transcends the old, dated scientism that can only "worship our brains."[26] He opens our eyes to reality. The Proverbs call his complex gift "the mixed wine of wisdom."[27]

Positive transference is one important part of our experience—however limited and oblivious—of the Triune God. We practice and encounter this kind of transference continually. When we stop for stop signs, or follow our doctor's prescription, or learn from a teacher, or pay our bill in a restaurant, or trust the pilot by boarding a plane, or, most especially, serve someone else who needs our help, we inhale and exhale God as Spirit—the Triune God who is indeed positive.

Negative transference is evil's twisting, violation, and seduction of healthy, natural transference. Unfortunately, it too is universal; unbidden, it pollutes us all. Whenever we condemn or reject others—as persons—we reveal our own sins. We live a lie, displacing our own personal guilt onto those we judge. Shunning humility, we pretend moral superiority and project onto those around us our own internally generated falsehood. We relate to others by negation; we gasp our own spiritual poison gas from the ultimate pollution—*agape's* absence.

To Be Ourselves

Negative transference, then, brings us to the next point. Bar-Jona was locked into Jona and Jane. If we only have human parents, then we remain psychologically dependent on them, positively or negatively—and inevitably both positively *and* negatively—throughout our lives. We may shift our parent-feelings onto many other individuals in our lifetime, but even this later projection or transference leaves us essentially tied to that original pair.

As a result, we live out our years unconsciously repeating our childhoods. We worship our parents or we murder them. We become just like them or obstinately different—carbon copies or blind

erasings. Either way, in imitation or rejection, we remain imper-
fectly bound to imperfect human parents. As the philosopher Georg
Christoph Lichtenberg observed, "To do just the opposite is also a
form of imitation."[28]

Through his Heavenly Father, however, Jesus offers us the opportunity to be ourselves, our *best* selves, the selves we were created
to be by the God who got our fathers and mothers together in the
first place. We can fully accept them and affirm the best in them,
our Jonas and Janes; we are freed from either deifying them or
cursing them. In Christ's wisdom we respect and love them, gaining
insight from them with discernment. We honor them by learning
both from their strengths and their weaknesses.

Christ gets us beyond our sexual stereotypes into "the mystery of
Godness,"[29] so infinitely and wholly "other," beyond our sex-role
fears, prejudices, and confusion as his universal perfect *agape* love
is beyond our puny, insignificant experiences. To Abraham, the "father of the faithful" for Jews, Christians, and Moslems, God announced his name as "El Shaddai." Just as the name *El* in Hebrew
denotes God, *Shaddai* from *shad*, Hebrew for a woman's breasts,
denotes his mothering qualities. As Oswald Chambers' wisdom perceived him so maturely, Christ's Father is *"El Shaddai*, the Father-
Mother God,"[30] the perfect divine Parent.[31]

With or without professional counseling, according to our personal need, the solid rock of Christ-in-us gets us past our Bar-Jona
emotional infancies, past our childish spiritual dependencies, past
our continuing "chutzpah" adolescences into maturity for ourselves
and others.

Then, in Christ, one with his Father and the Holy Spirit, we can
take a step further. We can share a parent's function to help someone else grow. Like Peter, we are given "the keys of the kingdom"
so we can open the door for others, too. We "bind and loose," loving
people with the same appropriate wisdom by which we have been
loved ourselves. We are given the pastoral authority that Jesus gave
Peter following his unforgettable Great Confession.[32]

If this phrase "pastoral authority" is too "churchy" for you, give
it another name. The AA group with whom I originally shared these
insights became inspired relating this "pastoral authority" to the
psychological reality they realize when, having been helped by AA

themselves, they become an AA sponsor for a newly recovering alcoholic.

Whatever you call this loving, parenting phenomenon, whether it helps people start the journey or encourages them along, its psychological essence is the same. Psychiatrists call it reparenting. You may call it confession, pastoring, counseling, evangelizing, witnessing, preaching, teaching, discipling, nurturing, training, spiritual direction, equipping, "becoming an agent of healing," "soul friendship," mentoring, or facilitating. You may call it nothing more than friendliness, sympathy, caring, or devotion. You may think of it only as listening or helping. Whatever you call it, its root is the same. We experience pastoral authority far more than we name it so.

You may not even recognize yet the Divine Identity that your concern for others serves. But whether you acknowledge his Name or not, when you lighten people's loads, aid those around you, and make life easier for someone else, you are the agent of the Trinitarian relationship.

Jesus commends you: "For I was hungry and you gave me food. I was thirsty and you gave me a drink. I was naked and you came and looked after me. . . . In prison and you came to see me there."[33]

In him we keep opening doors for each other, binding up wounds and loosening grave clothes, swinging wide the entrance to the kingdom where people relate to each other like Jesus and his Father. In Christ's name, we stop cutting each other down and start building each other up. I am convinced that all human compassion springs from this one relational Source.

To help us become what we are, therefore, the Bible reads forever contemporary, even more psychological than modern psychology. Biblical dynamics create and describe love's authentic heart, whether we so identify it or not.

The Phenomenon of Love

Back to Simon Peter's growth, then. How did he turn from a wishy-washy, squishy-squashy, jello-fellow into a rock-solid, authoritatively loving pastor? By the Holy Spirit. By the relational essence of Pentecost progressing within his attitudes. By the long, slow process of learning to look at Christ's death and Resurrection, according to the Scripture, as the most important thing that ever happened.

Compare Peter's attitude in his immature transference during the Confession story, with his thinking later when he wrote his First Epistle. In this first story, as soon as Jesus' Son-of-God identity was announced, as soon as Simon's Bar-Jona family problem was pinpointed, as soon as the whole church's pastoral potential was promised—Jesus immediately began to teach his disciples about the way it would all happen: his upcoming cross and Resurrection. He started at once instructing them in the inevitability of human suffering, starting with his own for us all.

And Peter? Old Simon Bar-Jona? His philosophy of life did not include suffering. Even more basic, his theology of God—his understanding of love—did not include suffering. So, divine wisdom having punched his negative transference button, horrified by Jesus' hard but precise realism, Bar-Jona sputtered, "Oh no, Lord, this should never happen to you!" Whereupon Jesus, sensing the seductive self-pity in Peter's sentimental gush, rebuked self-pity at the source:

"Get behind me, Satan; you think like men and not like God!"

But through the years that followed, Simon Bar-Jona kept growing, from his blind transference and vacillating instability into rocklike maturity. How? By learning to "think like God." By learning to focus every thought into the one reality of the death and resurrection of his Lord.

And so will we. "Denying ourselves" and "taking up our cross" means that in all our disasters, little and big, we identify our agonies with Christ's. We transfer our transferences onto him. We come to trust that, just as God on the third day brought resurrection from Jesus' suffering, so also will he bring triumph from our own calamities—in his own way, time, and particular purpose both for us and others. We have solid, rational ground for believing that things *do* turn out for the best.

Peter, this volatile tumbleweed of a man, demonstrates our potential as well as our difficulties. He teaches us his deep-down positive thinking for the problems in our individual selves, families, organizations, and society. He spotlights the good possibilities inherent in our particular pain now. All this keeps happening because God has a wonderful plan for your life and mine—a plan that includes our troubles and our tragedies.

2

The Psychology of the New Birth

Foundations for Relational Growth

~❧

---
1 Peter 1:1–2:10

He would like to start from scratch.
Where is scratch?
—*Elias Canetti*

*M*ost of us yearn to look at life from the sunny side. We long for some realistic path beyond our negativity, our dark expectations, our anxious habits of apprehension and doubt.

Yet when I was a lay student in theology forty years ago, the seminary's prime whipping boy was Norman Vincent Peale and his *Power of Positive Thinking*. The faculty charged that Peale purveyed unbalanced doctrine. They said he failed at dealing adequately with evil—particularly the personal evil within each of us—and they blasted his "theology of success" theme, pointing out its "success as idolatry" danger. Contrasting Peale with the apostle Paul's doctrine, the faculty's standard one-liner went "Paul is appealing, but Peale is appalling!"

· · ·

Academic theology's favorite villain now, in a repeat mode, is Robert Schuller with his *Possibility Thinking*. Same fight. Nobody loves these men but the people. It's not my place to resolve this theological dispute; my guess is that Drs. Schuller and Peale have something to teach the seminaries and vice versa. But the broader context of the controversy should not be missed. It hinges on the basic connection between thinking and living, cognition and action, attitudes and experience. On a personal level, it rides on the question of how our view of ourselves affects the outcome of our lives.

Peter and Positive Thinking

Some forty years after Simon Peter's Great Confession, he wrote his First Epistle. Today, in the middle of our traditional thought patterns and shallow understandings, this four- or five-page document sets off sequenced bombshells. It bases "positive thinking" on solid theology and gives "possibility thinking" its profound depth. And it speaks to us, not from a negative and pessimistic mindset, but from a positive, affirming, and optimistic one.

The entire Epistle takes the view that each of us, through the death and Resurrection of Christ, is someone of incalculable importance. In Christ, we each carry within us a unique, unrepeatable, and original destiny that, by paradox, is also available to everyone universally.

Not despite our tragedies, but *in and through* them, our lives can turn out to be inimitable adventures, full of drama, excitement, and hope. Our limitations, difficulties and failures—all our personal sufferings—carry within themselves the incredible potential of Christ's overcoming.

In the face of this basic biblical promise, why do we cling, obstinately and irrationally, to our gloomy reasoning? What makes us such stubborn cynics? Why do we sink into such negative perspectives about our family-and-work frustrations?

My own temperament, by nature, tends toward critical analysis, dark glasses, and negative thinking. I'm a worrier. You name it— from my own health to the high crime rates—I worry about everything. Then I hear that worry is a sin, so I worry about that, too.

For me, positive thinking is a battle. My emotions too often fight against those solid rational grounds for believing that things do turn out for the best. My feelings try to argue down the incredible potential of Christ's overcoming. I need to get at my emotional roots and get a commonsense grip on how my reason can hold the reins controlling my responses and reactions.

John Peer's cracker-barrel (if tongue-in-cheek) collection of *Logical Laws, Accurate Axioms, Profound Principles, Trusty Truisms, Homey Homilies, Colorful Corollaries, Quotable Quotes, and Rambunctious Ruminations for All Walks of Life* includes Jaeger's Fact: "Tell a man there are 300 billion stars and he'll believe you. Tell him a bench has wet paint on it and he'll have to touch it to be sure."[1]

Untangling the Mess of "Born-Again" Language

The notion of the second birth, which Jesus first introduced to Nicodemus, constitutes the beginning theme for the whole of Peter's first letter. At least seven times in the first chapter and a half, directly and indirectly, the Apostle assures us that Christians have been born again in the death and Resurrection of Christ.[2]

In the first chapter, for instance, Peter tells us that God "gave us new birth" and that we "have been born anew." In chapter 2 he advises us "like newborn babies [to] crave spiritual milk so that by it [we] may grow up."[3]

The message is unmistakable: Each and all Christians have, in fact, been born again—birthed anew spiritually. The Holy Spirit has been implanted in our hearts. A new nature has been given us. Jesus Christ has come to live his triumphant life through us. He himself, by his Spirit inside us, is the new birth.

"Born-again," for many Americans in our day, looms as a term full of misunderstanding. It's a password, an open sesame, yet sadly also a label and a stigma. Why? Perhaps because so many born-again people, without facing the reasons, become obstreperous about it.

In fact, as a product of evangelical groups and an evangelical denomination—from the inside, therefore—I have concluded that *the greatest enemy of evangelical awakening in our nation is our evangelical culture.*

By "culture" I mean collective atmosphere or organizational ambience. A culture is the way a group of people—a country, an ethnic population, a civilization—has grown together; the word refers to the sum of its collective parts. What I term "evangelical culture," then, is the particular psychological environment that has grown up around evangelical religion—the surrounding envelope of spiritual maturity (or lack of it) that is found both in our leadership and in our membership.

In evangelical culture, our strength (our emphasis on being born again) has become our weakness (becoming proud of it, self-inflated spiritually and self-satisfied, as if the new birth were our achievement). More biblically, we should instead allow our weakness, our need of being born again in the first place, to become our strength, recognizing our daily need for the new birth not only as a past event, but also as a continuous process of growing. After all, "Christ's strength is made perfect in our weakness."[4]

Instead of this daily growth, unfortunately, we have all too often remained psychologically and spiritually unaware, blind and shallow, relationally unreal. Unconsciously we have contaminated ourselves with show-business psychology, built around "stars" such as orator-preachers, evangelists, musicians, performers, and "personalities."

This gospel entertainment culture traces itself back at least to the American frontier's rural isolations and to nineteenth-century revivalism, and possibly much earlier. No doubt it sheds light on why we evangelicals have so stridently condemned worldly entertainments like drinking and dancing.

Psychiatrists, remember, have named the behavior described in Romans 2:1—"At whatever point you condemn others you automatically condemn yourself, since you, the judge, commit the same sins."[5] They call it projection, transference, or displacement. Unknowingly, we religiously entertained evangelicals feel guilty about our superficial human relationships, our lack of love. So, blindly, we displace our own guiltiness onto the entertainment of others.

But cruel attitudes toward others unconsciously reflect cruel attitudes toward ourselves. Murder and suicide form two sides of the same coin; destructive thoughts toward others mirror our own self-destructive behaviors. Critical temperaments, slashing out at people around us, reveal first of all self-cynicism: condemning, we are condemned; judging, we are judged. Jesus' cross spotlights humanity's uncontrollable projections: How often have our rigid evangelical negativisms proved, ultimately, self-defeating?

Only when we are "poor in spirit" do we judge ourselves, rather than sit in judgment on others. Only this "no condemnation" attitude within us triumphs over our transferences.

Our star system of gospel entertainment is not necessarily bad, unless we use it to paper over our guilt and hide it from ourselves while we keep playing spiritual one-upmanship. But that's the problem: Deep down, we all want to be stars, with our own fifteen minutes of celebrity.

But in Christ's kingdom, everyone stars; we help each other become authentic VIPs. We don't have to shove ourselves into a phony limelight.

So you're a born-again Christian? That's great. What other kind is there?

It's like saying, "I'm a United States of America Texan."

Every Christian is born again. There is no other kind. And this is precisely 1 Peter's positive affirmation.

Every Christian

The Christian life is Jesus Christ. Period. The Christian life is *not* Jesus Christ plus some particular kind of experience. Not Jesus Christ plus a spectacular conversion. Not Jesus Christ plus anything. (In this book, for instance, not Christ plus psychiatry.) The plus I add to Christ always becomes my way of feeling superior to other people. Which means I've plugged not into heaven, but into hell. I've connected myself not to sanity, but to its polar opposite. I can make myself a preposterous, proud Pharisee out of my own way of having been born again.

It's a beautiful exhibition of divine wisdom that evangelist Billy Graham has a wife whose conversion fits none of the conventional "new-birth" scenarios. Ruth Bell Graham is married to the great "hour of decision" apostle of crusade evangelism, through whom more people have had sudden and instantaneous rebirths than through any other preacher in history. Yet her own experience stands in surprising contrast to these dramatic conversions. The paradox is delightful.

Those who have the privilege of knowing the Grahams recognize how important Ruth is to her husband's life and ministry. Yet she cannot tell you exactly *when* she became a Christian. The daughter of Presbyterian missionaries in China, she came into her own relationship with Christ in a way that, from the outside, looked slow or gradual, almost unnoticed, without emotional fireworks.

Of course, from *God's point of view*, there was a "moment" when the great transaction took place. (You cannot be exposed to Ruth and Billy Graham separately or together and not be both grateful and inspired by that.) But from the *human point of view* that "moment" can very well pass unobserved or unrecognized. Ruth says, "I can't remember a time that I did not love Him and my earliest recollection is of deepest gratitude that He loved me enough to send Jesus to die for me."[6]

As surely as God raised up her husband for his role in world evangelization, I believe Ruth Bell Graham has been raised up, too. She has arisen not only for Billy, their family, and their ministry, but also as an ideal reminder for us all: The biographical details of "born-again" life will forever represent our infinite human variety.

In Your Own Way

To many of you who are Christians, who do believe, to whom Jesus Christ is your very own personal Lord, who have trusted him with your life, I say this to reassure you: On the authority of Scripture, *you have been born again.* Never let someone else's spiritual experience intimidate you. Whatever hurts you've suffered at the hands of human religiosity—and for many of us they are legion—remember that God himself is no bully. You don't need an experience like anybody else's. Whatever your Christian exposure or background— healthy or unhealthy—God made you uniquely you.

Religious cruelty is the worst kind. Without realizing what we're doing, unconsciously, we Christians throw our spiritual weight around to puff ourselves up and impress others. In the process, unintentionally, we cut other people down. Instead of affirming their uniqueness, listening to their story so as to give thanks for God in it, we imply they ought to feel as we do. Which to us means emotional idolatry and to them means spiritual brutality.

Theologians call this religious game playing "triumphalism"— and it's deadly in any form. In fact, I believe Billy Graham's greatness lies in his refusal to engage in this kind of spiritual one-upmanship. Consistently he points not to his own experience, but to Christ's cross.

It's a good lesson for us all. Love makes *the other person* feel important.[7] Feel your own eternal importance: If you believe in Christ as your Lord, you have been born again for a purpose far greater than you have ever dreamed.

Our Family Systems and a New Kind of Parenting

The idea of being born again carries within it the reality that we are given new parenting—a new Father and, therefore, a new family. This new parenting offers us a way to transcend the inevitable, often unconscious, snarls from our original family relationships. The new birth always remains, therefore, inherently and inescapably psychological. It offers us, and calls us to, psychological growth.

As I intimated, the work of Sigmund Freud, who started his pivotal writing in Vienna in 1895,[8] has had both good and bad consequences for the twentieth century. It has been bad in that it pushed along our collapse of personal morals, with so much attendant damage to so many people. But it has also been good, not just because individuals have been psychologically helped, but because, ultimately, psychology raises questions beyond itself.

I stand confident that, before the story ends, psychology will be a highway toward God. Secular psychology has shown convincingly that our very early experiences and foundational relationships have a powerful, perhaps unalterable, influence on the fabric of our lives. It valiantly tries to trace and unravel these thread balls of twisted and knotted relations between parents and children. Finally it runs headlong into the ultimate futility of undoing the past and the unexpected wisdom of Jesus the Psychologist: "You must be born again."[9]

Life Is Relationships

Why did Jesus, then and now, discuss our discipleship in categories modern behavioral science calls the most important to us emotionally? Precisely because two thousand years before Freud, Jesus knew that life is relationships.

Relationships lie at the heart of the commandments Jesus cited as the first and greatest, "Love the Lord your God with all your heart, mind, soul and strength," and also the second, "Love your neighbor as yourself."[10] And to answer the question of just who a neighbor is, Jesus told the Good Samaritan story, which shows that our neighbor is the person close at hand who needs help.[11] Is anyone closer at hand than our family members?

This relationship principle, personal and universal, pervades both the Hebrew scriptures and the New Testament. Consequently, the doctrine of the Trinity—the understanding that God is, within himself, relationships of perfect *agape* love—has never been more dramatically ahead of us, beckoning us on to fresh breakthroughs in psychological hope: reconciliations *of* our broken relationships, better interactions *within* our present relationships, and new priorities *for* all our relationships.

Seen in this light, Jesus' hard words about families and relationships begin to make sense. For instance:

> If anyone comes to me without "hating" his father and mother and wife and brothers and sisters, and even his own life, he cannot be a disciple of mine. The man who will not take up his cross and follow in my footsteps cannot be my disciple.[12]

What is so hard about Jesus' words? From his research in family therapy, psychologist Daniel Goleman concluded that, to uncover our unhealthy family schemas, we first have to penetrate our "vital lies." These are half-truths, hidden secrets, and unconscious deceptions taught by the family to keep it happy, special and invulnerable.

Therapy for the family begins when members start being honest about each other as human beings. This requires being open about ourselves and our false priorities. Human, realistic priorities for ourselves constitute, in Dr. Goleman's phrase, "simple truths" about ourselves and the way we are made.[13]

Jesus' words here contrast the vital lie of our family priorities with the divine truth that his cross, for us all, is the ultimate priority.

Ruthlessly Jesus demands precedence over *all* our up-close human associations. He claims supremacy above all our relatives, particularly those connections most psychologically intimate (including ourselves). This preeminence, beyond any human loyalties, soars as high as love above hate. Our allowing him such an absolute priority, by the free assent of our human wills, allows his Spirit to change the mixed-up confusions of our families toward orderly, loving maturity.

In Christ we are born into a new set of priorities that alone have power to transform all our relationships. As C. S. Lewis said, "When first things are put first, second things do not become less, but more."

Unconscious to Conscious Relationships

The second half of 1 Peter 1 sheds light on our interrelational blindness, contrasting our potential, as "obedient children" of a new and perfect Parent, with our only other option, to be disobedient children of disobedient parents, as in our "previous 'ignorance.'"[14] From our previous half-aware relationships we start moving toward more conscious ones.

In this particular passage three unusual Greek terms—word combinations used here and here alone in the New Testament[15]—spring out. Each points to the freedom that comes with our new parenting. Perhaps all three emerge from forty years of pondering that Great Confession interchange.

This first word, *anazosamenoi,* is found in verse 13. It is translated in the New International Version as "prepare," but the older and sexier King James translation, "gird up," comes closer to the image sketched out in the Greek.[16] It refers to the robes all Orientals wore back then and the necessity for people to wrap them up around their loins and waist to be able to run, thus fashioning a sort of multilayered exercise belt or jockstrap. This energetic word compound graphically pictures alert self-control. The verb conveys a Marine drill sergeant barking, "Suck in your gut!"

But the next words tie the apostle's thought, not to the gut, but to the body's *reproductive* zone, the sex organs, and then to the body's *mental* processes.[17] The King James translation says: "gird up the loins of your mind."

The second term is *aprosopolemptos*. This word from verse 17 is translated "impartially" in the NIV. Verses to come will describe this new Father, to whom we have been born, as just, merciful, and of unchanging availability, but first he is depicted as "without partiality."[18] To counter both parents' and children's preferences, prejudices, biases, and unfairnesses, Peter has coined a portrayal of our new Father's alternative: The God we worship is the Spirit of parent-child relationships unsullied by *favoritism*.

Third is *patroparadotou*. This word from verse 18 means "handed down to you from your forefathers," or, more fully in context, "you have been ransomed [with the precious blood of Christ] from your *futile ways such as come down from your forefathers*."[19] It points to the attitudes we have absorbed from our parents. Then the thought completes itself with two other words speaking of the various "twists and turns" on the paths of our lives—our behavior, "way," or conduct.[20] We could restate this whole "kinks in our personalities" concept, as Peter does, relationally: "useless personality patterns handed down through your parents and your original family's psychological systems."

Beyond Original Families

I have a theory about Simon Peter's own useless personality patterns, specifically about his unstable crowd-prone impetuosity. I theorize that Simon felt himself closer to Jane than to Jona. To me, his personality seems tied more strongly to his mother than to his father; he is anything but a loner. I also theorize that he had another brother or sister whom, he sensed, his father favored. (We know he had a brother, Andrew, but he may have had other siblings, too.) Call this Hypothesis 101. According to my theory, Simon always feared, somehow, that he had never had his father's approval, had never measured up, had never sparkled in Dad's eyes. And all this feeling got layered, forgotten but not forgotten, down in Simon's unconscious mind.

As for favoritism in the other direction, child to parent, I think Simon preferred Mama—classically Oedipal, psychiatrists would say. Simon felt more secure with his mother. Feeling rejected by his dad, blindly he rejected back, favoring Mother without realizing it. Or perhaps Simon himself set off the whole cycle, initially prefer-ring his mother and thus triggering his father's reserve.

This theory, particularly if you include the lone-male father ste-reotype and the group-nurturing mother stereotype (our historic sexual-pattern conventions), would explain Simon Peter's defense-lessness against peer pressure. When peer pressure began closing in on him, pushing him one way or the other, he overreacted out of his overdependence on his mother. The crowd's opinions, to his subconscious, represented Mama. Peer pressure, then, was Mama pushing him; without her support (because he didn't feel his fa-ther's) he was lost. Fear of his father, or estrangement from him, translated into fear of not being "in" with people.

The night Jesus was betrayed, on three different occasions, Peter denied he knew his Lord.[21] He couldn't withstand the sway of the crowd. His same problem surfaced again many years later in the dispute with Paul over whether Gentile converts ought to be cir-cumcised. He couldn't stand against the gang by himself; his fear of his mother's abandonment crippled him. Simon Bar-Jona acted spoiled. And, like many spoiled children, he came off simultane-ously as loud, pushy, and insecure. We call his syndrome by a famil-iar name: Mama's Boy. It nearly ruined him; Simon heard roosters crow a lot.

Whatever you think of my theory, and I admit I may be transfer-ring my own psychological speculations onto Simon, I'm convinced this problem is not unique. Do you notice the pattern on televised Sunday NFL games or Monday Night Football? When the camera swings to the sidelines or to the bench, featuring the hero of the last great quarterback sack or that gravity-defying touchdown catch, what's the good word? You're right, you've got it: A wave to the camera and, "Hi, Mom!"

I keep wondering, Where's Dad?

But the new birth starts all us spoiled Mama's boys toward becom-ing a new kind of Papa's men with a new kind of inner strength, the kind of strength that suffers—willingly for others—on a cross alone.

The New Freedom

From a shackling past, this Heavenly Father change in us begins producing a fresh kind of freedom . . . the liberty of being obedient children in a new family. This new family connection starts Simon relaxing with his dad—no longer driven to change Jona, to die for his approval, to love him in hate, to continue the war. Each generation, in peace, accepts and forgives the other's imperfections, unchained by a higher Parent-Child love.

That's what people began to sense when Peter stood up at Pentecost, speaking fearlessly to the very ones who seven weeks before had crucified his Lord; they recognized in him and his companions a new, bold, inner authority. These apostles became spiritual astronauts, transmitting back to earth their transcosmic flight, calling all humanity into a new orbit.

They reported the flight before they'd even started studying it: They had seen, in the man Jesus' face, realism beyond Mother Earth or Father Sky, realism beyond life and death as we know them, realism for us humans beyond extraterrestrial exploration. They had seen the Ultimately Real.

Depression like mine, as I told you, sees life through dark, dark glasses. These men, with struggles just like ours, had seen the living, human Light.

Have we in the church today *even begun* to grasp the Scripture's unrelenting, inescapable psychology? Listen again to some of the language about parents, children, our scrambled relationships, and our promised new birth:

> So God created man in his own image; in the image of God he created . . . male and female.

> But to all who did receive him . . . he gave the right to become children of God, not born of any human stock, or by the fleshly desires of a human father, but the offspring of God himself.

> For if you forgive other people their failures, your Heavenly Father will also forgive you. But if you will not forgive other people, neither will your Heavenly Father forgive you your failures.

> Forgive . . . not seven times, but seventy times seven!

Be as ready to forgive others as God for Christ's sake has forgiven you.

The Jerusalem that is above is free, and she is our mother.

First be reconciled to your brother, . . .

Now that you have purified yourself by obeying the truth so that you have sincere [unhypocritical] love of your brothers, love one another deeply, with all your hearts. For you have been born again.[22]

The liberty of the new birth grows within us as we realize that God's forgiveness establishes the difference between an all-loving God and incompletely loving parents, and empowers us to forgive our parents for being human, or for trying to hide it. We are freed, increasingly, into unhypocritical love.

Whatever falsehoods our subconscious minds may surface to us, the new birth tells us the truth. The Family of God is a brand-new psychological system, a reborn relational reality, an intergenerational saving therapy. In this new family, nobody is a nobody. Through your new Father within, you are somebody very important—inimitably distinguished at this present moment and forever more.

Growing from Insecurity into a Positive and Powerful Identity

Simon Peter knew out of his own gut that our fundamental problem is insecurity. In a fallen world we will never get away from that. We'd better get in touch with it: We're all vulnerable.

Life is never a question of whether I'm going to feel insecure or not, just where. I may get apprehensive here in my office, wondering what you'll think of my writing, or in my car when I leave here wondering if a policeman will stop me on the highway. Here, there, or wherever, I'm going to spend my life coping with a lack of self-confidence. We all, in various ways, have persona non grata feelings. We are ashamed. We are not acceptable. We are not welcome. We bury, beneath our bravados, this hidden sense of being persons without a place, without credentials, without acceptance, without significance. Deep down in our secret selves, we all quake with "unimportant nobody" anxieties, with scared, self-conscious fears.

Three phrases from the first chapter of 1 Peter contain promises about our new birth into new and living hope. I have found that these three reassurances contain an antidote for insecurity, depression, and despair, a proven remedy for negative thinking. These verses promise that "nothing can destroy or wither" our resurrection relationship with Christ: It "is kept for you in heaven," "under the protection of God's power."

And that *is* security. It addresses our pit-bottom fear of death, nothingness, insignificance, mortality, meaninglessness, futility. I have been born into an everlasting relationship with an everlasting Father. Gradually I am becoming aware that Christ himself within me is the essence of my maturing. My personal relationship with him grows. For the rest of my life I walk forward into new and ground-gaining stages of this maturation. My growth may proceed on a jagged curve, first up, then down. Still, I stand more firm and solid this year than last, and more steadily strong now than before.

Every experience, sad or glad, cultivates our real and inward advance. As we grow, we become more stable and secure; our growth produces assurance as a by-product. Making headway progressively, we develop our own identity—powerful, common to us all, yet unique to each one of us.

And what is that identity? It is spelled out for us. Our identity is as "priests":

> You . . . are . . . to be a holy priesthood, offering spiritual sacrifices acceptable to God through Jesus Christ.
>
> . . . But you are a chosen people, a royal priesthood.

Everybody a Priest

Grasping the import of "priests" in twentieth-century language comes hard. How can I bring you today the sense of power and significance this "priest" word brought to Peter's first-century readers? Priesthood to them represented major influence, command, and authority.

Remember two things. First, the *only* commonplace politics then, in both Jewish and Gentile societies, was the sacral state, the government whose control was buttressed by an official religion.

Priests carried enormous social clout. They got things done; they were the movers and shakers, the strategic people to know. They established the cultural climate. Priests held the smooth inside levers of public power; they were capable, for instance, of getting Jesus crucified on short notice. Today the ordinary priest probably runs a weak second in perceived social impact to teachers and other secular professionals, business and administrative executives, political and governmental officials. Not then. Priests, in that day, rode high as *very* influential people.

Second, remember that neither Jesus himself, the carpenter, nor Simon, the fisherman, nor any of the other disciples represented these "professional priests" in their own Jewish politico-religious hierarchy. According to the Jewish religious establishment, they were like you and me, ordinary lay people.

Now consider something else: Priests, to Peter's Jewish readers, meant the designated order of men who performed sacrifices of animal blood to cleanse away sins before the altar in the temple. This ancient idea of priesthood allowed the priest, and only the priest, legitimate standing in God's presence. But followers of Christ's way believed that priestly function had ended once for all in the shedding of Christ's own blood as a sacrifice for our sins.[23]

No longer, Peter is saying, do religious sons and daughters (lay people) have to live in fear of the priests, the religious fathers. The Son's being Resurrected by the Father means favoritism finished, hierarchies healed, relationships reconciled: All of us have equally legitimate standing before God; we are all priests.

And that's why the apostle psychologized this spiritual-hierarchical word to its central core: Priests are leaders who represent God to other people and represent other people to God. Or, phrasing it another way, priests lead by serving God and people in spiritual realism and human integrity.

Peter described the *whole* Christian church as priests. He spells out our specially chosen priesthood identity, picturing Christ's twin-focused stereoptic vision of the new humanity: In the first view, our universal consecration ("a *holy* priesthood"); in the second, ("a *royal* priesthood") our universal leadership. Each of us is a priest. Perpetually it remains an explosive concept: *universal priesthood.*

Peter's growing inner awareness of, and confidence in, his own leadership capacity constitutes his new-birth legacy to all us nobodies (in times past "not a people") who steadily and increasingly realize we have become somebodies ("now . . . the people of God"). And what is the visual vehicle Simon uses to convey our new, priestly somebodyness? He gives us the verbal picture from his own Great Confession dialogue forty years before. It's Peter's own new identity in us all; he says we've all become stones, we've all been made rocks.

Rocks. But not *the* Rock. *Christ*—not Christians—is the rock on which the church is built. Simon uses five verses to make sure we get the point. You remember: It's the section that begins "As you come to him, the Living Stone—rejected by men but chosen by God and precious to him—you also, like living stones, are being built into a spiritual house" and then goes on to call Jesus the "cornerstone" and "capstone" of the faith.

Peter's graphic illustration depicts nearly four decades of his gradually becoming convinced of what Jesus' words and deeds meant for his life . . . and for ours. Those words and deeds, and everything since then confirming them, have now finally persuaded his Simon-Jona-Jane insecurity that he is, in fact, somebody very important, not a peer-pressured, crowd-shoved jelly-legs.

That intimate assurance, Peter's own by-now-well-put-together steadiness about himself, no doubt explains how he can convey to his fellow Christians these heavy power titles of "stones" and "priests." He is by now, like Christ, so confident of his own leadership that instead of clutching authority to himself, he wants to give it away to others. Spiritually grown, he at last knows for certain he is special; for that settled reason, he longs for all other people to know that *they are special,* too. Later in this book you see just how this everyone-a-priest churchly democracy relates to Peter's apostolic authority.

Peter's verbal pictures—"him, the Living Stone . . . you also, like living stones . . . built into a spiritual house"—portray the new birth as not only individual, but also social, not only single rocks, but also, together, a house. It's the same idea Jesus painted of Peter himself so long before.*

---

*Why does Peter use the word *stone* instead of *rock* in referring to his—and our—new nature? To me it seems apparent that Peter's *modesty* forbade his using *petros*

Twice here, in fact, Peter uses the very root verb from the Great Confession story, "to build a house, to construct, establish." Three times he uses the word "chosen"; three times the word "laity, people of God."[24]

With such repetition, the apostle hammers at our universal priestly identity. We have now become *personae gratae*, acceptable persons, persons with grace, an elect race, a holy nation, God's own special people. "His wonderful light"[25] has overcome the darkness in our psychological histories by the brightness of a complete and perfected mercy. This is the promised kingdom with keys, a mutually reinforcing community of gloriously forgiven somebodies.

On Baptist Quiz Games

It is possible for you to be born again and not be fully aware of it or completely sure about it. Baptists sometimes play a game, often without much awareness of its being a game, by asking each other, "When did you get saved?" Which, of course, is our code word for the question, "When did you get born again?" Sometimes the question is asked so aggressively, so soon after first introductions, that it's almost like a Baptist inquisition.

The safest way to answer, of course, at least in our evangelical culture, is to have the date, time, and place firmly in mind and on the tip of your tongue. But that can be a problem for people whose experience hasn't fallen neatly in a time-date-place cubbyhole. Let me tell you my own story, for instance, starting with the very dramatic change Christ made in my life when I was a college student.

I had been a rebellious teenager throughout high school. Granted, mine was sort of a tame *Baptist* rebellion, as rebellions go, but for me it was a genuine, first-class adolescent revolt. Then I was confronted through people in the youth program at our church, and my life turned around dramatically. A whole new devotion to Christ

---

or *petra*, the Greek words for "rock" which Jesus had used in Matthew 16:18. Since Peter is so clearly spelling out for us that Christ himself is "the Living Stone" (2:4), he couldn't very well choose his own name (even if it were new) as a description for his Lord. Therefore, he uses a synonym for "rock," the parallel word *lithos* or "stone," except in 1 Peter 2:8, where he uses *petra* as the "stone rejected."

replaced my wildness, and soon I was witnessing, singing, preaching, and evangelizing, all as a layman. Some of my readers who heard me speak in those years might remember my personal testimony. It focused on this dramatic collegiate transformation.

I certainly wasn't misleading anyone; the story was totally accurate and wonderfully true, even though I may have been unconsciously influenced by the fact that sensational conversion stories sell better to Baptist crowds. But all this time, a question secretly bothered me. Exactly when *had* I been saved?

I remembered my childhood experience from years before, but I wasn't sure of its authenticity. Episodes of depression made the question emotionally acute: How could I be certain I was born again? Had it happened when I "walked the aisle" as a young boy? Or when I "rededicated my life" as a college student? Or on another college night after reading the Scots Presbyterian preacher James Stewart's *The Gates of New Life*, when I had prayed, "Lord Jesus, if I've never received you before, I do now"? For each of those occasions today I'm thankful. But despite them, there were times (usually when I was depressed) that I would become unsure, sometimes really tortured as to just when I was saved.

Many years passed, and I went on with my life—working in the family business, continuing to preach, my depressive episodes getting worse. Then, finally, the psychiatrist. Did that man, now my dear friend, ever have a more resistant patient? More pious? More proud? But at last, humiliated that I had been so slow, I started hearing what he was saying: "Howard, if you ever want to be a well man, you're going to have to start talking to your dad about how you feel."

I did and I improved.

Later came a vocational crisis: Should I stay in the family business or not? This was followed by a severe depression—not as bad as before, but bad nonetheless. In its midst my Oklahoma oilman friend Keith Miller gave me *My Utmost for His Highest*, by the pioneer biblical psychologist Oswald Chambers. Chambers challenged me with two powerful insights: His "white funeral" concept of death to self—deliberately choosing to yield myself to God rather than to my idolatrous ego, and his penetrating observation that "a great many Christian workers worship their work."[26]

This hit home. I realized—and my beginning to think psychologically had prepared me for this realization—that my Christian work, my lay ministry, had become my idolatry, my unconscious way of competing with Dad. He was a big-shot groceryman; I'd just become a bigger-shot lay preacher.

So for my own version of a "white funeral" I knelt beside the green ottoman in the guest bedroom at our family ranch house and prayed, "Our Father, I commit to you my work. Little or big, it's yours to decide. All I want is the life of the Lord Jesus manifest in my mortal body."

As soon as I prayed that prayer, knowing I had done business with God at a deeper level than ever before, the thought hit me, pure, clear, and calm: "Why, this is exactly the same as it was when I received Christ for the first time as a nine-year-old boy!"

Since that day, I have never worried about when I was converted, and I have never again been so badly depressed. I've been through some vicious low spells since then, but never again that dark or heavy. And from that particular extended pain, I learned two interrelated lessons:

First, even if we lack perfect assurance, God always intends a good purpose from our pain, one which will become clear on his own patient schedule. If you struggle with doubts about your own experience, my words to you are "hang in there." You may never know exactly "when." But you can, as I did, grow into a deeper confidence that you are Christ's, that you really have been reborn in him. (You might, in addition, ask yourself if there's anybody you're holding some hard feelings against.)

Second, our relationship with Christ inevitably involves our relationship to people—especially those who are closest to us. My experience as a nine-year-old, for instance, was all mixed up with Mother and Dad. Mother took me to the Sunday night evangelistic service where I trusted Christ; Dad also went with me a few Sunday nights later when I was baptized.

So today it all makes sense: How could a God who *is Love* grant the deeper spiritual composure I craved when such contradictory tangles and unreal denials characterized my deepest inward attitudes toward the two people whose love gave me my physical origins and my spiritual heritage? My assurance with Christ cannot be separated from reconciliation, forgiveness, health, and love in my relationships with my own personally important other people.

Shortly before my "green ottoman prayer," I received clear insight that Christ had died and risen again specifically to handle my relationship with Dad—and every other complicated relationship, too. Whenever we know anyone well, is there any relationship that isn't complicated? Chambers says every human relationship is potential hell.[27] It's enough to drive a person to Christ. But after that insight in 1961, I had the years I felt best about in the business and in my *entire* lifetime's relationship with Dad.

So, how do I answer the quiz question now, "When did you get saved?" The last time anyone asked me, I enjoyed my unselfconscious answer: "At Calvary." And the next time someone in a Baptist foyer asks me, "When did you get born again?" I think I'll say (referring them to 1 Peter), "That first Easter morning, through the Resurrection of our Lord Jesus Christ from the dead."

To trust this reality is to be "born again" day after day, growing in the positive process of becoming priests and pastors to each other. Such progress within us, individually, offers an adequate and practical hope that the world's marriages, families, and organizational systems can be changed.

3

How to Live with Each Other

The Painful Truth

◦❧

1 Peter 2:11–4:19

Every time I see a "Yield" sign on the
highway, I feel sexually threatened.
—*Lily Tomlin*

*O*ur inward healing brings with it growth in all our relationships. After my deepened 1961 faith commitment, I
began in a new way, not only to get more in touch with my own
feelings, but also to get more in touch with painful stresses between
other people in our family, the company, and wider religious circles—destructive tensions to which I had been blind.

I then—unconsciously, I realize now—began trying to act as an
agent of healing with, for, and among these others. I began to learn
that an ongoing new birth means, not just newness about sermons,
stained-glass, and choirs, but perhaps, even more, in relationships,
in our everyday run-of-the-mill tangles, tempers, and torments.

To say it another way, I began to be more politically aware. But
not as that might sound to you—not city, state, or national politics.
As a matter of fact, after that 1961 Ranch prayer, I resigned from
two Washington positions involving government.

No, my new awareness was for the up-close politics of our marriage, our family, and our company. For instance, in my job as a
grocery company vice president (my position since 1951), with

Dad's pleased agreement I decided to take over personally, at head-quarters, our firm's merchandising—both for my sake and for the sake of other executives involved. It proved healing for everybody. My new relational-political awareness thus produced what I mentioned: My best years ever with Dad and the company.

How do we function in the ordinary nitty-gritty arenas where human personalities rub up against each other and generate sparks over who leads and who follows, who gets what (and why), and how things change for the better? How do we apply, practically, this new secure and important identity we've been given as priests? How do we move past the self-delusion that we love others when what we actually want is to control them? How do we practice peacemaking, not only among races and nations, but also close-in at home, and at work?

This, unfortunately, brings us back to the question of suffering. To be honest, suffering isn't my favorite thing to talk about, much less to do. On my slack-brained days, I feel it would be nice if I could grow as I relate to others with no distresses, no afflictions, no chastisement, no instruction, and no discipline. And I would certainly rather live without having to give in to other people—in my own family or outside it. I don't like being told what to do, and I've never enjoyed being corrected. Who does?

But, as Peter began learning immediately after his Great Confession, Jesus thinks in a drastically different way. Over the years, Peter must have pondered the frightening significance of that black moment when Jesus turned his back and retorted, "Get behind me, Satan!"[1] You wouldn't forget it, either. Not that. You'd keep wondering—as Peter wondered: Why did Jesus blast me just then? What did I do wrong? What did he mean?

After all, Peter had just been responding naturally to Jesus' prediction that he must suffer and die. Even after acknowledging him as the Son of God, Peter obviously hadn't been able to fathom Jesus' talk about sorrow and pain.

It took Peter many years to understand what Jesus was saying, but he finally got the point, and his mature understanding of how Jesus intended for us to live together in the friction of relationships—and how that way of living can transform those relationships—forms the gist of the next two and a half chapters of his first Epistle.

The Hot Topic of Submission

The next chapter and a half of the Epistle leaves many educated believers today embarrassed. That's because these passages involve the subject of our mutual submission, which is about as misunderstood and distorted, unpopular and hated a topic as I can think of, especially when it comes to male-female relationships. Feelings on this question have gotten so tense that genuine communication has almost stopped. People have chosen between being fundamentalist and antifundamentalist, traditionalist and revolutionary, right and left. Even those who try to take a center path feel the heat.

(Years ago a right-winger blasted my centrist position on governmental politics: "The only certainty about the middle of the road is that you get run over!" Which reminds me of John Peer's Law of Enough Already: "The more you run over a dead cat, the flatter it gets."[2] Well, no need to fear. There may be flattened cats on the left and right and even in the center, but Truth is no dead cat. As the Presbyterian writer Ben Patterson says, "The Christian life is not the middle way between two extremes. It is the narrow path between two precipices."[3])

On one side of the submission issue stand those who approach the biblical teachings legalistically and interpret them literally in terms of who, with divine approval, may do what. This mind-set commends itself to us in that it takes the Bible seriously, and many people manage to live creatively and productively inside its strictures.

But you know what tends to happen with the literalistic approach. Too often it solidifies into a rationale for domination and autocracy. It becomes a club wielded against those who are supposed to submit: women, citizens, congregations, employees. And the "submitters" in turn often use submission as an excuse to forego responsibility: "I was just following orders."

At the other extreme on this question stand those who, often in reaction against the abuse of the submission passages, choose to discount or ignore them. Many New Testament students hold these particular Scriptures to be culturally conditioned and therefore irrelevant today. By cultural conditioning they mean that Peter wrote in a patriarchal, nondemocratic age, and that we can't possibly expect him to be intellectually progressive on this kind of issue now. So keep preaching the Gospel, they say, but take those submission passages with huge grains of salt.

Some go so far as to dismiss the submission sections entirely. Their belief resembles that of Martin Luther's on the Epistle of James. The Wittenberg reformer's enemies often used the Book of James and its emphasis on human works to counter his concept of salvation through biblical faith. In response, Luther summarily demoted James's Epistle to a lower grade, branding it "an epistle of straw." Just so, today some scholars straightforwardly downgrade all the submission portions of the New Testament.

Their viewpoint, of course, raises the question of how much of the Scripture they thereby consign to straw-dust. Big portions of Paul's writing would have to go—at the least, sections of Romans, Ephesians, and Colossians—in addition to chunks of Hebrews and, no doubt, the substance of 1 Peter.

But an even more important problem of the "culturally conditioned" argument is that it misses the broader context of what Peter and Paul both understood so clearly about the whole biblical revelation—an understanding that is inextricably tied to the very nature of God himself.

The Trinitarian Paradox: Authoritative Submission

Both Peter and Paul understood that, in the man Jesus, humanity had at last glimpsed the true nature of *divine authority and power.* More explicitly, Peter and Paul intuited the perfect Triune relationship—of *agape* love—at the center and the circumference of the universe: the Father, the Son, and the Holy Spirit.

Even though the Church would not philosophically spell out the doctrine of the Trinity for several centuries, trinitarian dynamics permeate all the New Testament. Only the Trinity explains the New Testament's near-at-hand politics.

Peter and Paul grasped viscerally (by inspired intuition) the *organizational implications* of a God who is Triune: the Father over the Son, the Son under the Father, the Spirit uniting Father and Son in full equality—as fully one as if they were not three, as fully three as if they were not one.

This open mystery, this human enigma, this seeming paradox combines two virtues we otherwise see as irreconcilable: hierarchy and equality. In eternally authentic love, hierarchy (the Father) and equality (the Son) are not opposites. Instead, they are incredibly one, held together by a mediating reality (the Holy Spirit) that stands on equal footing with both of them.

Christ came to reproduce this dynamic paradox of Triunity in us, which explains why the universal priesthood idea was so essential, as Peter's conceptual preface, before his teaching of submission. Peter, in presenting submission as a key to living together, thinks synergetically—he presents us with *authoritative* submission.

This paradoxical principle rests at the core of all healthy biblical interpretation, for it springs from the heart of the Trinity, from the fully divine, fully human nature of Christ himself, from his Servant-Leader character and psychology.

So first, theologically speaking, I believe that discounting or dismissing the New Testament passages on submission constitutes a serious mistake. Many "culturally conditioned" Bible teachings obviously do require translation into contemporary principles. And we must always beware of literalistic and legalistic approaches to the Bible, remembering that just such a negative mind-set produced the manipulative spirit of the Pharisees, an unconsciously sick submission to religious tyranny. But to brush off the submission passages as unpalatable and offensive today is to throw away the very relational key Christ died to give us: a key to relationships based in the very nature of God himself. Christ is the suffering *Servant*-King: The submission passages of the Epistles *implement* the servant passages of the Gospels.

Second, in a psychological sense, our twentieth-century readiness to reject biblical submission out of hand increasingly strikes me as uninformed, provincial, and arrogant. Do we really suppose that we know better *now* than the New Testament writers did *then* about how humans can live with one another? After all, if we know-it-all moderns have insights so superior to the Source Book on how to get along, why doesn't our vaunted brilliance pay off by curing our marriages, families, jobs, and public lives? Our easy dismissal of the biblical models would carry more weight if we got along better on our own.

Too Simple, Too Fast, Too Cheap

That same reasoning—both theological and psychological—applies to the way we approach the question of who submits to whom—who leads and who follows. This, after all, is the essence of institutional change—social change, political change, change on our jobs, change in our marriages.

Do we think our twentieth-century fascination with the ideal of revolution as a quick route to change is something new? Jesus could have been a Zealot, a Jewish revolutionary; he had one such malcontent among his followers.[4] But Jesus thought through things too clearly for that. Instead, he modeled and explained a positive way of relating to others that, when followed, becomes *truly* revolutionary in its transforming implications and is actually capable of breaking the old patterns of might and right with new patterns of organizational love.

Quickie shortcuts to institutional transformation inevitably fail. Revolution against autocratic leadership, as in yesterday's France or czarist Russia, is followed by yet another type of autocracy, as in Napoleon or Stalin. Stereotypical revolutions produce stereotypical tyranny. Their change is too simple, too fast, too cheap. Instead of bringing about real change, they end up producing only more of the dictatorial same. The Russian revolution produces the Gulag; the French produces Waterloo. Office intrigue may succeed at getting the boss fired, but the ambitious employee who takes the boss's place can turn out even bossier.

Institutional change that is Trinitarian, instead, following the Servant Christ who suffered *under* Pontius Pilate, always starts from underneath, from the bottom, from below. It hinges on *chosen* humility; rather than the servant's overthrowing the leader, the servant-leader underneath chooses to *be* the servant. This new influence, from below, of Triune love, enables the leader above to change into a leader who serves. Christ died to give Pilate, along with all the rest of us, the chance to begin again.

Leadership transformation on top starts from servant-kings beneath. The Holy Spirit—authoritative yet submissive—is this servant-leader character within us, leading us but also serving us. The leader Father could not be Triune without the servant Son and the uniting Spirit, who coordinates both the others into one.

Authoritative submission is inherent from first to last in Peter's understanding of how we live together in positive, constructive ways. We stand so rock-solid in our priestly identity as somebodies, with the divine gift of leadership, that we can serve others without fear of being nobodies. Servant-leadership reveals itself as the solved paradox of Triune love: The leader leads only to serve; the servant serves only to lead.

Demolishing Sexist Stereotypes

Authoritative submission as Peter describes it applies to all relationships, not just those between men and women. Today, however, the submission topic makes the loudest noises and starts the biggest fights in the arena of male-female relationships. It need not be so; we dare not let our historical male tyrannies—even our hellish misunderstanding of these very scriptures—shackle us.

In every single one of us, as well as in us all collectively, the *male principle* and the *female principle* are both indispensable. The two together unite in each individual to form our full sexual (male or female) identity. The traditionally defined masculine principle is authority; the feminine principle is submission. But social peace and psychological health require them in consensus, joined (appropriately for each sex) in every individual.

Harvard educational psychologist Carol Gilligan's research into differences between male and female moral development confirms this need for a complementary relationship between male and female. In her landmark book, *In a Different Voice*,[5] published in 1982, Gilligan observed that while males incline to talk of moral development in terms of *rules*, females tend to speak about it in terms of *relationships*.

Gilligan's psychosexual insights shed light on our broad modern despair: We can't solve public problems simply by adding more laws, regulations, prisons, lawsuits, and courts. Beyond that, however, Dr. Gilligan's findings underline the fact that the male principle and the female principle demand each other. Rules grow out of relationships and relationships depend on rules—and individuals and institutions need both.

This psychosexual reality also lies at the heart of Peter's authoritative submission teaching. Nothing spotlights our moral, behavioral, and spiritual immaturity more clearly than our failure to understand what he is really doing in these passages. For Peter writes knowing full well that "submission" is the traditional "feminine" stereotype and "leadership" the traditional "masculine" one—and that all of us need both. Not only does the Apostle refuse to succumb to popular patriarchy; he goes further and destroys it. Fearlessly he grasps the sexist stereotypes and turns them upside down:

Submission, the traditional feminine role, is not just for servants and women but for all Christians. Leadership, the quality traditionally consigned to males, belongs not just to male autocrats but to all of us universally. Institutions, which by their social or communal nature are stereotypically feminine, inclining toward matriarchal idolatry, become transformed for the good through love—creatively suffering, constructively therapeutic, authoritatively submissive love.

Since the "submission" of Christ's cross was stereotypically feminine but the "leadership" of his Resurrection stereotypically masculine, the two events, together, forever demolish sexist stereotypes. Far from advancing a historically decadent patriarchy, the teaching of this Epistle now looks breathtakingly advanced. Peter realized, exactly and deliberately, what he was doing; he made war against sexism nearly twenty centuries ago.

Far more than conventional modern authorities, Peter had become aware of the sexual insecurity of males. His choice of words about Sarah and Abraham, much stronger on the subject than anything in Paul, probably reflects his autobiographical insights and his awareness of his own personal needs as a married man.

He had observed firsthand that marriage is a feminine institution. When our roving male instinct agrees to settle down and restrict itself to one woman's nest, it agrees—organizationally—to commit itself to that woman's territory and influence: The home is the woman's domain.

So for the feminine institution of marriage to hold together, Peter knew that wives need to live by the principle of the strong helping the weak. Since the male tends to be the lone buck wandering away, leaving the doe with the fawns, the woman's authoritative submission is for her own welfare. The wife is also the more secure of the

two mates psychosexually—in her own individual gender identity—
by the monthly reinforcement of the menses, and/or by childbirth.

She can use these powers—her greater institutional and psychological strength—to give her sexually less secure husband reassurance and confidence. Her freely accepted pain of submission to him
in their marriage frees him for his mutually painful submission in
the marriage to her, as well as for his further submissiveness in
work and society elsewhere. She is the weaker vessel physically,
but *not* the weaker sex.

Peter's particular choice of words about husbands jumps out at
us, confirming that a Trinitarian organizational model was in his
mind. The husband is to live together with his wife according to
knowledge about God's Triune, relational nature, assigning his
spouse honor. They are to share a *mutual* hierarchy, living as *joint
heirs* of the grace of life. He gives us, therefore, a statement on
sexual equality as strong as any feminist could want: Men and
women are to be "heirs equally."[6]

While dismantling both matriarchy and patriarchy, a flexible
Trinitarian psychology (authoritative submission) affirms both
sexes without worshiping either. Contributing their indispensable
strengths to each other, both sexes progressively grow more pliable,
yet more established. Leadership is the stereotypical male principle, followership the female. Both principles, operating resiliently
within each of us, draw us toward fully developed health. These
male and female principles work together—in completeness—only
under Christ. Submission to him makes us unafraid of followership,
with and toward each other, precisely because his flexibility roots
itself in our one Father's primeval wellspring of leadership.

Authoritative submission confirms our experience with a Triune
God. When I took over company merchandising—after my deepened 1961 commitment—I freshly asserted my company authority.
But I did so only out of my new submission, from underneath, to
serve my father's leadership. My fresh spiritual growth was giving
me a new inner power relating to people—power that was internal
and qualitative rather than external and quantitative. In fact, I
missed the large numbers of people to whom I had preached . . .
their absence to me was painful. But I could sense—in my interior
life—that through this pain I was slowly growing toward my Christlike, true, authentic self.

Having laid a foundation, then, let's trace Peter's subtle logic through the Epistle's core. We proceed by asking four questions on authoritative submission as a key to living together: "Why?" "How?" "If?" and "Where?"

I. "Why?"

"Why?" implies both motive and goal.

First, motive.

Everything so far in the Epistle's psychology has spelled out our motive in this new and dramatically different way of relating to each other—in authoritative submission. For both those inside the believing community, and for those outside, the motive is the same: that basic spiritual reality traditionally known as faith. And how does our faith grow in its motivational power?

In an earlier era much like our own, an era of widespread disillusionment with revolutionary violence and its social benefits, the nineteenth-century English poet William Wordsworth described a spiritually mature person as "one in whom persuasion and belief has ripened into faith and faith become a *passionate intuition*."[7] In this description of a basic, relational, feel-it-in-our-bones faith, Wordsworth focused on the precise inner reality that underlies all the behavior described in this central section, the Epistle's heart.

And this reality, in turn, brings us straight back to our prior question of sex roles and submission, for such intuitive faith is fearlessly feminine. It *chooses* to yield to God, to submit, to surrender. It fulfills the prophet's vision: "For your Maker is your husband, the Lord of hosts is his name."[8] And again, "As a young man marries a maiden, so will your Builder marry you; as a bridegroom rejoices over his bride, so will your God rejoice over you."[9] This intuitive relating, this spiritual yielding, this instinctive trust in our Maker, produces big changes in our conduct—changes that loom as phantasms to eyes blinded by sexual stereotypes, changes that all of us, both male and female, dread as weak or feminine.

Christ makes males more male and females more female, paradoxically, by releasing each sex from its fears of its own and the other's strengths. Women grow unafraid to lead or to follow; men grow unafraid to follow or to lead. Differences between the sexes, in the process, are not minimized but heightened. Since each of us is created sex-specific, our spiritual and psychological development enhances that specificity by accepting and transcending it. We become more fully what we are. Our individuality's settled male or female identity rises beyond blurred and unconscious androgyny to deliberate, conscious flexibility: authoritative submission.

Margaret Mead explains not only why we read femininity as weak rather than strong, but also why relational faith demands its strong weakness, when she observes that "because of their age-long training in human relations—*for that is what feminine intuition really is*—women have a special contribution to make."[10]

Not only does intuitive faith—faith perceived as relationships—not panic at the feminine; it actually embraces it. Visceral faith makes sense precisely because it reproduces in us Christ's creative obedience, including obedience in human relationships.

When faith grows into a passionate intuition, when it turns relational, then it becomes credible. And that credibility—that rational believability—brings us from the *motive* for authoritative submission to its *goal*, which is authentic witness or evangelism.

The words *witness* or *evangelism*, like the term *new birth*, tend in our society to be loaded terms. To many people they evoke stereotyped images of TV preachers with their show-biz pompadours and flamboyant fund-raising. Even we others think of witness or evangelism in terms of their more overt forms: mass evangelism, personal witnessing, Christian education, literary or media outreach, or church-sponsored social service programs.

Peter's psychology gives us a view of evangelism much broader and deeper than any of these activities, important as they may be. He depicts our witness to those around us as a deep, underlying purpose of our life in Christ, as well as the natural outgrowth of a reproductive, virile faith based, unafraid, on passionate intuition. In these central two and a half chapters, Peter opens up the heart of the church's strategy for reaching out to everybody. It pivots on the practical, down-to-earth plan of our living *convincing* lives in interaction with others.

Nothing fancy. No souped-up techniques. Just ordinary life as it was then, as it is now.

At least seven times in the Epistle's inner core,[11] Peter points to our mission of outreach. In each case, he describes it not as special activity but as fundamental conduct and character, not as something we *do*, but as something we *are*. Evangelism is God's sovereign work "when he visits us,"[12] but it builds on the previous framework of our "turning up and down, back and forth." Conduct. Manner of life. Personality patterns. Psychology.

Particularly, Peter envisions that our *positive thinking* about all our troubles within, or our opposition without, will *intrigue* those who do not believe; that's why he advises us to "always be ready to answer anyone who asks you to explain the hope you have."[13] The Apostle envisions us as being people whose personality patterns are so convincing to skeptics that our witnessing and our evangelism is not hard sell but merely *explanatory*. We are to live persuasively. Then we are to stay available, modestly, to answer the cynic's questions.

Afflicted today by the "cult of verbal Christianity,"[14] most of us see evangelistic witness as *mere words*. The Apostle describes something different: attitudinal witnessing, wordless ethics of quiet example, the Good News influencing the unconvinced by almost unnoticed, daily, pedestrian relationships.

Did Jesus practice what he preached? No, he preached what he practiced, which is a lot harder to do. In Christ's vision, the verbal proceeds from a growing authenticity in our manifestation of *agape* love.

"Loving" people far away—whether through witness or evangelism, missions, or social service—becomes contaminated when we have fled our calling to love those close to us. When we ignore reality in our familial and vocational relationships, we end up unloading these relational malfunctions on our more distant relationships.

I may go to the ends of the earth to spread the Good News. But if I take with me my unresolved hostilities and unforgiven resentments from my childhood, adolescence, and adult life they will haunt me there, poisoning my impassioned good works. I will project or transfer into those faraway efforts, not unfeigned love but my own problems, sin, and sickness—all unintentionally.

Jesus wrestled right to the end, obedient to his Father, with his own human family relationships. During the days just preceding his final week, he went through a tense scene (over his schedule) with his brothers.[15] So, too, in our own ways, will we; otherwise we quit growing and turn phony. Chambers has written, "The deadliest Pharisaism today is not hypocrisy but unconscious unreality."[16]

Intuited Triunity incarnates our yielding relationship with a relational God into our authoritatively yielding relationships with each other. In the flow of everyday practical activities, we become "ministers of reconciliation."[17] The mind of the Triune Christ works in us—beyond our sexual stereotypes—progressively changing all our organizations, our institutions, and our structures, starting with our families and our marriages and moving out from there into jobs, spare-time activities, and governments.

II. "How?"

In such different institutions as family and government, living together in society requires the selfsame principles as living together in marriage. And vice versa. Marital intimacy demands no different thinking than in the politico-social order of our city halls. If it won't work in Washington, then forget it for breakfast tables and bedrooms. But if it can renovate our marriages, it can surely renovate Congress. The psychological and social principles we need for both institutions are identical, for in the final analysis the principles are not principles at all. They're descriptions of the nature of God himself—the Trinity.

Which brings us, inevitably, back to Christian submission, for it explicitly dominates chapters 2 and 3 of 1 Peter and implicitly chapter 4. The apostle introduces it in three divisions: Submission in society, submission in work, and submission in marriage.

The word *submission* raises grave questions. But positive thinking demands this word. Otherwise there is no way to think rationally about the *underside* of words like *order* or *leadership* or *teamwork*. How else do we adapt to or adjust to each other?

If you reject the word *submission* for its obvious dangers, you never actually describe what happens when we "get organized." It may be a perilous concept, but less so than to be blind to its continual reality all around us or to fly off unconsciously in all directions at once.

Negative thinking demands words like *rebellion* or *revolt*. These negative words bring us, of course, to *anarchy*, which literally means "without leaders." Herbert Marcuse, a prominent figure in the 1960s' countercultural revolution, spoke about "the power of negative thinking."[18] Traditional revolutionary movements, which inevitably depend, ironically, on submission from *their* followers, lack positive concepts for subsequently organizing their institutions, to replace those *against* which they revolted. Predictably, they turn totalitarian.

"Continuous rebellion," in fact, formed Mao Tse-tung's prescription for China's youth in his last-gasp mid-1960s Cultural Revolution. His idea emerged logically as the end point of negative thinking. "Continuous rebellion," however, carried within itself the unpleasant little problem of staying unendingly bloody. It ripped China apart. If you don't like submission, you might think of Mao's "continuous rebellion" as your other organizing option: "Father-murder as the ultimate social strategy!" It's more fun for the younger generation. More fun, that is, unless the unwilling-to-submit older generation, as in China's more recent Tiananmen Square, declares war.

By contrast, submission modeled on the Trinity demands the consent of the governed: The Son consents to the Father's governance by the enabling of the Holy Spirit. The Cross tells us it will never become too easy. The Resurrection tells us it will always triumph at last.

Work and Government

Working for and with my parents all my life has forced me to think a great deal about faith, families, and organizations. And the most important lesson I've learned about myself across these years is simple: I have an enormous capacity for self-deceit.

The "submission principle" drives my self-deceit into the open. I've learned more about God's *agape* love from Dad and Mother than from anyone else, unless it's my wife and children. And if you'd asked me, before I went to the psychiatrist, if I loved my Dad I'd have replied—insulted—"Of course!" But then I hadn't focused adequately on the lonely pain that was Dad's—the pain of being in charge. For the buck always stops somewhere; someone has to be the boss.

A friend, during that long-ago period, confronted me. Why did I so regularly get to work late? Why? Well, I'd never thought about it, except I knew it irritated Dad. "Howard," my friend said, "did it ever occur to you what a good way that is to hurt your Dad? To get at him? How better could you tell him that the grocery business, which means so much to him, isn't all that important to you?"

Could it have been, unaware, my parent-hate? My father-murder?

Even today, in our family, business, and operating foundation, unsettled conflicts from my unfaced childhood spew problems into my organizational present. They contaminate the agendas, not only with those who lead me, but also, just as surely, with those I lead. Adolescent revolt still infects me in my sixties!

Jesus didn't go through adolescent revolt. Instead, he went through adolescent authoritative submission. The story is obviously significant, the only glimpse we have of Jesus between his birth and his adulthood.

You remember: Age twelve, sitting in the Temple in Jerusalem with the Teachers, hearing them, questioning them, amazing them; his parents' meanwhile losing him in the big city crowds, their three-day searching before they found him, his frightened mother's rebuking of her Son; his calm explanation to her of his being about his "Father's business," (a positive assertion of preteen human *authority*); his then returning home with them, where he "was *subject to them*" (the same word Peter uses for "submit"[19]). His was an *authoritatively submissive adolescence*. Later, finally, he became "obedient unto death."[20]

If Jesus' path went through constant submission, none of us will stumble along toward full psychological health any other way. When St. Francis listed the principles for his followers' spiritual growth, he said, "Do the will of another, and not your own will."[21]

Such a healthy mutual submission—authoritative submission—can make government "of the people, by the people, for the people" work. It creates that flexibility between voters and officials by which democracy functions. Without it, force becomes the sole source of societal authority—sheer naked "power from the barrel of a gun." Witness our current street gangs; they illustrate. Or echoes of "Kill the Cops!" producing police brutality. By contrast, social interaction turns peaceful, personal, and human within mutual submission.

Our problem—let me be more direct . . . my own problem—even talking about submission lies in our confusion about the meaning of the word. We think of it either as being *obsequious,* which Webster defines as "much too willing to serve or obey; overly submissive; fawning," or else as being *servile,* which "suggests the cringing, submissive behavior characteristic of a slave . . . abject." But notice that Webster uses the submission word itself describing both these "fawning" and "abjectness" caricatures.

One prominent religious leader, in obvious resonance to my message, said after hearing me, "Howard, can't you find another word beside the word 'submission'?" I more than understand his concern; the warning he gave me pains me today by its realism. For whenever we lose the paradox of submissive authority, we lose submission's mutuality. Which loss means, not servant-leadership, but tyranny. For we all resist paradoxical thinking: It's not male and "analytical," it's female and "intuitive."

Yet I observe that the pivotal "consent of the governed" clause in our own Declaration of Independence comes to us from this very submission—or female—principle. Democratic elections, every two or four years, give us opportunity to vote for Congressional or Presidential candidates to whose authority we choose to submit. We may elect to vote for the challengers and against the incumbents, to change governments, to "throw the rascals out." But when we do, we "consent to be governed" by the rascals' replacements. In both cases, before and after the rascals' departure, one constant remains: the principle of submission. The entire timed process of our elected representative government encapsulates, in sequence, the paradox . . . the tempo, the pulsation of authoritative submission. For—let us be honest about both words' psychology—to consent to be governed is to choose to submit: *consent* is submission; *government* is authoritative.

III. "If?"

I like the Bible's intellectual integrity. It faces squarely the implications of submission, playing no games. The "white funeral" goes on all day every day: "For Thy sake we are killed all the day long."[22] Death to self remains a lifelong, never-ending process. Peter refuses honestly to ignore one inescapable fact: Submission is filled with suffering, and that suffering is primarily psychological.

Nevertheless, after reading that truth, we try to get around the suffering angle. Sometimes we twist healthy submission into a facile technique for getting our own way and manipulating people (often a fundamentalist trick). And sometimes we run the parallel—but identical—risk of turning leadership for social goals into a runaway bulldozer, crushing the few in behalf of the many (often a liberal trap). Both errors fight wholesome Christian obedience, which alone makes suffering healthy for ourselves and therapeutic for others.

Traditional "feminine" submissiveness, with its inevitable emotional hurts, becomes a model in social interaction, not only for females but also for males. Phenomenally, Simon's new birth security has grown; his macho swagger is a necessary crutch no longer. Now he is the self-confident, rock-solid male; standardized pictures have ceased to fit. Gone are the hackneyed swearing, the domineering put-downs, the cruel dirty jokes, the compulsive innuendoes, the one-of-the-boys bluster, the tough-guy façade, the subtle sexual braggadocio. Dying to his machismo, forsaking his masculine conceits, he has found himself anew. No longer does he need to *prove* his manhood; he *is* a man, a secure human male.

Submission's suffering, Peter has discovered, is essential for growing up. His own welfare has demanded it. Losing his life for Christ's sake, he has found it.[23]

But never to us, male or female, does this mean the melancholy victim's suffering for suffering's sake. Wisely intentioned Christian submission means neither masochism nor self-flagellation nor self-deprecating martyrdom. Rather, its pain is constructive and curative both for self and others. Christ in us alone knows how to love our neighbor as ourselves.[24] His cross is never self-destructive; it is only self-fulfilling.

Our *healthy* suffering is linked to Christ's in every one of Peter's relevant observations.[25] For example:

> To this you were called, because Christ suffered for you, leaving you an example that you should follow in his steps.

> It is better, if it is God's will, to suffer for doing good, . . . for Christ died for your sins.

Therefore, since Christ suffered in his body, arm yourselves also with the same attitude.[26]

In an age of televised fantasy, instant gratification, narcissistic heroes, chemical dependencies, pop-psychology fads, escapist addictions, and sexual confusion, we desperately need to hear these words. Maturity's insight embraces healthy—and declines unhealthy—submission and its suffering.

How Each Sex Wins

Given the fact that not all suffering or submission comes from a healthy source, the recent women's movement in America obviously springs from a great need. It declines unhealthy submission and asserts healthy authority.

But with all its great strengths, courage, and accomplishments, too often today's feminism buys into revolution's negative thinking. Refusing traditional feminine submission, it opts, instead, for traditional masculine assertiveness—trading one stereotype for another.

Unfortunately, since *men* don't like submitting to other people either, we now have a polarized society where healthy submission is out of style for both genders. So the "service society" abhors giving service.

Clearly, if any nation anywhere rejects traditional "feminine" submission, sooner or later that nation will destroy itself. If everyone expects to be served, and no one expects to accommodate others, its institutions, family systems, and social fabric will disintegrate.

I grow more and more convinced that our national hope at present lies in 1 Peter's vision, that, under Christ, American male leadership begins accepting traditionally female submission for itself—even though it hurts. Perhaps then, once more, American women will agree to do the same.

Don't be afraid. Ours is the promise of Abraham, Isaac, and Jacob, a universal promise, the promise of the ages. Remember the Genesis story of Isaac and Rebekah's twin sons, Jacob and Esau? Remember God's hair-raising words about that diametrically different pair: *"Jacob I loved, but Esau I hated"*?[27]

Hated? That's a scary thought, being hated by God. Besides, God is *love.*[28] How could a loving God hate?

The answer, of course, is that God hates what destroys us. Jacob is a picture of faith, Esau of antifaith. Jacob portrays obedience, Esau rebellion; Jacob was patient waiting, Esau impetuous haste; Jacob showed strong humility and peace, Esau traditional authority and war; Jacob embraced spirituality, Esau materialism; Jacob family loyalty, Esau its heedless forsaking.

But wait—there's one more—one that explains all the rest:

Esau represents rejection of the feminine.

Jacob represents its acceptance.

The twins' mother, Rebekah, was the drama's key player, following God's purpose revealed to her, fearlessly asserting spiritual authority. Her plan, thwarting her husband's favoritism and securing Isaac's blessing for Jacob, depended on Jacob's submitting and obeying her. And he did.

But in Esau's relationship toward Rebekah, rebellion's sad history got acted out in the bitter disappointment of his pagan marriages, their mother-son relationship further souring.[29] For men's sake in specific, God hates mother-murder too. The blessing of Jacob—finally, by Isaac—portrays psychological health: the unity of the parents and the healing of the generations. The whole narrative breathes Triune intimations and relational undertones.

"Trickiness" in the story represents *deceit* in us all, competing for parental approval with its prospect of established temporal and religious power; *immaturity* in both older and younger generations, offering—if acknowledged—reconciliation and growth; *feminine intuition*—reaching even past favoritisms, controversy, and contamination to promote familial welfare and long-term relationships; and *divine purpose*, wisdom, and sovereignty, revealed to submissive feminine initiative ("Rebekah went to inquire of the Lord") that uses even our sins for a good outcome.

"Jacob I loved": the Jacob whom God loved was "a quiet man, living in tents." By contrast, Esau was the rough, rugged, tough outdoorsman, "hairy . . . a skillful hunter, a man who lived in the open."[30] So much for male stereotypes: "Esau I hated." God hates rejection of the feminine. The macho man is doomed.

Suffering, in our submission, remains inevitable in a fallen world. Our only option is whether or not we make our traumas affirmative and praiseworthy, profitable for our benefit and others' welfare. Christ's devastatingly positive thinking shatters us, for it embraces "the *incredible all-rightness* of everything there is."[31] This "incredible all-rightness" includes the hard as well as the easy, the sorrows as well as the sunshine, the moans as well as the music.

Christ's confidence not only envisioned his cross, but also looked beyond it: "For the joy that was set before him [he] endured."[32] And that is why, in a bright and steady hope, we can identify our lesser wounds with his. Out of every negative experience of vexation, disquiet, or heartache—little or big—we can endure, wringing creative potential. Doing it won't take away the pain, but it speeds up tasting the joy.

IV. "Where?"

The biblical principles of new birth and new growth offer us hope and health for both personal and institutional renewal. But such change occurs only if we understand its principles well enough to keep reminding ourselves and each other that we *never* finally arrive, and never all at once.

Instead, we will probably go right on here in the land of our familiar living, from car to job to home, from day to week to year, in the same old relationship structures. But in the midst of these structures, a growing spiritual freedom from insensitive or self-defeating habits will provide us more and more psychological liberation.

Now, for the first time we don't have to stay tied to our earthly parents or our original families, either blindly blotting them out or else copying them dimly, unthinking. Every day we can be born again to increasing self-control, becoming our *true* selves. (By "losing" self we find it: the more God-control, the more self-control.) And this happens not only within ourselves, but within our current structures—as we live together in our existing relationships.

Why does our life together get so regularly stressed? Because with all the people with whom we live and work, we develop certain negative practices or patterns that are rooted, not only in long-established individual personality traits, but also in counterproductive routines within each relationship. It's the sick little kid in me struggling to get along with the sick little kid in you.

These negative patterns spring from undealt-with childhood problems. If my childhood programmed me into subservience to an idolatrous parent or family, I will practice a similar reflex of idolatrous subservience in organizations as an adult. If I grew up in self-idolatry, in spoiled rebellion against one or both of my parents, I will repeat those knee-jerk inclinations later, unconsciously, with my spouse, family, and organizations. Ditto for you, too.

Given these fearful repetitions, apart from grace and truth, every institution on earth decays and turns idolatrous. It starts with marriage. I expect my spouse to bring me what no human can provide. Then I bring the same immoderate expectations and overblown devotion to my family, workplace, or government. Yet no mate, clan, job, or state is worth my ultimate trust. No one but God deserves *complete* submission.

In a book called *To Resist or to Surrender?* the Swiss physician and counselor, Paul Tournier, spoke directly to these loaded day-to-day decisions about when and when not to submit to others. He wrote that when a person who normally surrenders instead resists, or when one who usually opposes, yields, watch that situation carefully: God is at work.[33] These kinds of decisions arise from prayer.

In these present family and organization systems, the full potential of our health-giving human capacity gets released as we develop the habit of submitting to our Maker. I used to think that the old hymn was just for evangelism in revival meetings:

> *Just as I am, without one plea*
> *But that Thy blood was shed for me*
> *And that Thou bid'st me come to thee,*
> *O Lamb of God, I come, I come.*[34]

Now I know better. That hymn is for every day. All day every day. Whenever I'm stressed out, in my heart I'd better learn to sing it silently.

Submitting to God and resisting the devil: the day-to-day drama of our lives lies in trying to differentiate. As best we can: we never, on earth, get it perfect. But it's the ultimate warfare's excitement: It gives our garden-variety lives moral meaning, transcendence translated into the here and now.

Chambers calls the Spirit's work within us "moral originality,"[35] a spontaneous empathy, a thoughtful integrity. Triune love is tough, perceptive, and unconquerable. Gradually obedience to this Higher Parent produces in us a growing discrimination. We are free to suffer, but equally free to decline if the suffering is unwise, unhealthy, or unnecessary. Such courage and wisdom come to us on schedule—never behind time, never in advance, always leisurely and quietly, always stretching us out into the future.

People around us likely won't see any spectacular, dramatic change. They will only notice that we are easier to live and work with, less intent on having our own way, and more fun to be around. More positive. More grateful. More upbeat.

But we ourselves will experience these changes as the true excitement and lasting joy they are: in God's own timing, real inward growth. Sometimes leading and sometimes following, our progressive adaptability to others comes from an increasing ability to put ourselves in the other person's shoes, to feel what he or she feels. We will gradually find, springing up in and around us—often seen only in retrospect—less argument and more harmony, less war and more peace.

Choose Your Suffering

Our healthy adaptability to others depends on our discernment about when or when not to submit, when and when not to suffer. Peter's Epistle, in fact, shapes up as one of the Scripture's pinnacle statements on suffering. Some tie its emphasis to first-century persecutions, which to a degree makes sense. But that long-gone history does not even begin to explore its practical insights for us today, whose sufferings may be less dramatically intense but remain for us mountainously real.

At least five major sections in the Epistle treat the suffering theme. It gives us clear-cut distinctions—of legitimacy and necessity—between various kinds of suffering and helps us think about our own pain rationally, perceptively, and analytically:

Sometimes we suffer "for righteousness."[36] This kind of suffering carries a specially blessed reward.

Sometimes we suffer because suffering is the human condition.[37] The old hymn writers wrote with realism: Life *is* "a vale of tears."

Sometimes we suffer from our own sin, stupidity, and ignorance, from spiritually illiterate negligence, from stubborn, bullheaded rebelliousness.[38] This kind of suffering is needless.

Sometimes we suffer for no apparent reason at all.[39]

"Why?" is the ultimate human question; it is never wrong to ask it. Jesus cried "Why?" at the climax of Calvary's passion—his shout of bewildered, despairing abandonment. But no sooner had he asked it than he cried again, "Father, into Your hands I commit my spirit."[40] The intimacy of the "Abba" reflex: questioning followed immediately by commitment.

By contrast, when we suffer without such commitment, when we interrogate the universe with angry "Whys?," shaking our fist in the face of God's silence, we only compound our pain and impede our healing. For whatever we think, God is not silent. If we stop whimpering and listen, he speaks to us clearly in Christ.

Whatever conception we have projected or transferred onto God, our picture of him inevitably becomes infected by our impotent childish rage at the family systems from which we came or some other family or organization system later. We blame God for all our parents' or leaders' sins, ignoring our own. Unconsciously we thus judge mother or dad, past or present, personal or social, oblivious to the inward fact that in so doing we deify them negatively. Believing the worst about them and about our heavenly Parent, we continue to hurt Him further, not to mention our earthly parents, our own family, and our society now or in prospect. Saddest of all, we continue to hurt ourselves.

Avoidable Suffering

One of the Epistle's central themes in this section is *avoidable suffering.* I list its commonsense principles:

(1) *Turn away from evil to avoid suffering:* "Whoever would love life and see good days must keep his tongue from evil and his lips from deceitful speech. He must turn from evil and do good; he must seek peace and pursue it."[41]

(2) *Be aware that most of the time you will not suffer for doing good:* "Who is going to harm you if you are eager to do good?"[42]

(3) *Don't suffer needlessly:* "Let none of you suffer as a murderer, a thief, an evildoer or a busybody in other people's matters."[43]

We need freedom from our martyr complexes, from our sick suffering that we will progressively escape as we grow spiritually. Healthy death to self-centeredness frees us from having to *look* holy, pious, "Christian," "perfect" or anything other than what we truly are: a normal, natural, male or female, full-scale human who is perennially in the process of being healed, becoming whole.

The life of faith is "conscious repentance and unconscious holiness, never the other way about," says Chambers.[44]* Conscious holiness makes us insufferable prigs. But, as we grow up, the Spirit works through our conscious willingness to change our minds, reproducing the mind of Christ in our unconscious, relaxing us about ourselves in the midst of all our relationships' stresses.

Presbyterian pastor Bruce Larson says there are two *sick* ways to handle suffering: "Why Me?" and "More, More!" In answer to the first, "Why Me?" question, Larson asks, "Why Not You?" To suffer is to be human. To the second, "More, More!" response, he asks, "Who Are You?"[45] Are you the Messiah? Or are you a happy one for whom he came?

Psychologist Myron Madden says, "Either we accept the atonement of Christ or else we repeat it."[46] My neurotic suffering, my "More, More!" represents layers of my mind where I have yet truly to accept Christ's atonement and am, instead, repeating it.

In the Christian life, nothing is ever perfect except Christ. My commitment is never perfect, nor will it be on this earth. Coach Henry Parish, our very wise Laity Lodge tennis pro, says, "We are always choosing between Christ and self-destruction." An attitude of "More, More!" simply showcases my self-destructive meddling in matters Christ has settled for me once and for all.

To Inflict Pain or to Absorb It[47]

I mentioned Peter's wisdom, "Let none of you suffer . . . as a *busybody* in other men's matters." In the Greek, that "busybody" idea

---

*The word "repentance" means *to change our minds*.

means, literally, don't *steal* the other person's *leadership*. To have your leadership stolen hurts. Which reminds me of Locopi's Law: "After food and sex, man's greatest drive is to tell the other fellow how to do his job."[48]

So a pertinent example of Peter's modern practicality comes from an article on Fairchild Industries not long ago in *Fortune* magazine. The article focused on a program at Fairchild in which retired executives went back to conduct management seminars for their younger replacements. The sessions were built around an unusual strategy—"Tell us the worst mistake you made while you were with Fairchild Industries"—which had for its purpose to create a climate of open, vulnerable self-revelation.

Fairchild's consultant for the executive seminar program was Mortimer Feinburg, professor emeritus of psychology at Baruch College of the City University of New York. Reviewing the sessions, Feinburg found a common thread in the problems described by the retirees: a rebellion against authority. "How do you cope with a boss in any organization without making yourself a lackey?" The manager who finds himself fighting authority should ask, "Is it my integrity that's at stake? Is it my ego? Is it my macho?" If it's dishonesty, that's a different thing. But if what the boss wants is just something to make himself more comfortable, do it. You have to ask yourself, "Am I attacking my boss to prove I can attack my father and get rewarded?"[49]

What Feinburg told Fairchild Industries about business is exactly what Peter told us about how to live with one another. "Think organizationally," the Apostle, in effect, has said. "Don't suffer uselessly, counterproductively, suicidally. Don't suffer as a meddler in other people's departments, a know-it-all in others' circles of responsibility. Don't suffer as a usurper of someone else's prerogatives. Don't suffer as a rebel against your boss's authority." It is a principle that is at once current, helpful, and therapeutic, even though it's painful. This Epistle is giving us a saving word. Ultimately, because life remains relationships and love alone endures, father-murder always winds up as self-destruction. At home. On the job. In the political arena. Everywhere.

Knuckling under to your boss may hurt: You are absorbing the pain between you. But by deferring to his authority you accomplish two things:

1. You avoid spreading your pain to your boss, who has more than enough pain now without your adding to it.

2. You contribute to the growth of your relationship with the boss, and to the growth of *your own spiritual self-control.*

Why do we rebel against authority? Because we feel—rightly or wrongly—that authority has rejected us. Rejection—being thrown away or culled out or discarded as unsatisfactory—has to be one of the most painful things that ever happens. To feel ignored, left out, not good enough, somehow inferior, hurts us all. In fact, rejection describes one important reason we find Peter's prescription for living together so hard. To be submissive to someone else, when we feel we're being rejected by them, is—of course—turning the other cheek.

Yet, rejection—those rebuffs that all of us have experienced from parents, siblings, teachers, spouses, families, bosses, government officials and friends—is exactly what Jesus took for us, once for all, on the cross. By it he gives us the psychological strength—in everyday life—to cope with the smarting of our rejection, overcoming it for ourselves and for others.

Peter, who had received his rock or stone identity from his unforgettable "You are the Christ, the Son of God" conversation, picks up on this rejection psychology when he calls us to authoritative submission. He applies the rock idea to what Jesus had done for him and was now doing in him. "The stone which the builders rejected has become . . . the corner stone."[50]

The pain Jesus accepted on the cross is the same pain that enables Him to hold the universe together, including our relational lives today. That's the message: Out of our rejections, He builds us up.

The psychology of faith says to us: "You are already somebody very important; you have acceptance; you have security; you have the significance of the cosmos in you. Nobody can shake it. It's not a theory or a doctrine or a philosophy; it's a Person. Keep your eyes on that Person, and increasingly he will share with you his own security. Then you will have the power to take the path of pain-absorbent, health-giving, authoritative submission."

PART TWO

❧

Relationships Renewed

Reparenting and Rechildrening

The family is a good institution because it is uncongenial.
The men and women who for good reasons and bad, revolt
against the family, are, for good reasons and bad, revolting
against mankind. Papa is excitable, like mankind. Our
younger brother is mischievous, like mankind. Grandpapa
is stupid, like the world; he is old, like the world.
           —*G. K. Chesterton*

The characteristic move of the modern
intellectual is the flight from home.
           —*Lionel Trilling*

The devil's boots don't creak.
           —*Scottish Proverb*

The poet Maya Angelou once said that even as a young
woman she never agreed with Thomas Wolfe's title *You
Can't Go Home Again*. Instead, she felt, you never truly leave
your home. "You take it with you; it's under your finger-
nails; it's in the hair follicles; it's in the way you smile; it's
in the ride of your hips, in the passage of your breasts; it's
all there, no matter where you go."[1]
           —*Andre Bernard, Maya Angelou*

4

The Joy of Flex

Ordinary People, Secular Church, Realistic Hope

c❧

---

1 Peter 5:1–7

He that will not apply new remedies
must expect new evils.
—*Francis Bacon*

*N*one of us live in healthy authoritative submission all
the time. So Peter's psychology confronts us—head-
on—about our universal human neuroses. The Yiddish scholar-
humorist, Leo Rosten, says, "I have come to the conclusion that
Americans treat 'neurotic' as a synonym for 'nuts'; that Englishmen
think 'neurotic' an adjective applicable to foreigners; and that Jews
consider 'neurotic' a synonym for 'human'."[2]

How, then, facing our own neuroses, can "religion" in America
be changed into a health-bringing spirituality that transforms the
nation? The next steps in Peter's psychology tell us how.

The apostle's how-to, on that potential for national change, starts
within each of us, within each citizen, whether we are churchy,
religious, or not. T. S. Eliot said, "Success is relative: It is what we
can make of the mess we've made of things."[3] Peter agreed, and in
his prelude to these next steps said, "Let judgment begin at the
house of God."[4] Starting with us in the churches, we've all contributed to the present—neurotic—mess.

Reparenting and Rechildrening

Psychiatry likes to say it is in the business of "reparenting." This strikes me as a very helpful definition. In fact, I use the term *spiritual psychiatry* to describe the process of authentic Christian growth because reparenting—the repair of the imperfect parents' damage in us all—is such a basic spiritual need.

Many modern psychiatrists and social psychologists recognize that reparenting goes on not only in professional therapists' offices, but wherever there are healthy adult relationships, as we tell each other our hurts and problems and receive back wise and caring counsel. Reparenting takes place wherever there is self-giving *agape* love, whether its Author gets credit or not, and whether or not we are conscious of the process.

But "reparenting" is not our only need; we also need what I have come to call "rechildrening." That is, in addition to replacing our faulty parent images, we need to replace our faulty child *responses* with healthier ones. Rechildrening is what we talked about in the last chapter on submission. If we are ever to learn how to fit in with each other in marriage, family, work, and society, its lesson remains essential. Its relational order is indispensable for healthy community.

I admit this distinction between reparenting and rechildrening is subtle—and that common psychological usage of the word "reparenting" often includes this "rechildrening" response. But I find that focusing on the fine-drawn connections between these two facets of development helps me immensely in my growth.

When I first accepted psychiatric help over thirty years ago, changes started taking place inside me and in my relationships. These changes began to affect all my thinking; the result was new levels of spiritual growth. Because so much of my life had been spent in various organized structures, I began applying what I was learning about myself to organizational relationships, grappling with what the Scriptures had to say about authority, submission, and servant-leadership. I even wrote a book about it, *The Velvet Covered Brick*.

As this growth process continued, life forced me into deeper reflection on the Scriptures, on relationships, and on behavioral science. During this time, I began to hear the word "reparenting" used to describe the psychiatric process. It made sense—and yet it didn't seem to describe fully what was happening in and through me.

Then I began studying 1 Peter's psychology and pondering our Lord's insistent calls to us to "be born again" and "become as little children." At that point I realized that, while my parent images were being revised, something else was also happening. My responses were changing; I was being rechildrened! And I realized that, for my fullest development, the two processes always need to go together.

Reparenting is the process of cognitively replacing our—often unfair—mental images of our own imperfect parents (and the damage they caused us) with a more healthy conception, a more exemplary model. In spiritual terms, this means replacing the image of our imperfect parents with the perfect heavenly Parent. In secular terms, it means replacing our distorted, incomplete parent pictures with a more adult, reasoned view of what an ideal parent should be.

Rechildrening means changing our own inner *response* to our own childhood's parent image. Whereas the common child response to imperfect parents is fear, rebellion, or overdependence (depending on what the actual parents are like), rechildrening happens as we develop within ourselves—and toward others—the attitudes of children of a perfect Parent: respect, humility, positive self-image, and healthy submission.

If reparenting corrects the *authority* damages within us, rechildrening corrects the *submission* damages as well. And the therapeutic outcome of these two dynamics is a healthy, flexible interplay between *authority* and *submission*. I call this interaction "pastoral flex"—an essential for healthy individuals living in healthy institutions.

The Trinitarian Model

We can restate these relationships in Trinitarian terms: The Father is *authority*, the Son is *submission*, the Holy Spirit is the *unbreakable flexibility* uniting them.

Reparenting improves our image of God. Rechildrening improves our image of ourselves and, therefore, our interactions with others.

The resulting wholesome flexibility manifests itself not only as individual psychological growth, but also as cooperative health in our varied institutions, from marriage to the government. This social aspect, in fact, stands as one of the distinguishing aspects of rechildrening as a process. Reparenting happens cognitively, within our own minds, though others may help us face the truth. Rechildrening happens socially, by means of our healthy interaction with others. And it has two results.

First, it results in *a fresh awareness that we are NOT God*; that we cannot control others; that laws or governments, external authorities, and especially our own human limitations, must be accepted.

Second, it results in *a new recognition that we ARE fully human* adults; we take charge of our own lives; we stand up to people we have previously feared; we forsake overdependence on others to attain healthier autonomy—or distance—in our relationships to them.

Reparenting relates us psychologically to the ideal parent, therefore spiritually to God the Father. Rechildrening relates us psychologically to the ideal self, therefore spiritually to Christ within us. Pastoral flex coordinates in us the life of the Father in the Son, our own good or bad childhood integrated therefore appropriately (but never perfectly) into a progressively maturing adult.

To summarize, then: Reparenting corrects the damage caused by the ways we were parented. Rechildrening corrects the damaging ways we responded to the way we were parented.

In the mysterious fluctuations of human relationships and institutional change, reparenting and rechildrening go together. It's the organizational way our new birth grows. The divine Parent in the Child, the Spirit of the Father in the Son, works in every human interaction to both reparent and rechildren us, continuing the process of the new birth, making us as He is in His inner nature.

In all our relationships, if we take time to look, one way or another, the Trinity comes to us in disguise and speaks to us there, showing us how to negotiate, how to give and take, how to flex. "Adapting to each other" healthily, we become "conformed to His image"[5]; otherwise we choose the loneliness and isolation of hell. But "joy is the serious business of heaven," says C. S. Lewis,[6] and our Divine Parent works relentlessly to make us his happy children.

Mountains That Move

But we cannot become happy children of this Heavenly Parent as angry and rebellious, superior and condemning children of the earthly parents he used giving us birth. Your "second birth" God loves your "first birth" parents the same way he loves you, since he is their Creator and yours alike. Reconciliation, forgiveness, and love within our whole society awaits reconciliation, forgiveness, and love between the generations in our personal households.

We ourselves don't know how to pull this reconciliation off, but somebody Triune does. He bridges the generation gap and brings peace to the battle between the sexes. When we turn our messed-up family relationships over to him, he teaches everybody involved, in his own way and time, how to become for each other "agents of . . . reconciliation."[7]

Because we're dealing with fully human processes, there are no shortcuts. We don't turn out reparented and rechildrened overnight. It comes through gradual changes, never finished in our lifetimes. Even in a hurry-up chutzpah generation, maybe especially in its breathless electronic speed, there is no such thing as instant maturity. Yet the irresistible springing up of this new and living organism (our reborn self) and its continuous movement toward completeness (already we are "complete in Him,"[8]) breaks open our old family systems, just like "living stones" cut through caked mud.

The faith that moves mountains therapeutically is not loud and showy, demanding attention, "sounding brass or tinkling cymbal."[9] It is a low-profile, noiseless growth in *agape* love. This series of slow or rapid changes succeeding each other in us is quiet, calm, and leisured; you don't realize your mountain has moved till its new location startles you.

You didn't move it. The Living Stone used you, unaware, in his leverage. He moves mountains with divine dynamite. Its *agape* blasts are silent, invisible, long-acting, and time-released.

In our closest relationships nothing less than such dynamite moves the giant mountains of superiority, suspicion, guilt, and fear between us—subtle, unspoken, hidden mountains, but, nonetheless, huge, forbidding, and massively real.

Looking back now, way back to the period before my "green-ottoman, white-funeral" prayer, and before my psychiatric treatment, I realize that for years I condemned Dad without knowing it. And of all ungodly and hellish strategies, I used a perversion of the Christian religion to condemn him. I was "more spiritual" than he was. In my unrealized and unfaced religious competitiveness, spiritual pride was my desperate sin. Preaching grace, I boasted, unknowing, about my works. You might never have recognized it. In the words of C. S. Lewis, I was "greasily humble."[10] But doing good, I underestimated my own evil.

Dad was running a business; he wasn't out doing public Christian service and evangelistic work as I was. In the terms of our Southern Baptist culture, he wasn't as "on fire" as his pious, priggish, but unaware son. The fact that he lived his life and operated the stores as a Christian stewardship, with enormous positive impact, using his gifts and talents faithfully, didn't faze me; he wasn't "touching people for God" as I was in my lay evangelism.

Therefore, when I submitted more fully to God in that 1961 prayer, I also wound up submitting freshly to Dad, without being conscious of it till much later. I went back to my grocery company office and found myself turning down invitations to go out and speak. I took on more and more responsibility in the business, which Dad had always hoped I would *want* to do.

What I had experienced was a combination of reparenting and rechildrening. In my relationship with the psychiatrist, I experienced reparenting, both through his taking me so seriously as a patient and in his calling me to get things straightened out with Dad. And in the whole process, finally focused in that particular prayer, I was receiving the Heavenly Father's perfectly timed, deeper reparenting.

Not, however, until I began voluntarily submitting to Dad, giving the company more priority as he wanted me to do, did I grow spiritually and psychologically in my own rechildrening. In developments within our family years later, when we decided that my brother, Charles, would run the Company and then that I would run the Foundation, Dad said to me, "Howard, you've changed."

Which I had. And I do not believe I'd be free from day-to-day company responsibilities now, free to concentrate on a strong operating foundation's work, free to do this study and write this book, if I had not in that particular stage of my personal history experienced both reparenting and rechildrening.

Reparenting and rechildrening go together. Inseparably they are one: "Who is really greatest in the Kingdom of heaven? Jesus called a little child to his side and set him on his feet in the middle of them all. 'Believe me,' he said, 'unless you change your whole outlook and become like little children you will never enter . . . .'"[11]

The Secular Church

As the unique institutional manifestation of Christ's body, the church holds staggering reparenting and rechildrening capacity. And fortunately for the church, the world, and you, most members do not need professional therapy such as I have had in order to release that potential in themselves or others. What we do need, however, is a clear vision for how the church fits into society and how we relate to one another within the church.

Years ago I read, "The church is the only institution in the world that carries within itself the seeds of its own reformation." And why so? Because Scripture serves as a continual antidote to the greed, jealousy, and pride, the irresponsibility and rebellion, the apathy and resistance to change that inevitably hamper human institutions. If history shows that obedience to the Word of God is the power behind that ongoing reformation—as I believe it does—then what does the Bible have to say about how the church releases its reparenting potential?

The answer that has emerged again and again, over centuries of reformation and counterreformation, is that it happens through the laity—that is to say, through those of us who are not church professionals—in the secular institutions of the mundane world. Through nonecclesiastic vocations, our latent church capabilities break loose in our politics, jobs, families, and marriages. We of the laity make up the church decentralized—the church in the world, the *secular* church.

Look at it another way: If to be a church member means professing a relationship with the one three-personed God who is relationship within himself, then the purpose of that one transcendent relationship is to change all our other human relations. Look at it a third way. The secular church is *all our various, ordinary day-to-day relationships.* In these relationships, transformed by our continuing encounter with the Triune God, the growing process of re-parenting and rechildrening goes on.

Quaker philosopher Elton Trueblood points out that Jesus' familiar pictures of the Kingdom as salt, light, and leaven (yeast)[12] all share the same basic strategy, *penetration.* The Kingdom permeates the world. How? By new attitudes within and among the church's ordinary people.

When Jesus tells us to go into the world and preach the gospel, he means it extensively: Yes, go into Europe, Africa, or Japan. But he also means it *intensively:* Embody God's message in your own world of business, law, architecture, medicine, education. He means it geographically, no doubt. But he also means it *vocationally:* Go into the worlds of art, entertainment, construction, communications, philanthropy, and live out the gospel *there.* We are to go into *all* the worlds. And, everywhere, we are to start with the way we relate to people. We as the secular church are called to live out the health of Triune flex in the excruciating personal tensions we inevitably experience with people who are over us, people who are under us, and people who are, somehow too painfully today, our equals.

Kingdom Growth

Because it integrates our childhood and adult experiences, the secular church offers us a comprehensive perspective of lifelong growth. Viewed positively, then, every relationship—not only of joy but also of pain—assimilates itself into the one process of our psychological and spiritual maturing. Our growth—both individual and collective, in this secular church overview—moves forward by the ministry of adaptability, a strong, settled adjustability, a firmly rooted resilience with each other. This forward movement perpetually consolidates within us the two ongoing psychological developments of reparenting and rechildrening.

These two aspects of growth, in addition, unite both the personal and the social. That's why my reparenting-rechildrening syntax, grammatically, is not perfectly parallel. This is deliberate. "Parent" is a singular word form; "children" is plural: personal reparenting and social rechildrening. Whereas psychiatry has often been criticized for concentrating exclusively on individuals, and evangelism has likewise been subject to the same criticism, the secular church sees us changing both internally, within ourselves, and externally, within all our various institutions. By it, secular organizations have the potential, for which we all yearn, of becoming nurturing groups. And that's an exciting prospect. It offers our nation realistic hope.

We, in our churches, believe that God is Triune, the Trinity—the One in Three, the Three in One. This means we believe that He is—organizationally—both centralized and decentralized. As One, he is centralized. As Three, He is decentralized. This paradoxical Trinitarian principle stands vital for all our organizational psychology—both secular and religious.

If you want only an "institutional church" faith, forget the Apostle Peter and his psychology. He thinks beyond institutional churches; he thinks Kingdom of God. Early on he started in about "every human institution." The Kingdom, simply put, is the rule of God in the world. It is present now, wherever and whenever *agape* love prevails. Though it will not arrive fully until the consummation, its reality is around and within us today, both evident and concealed, both visible and hidden.

Never confuse "religious" churches with the "secular" Kingdom. They overlap and reinforce each other, with the biblical vision infusing both, but they are not one and the same. Institutional churches are the church *centralized;* Peter's vision is for the Kingdom of God, the secular church, the church of One in Three, the church *decentralized.* Churches send us, their lay people, out into our everyday secular tasks to do the really hard work of the church—building the Kingdom in our down-to-earth gook, gut, grit, and grind.

And lots of us, who want reparenting and rechildrening happiness very much, are not very religious.

Elders and Youngers

Since everybody needs not only reparenting but also rechildrening for growing psychological health, the key to the church's reparenting/rechildrening potential obviously lies in the decentralized church, the laity. In that light, the Apostle Peter's choice of words in the concluding chapter of 1 Peter hits me as amazing. His words jolt me, startle me as nothing short of dumbfounding.

This Epistle is light-years ahead of the twentieth century not only organizationally but also psychologically. Closing the Letter, Peter addresses two groups, or—more correctly—two sets of *functions* within the same group of people. At first, he speaks to "elders." Then, just afterward, he speaks to "young men"—more accurately translated, "you who are younger." I like the more concise King James phrasing: "youngers."

"Elders" for *reparenting.*

"Youngers" for *rechildrening.*

"Elders" as the human-size manifestation of the Father.

"Youngers" as the human-size manifestation of the Son.

For many centuries we thought these two words connoted nothing more than relations between higher and lower church officials. Now we see they go much further—a secular world further, in fact. These two words describe—by the Holy Spirit—the church's trinitarian soul, its functional freedom, its relational character.

After years of studying, I am convinced that Peter's "elders and youngers" offers Triune reality to us all, and that both these psychological functions belong to every believer. Elsewhere I called this "the Pastor principle for every leader and the Church principle for every organization."[13]

Elders lead.

Youngers serve.

And each of us is both.

So two flexible postures within us describe this relational creativity: leadership or service; eldering or youngering; authority or submission. The happy, constructive flow of our relational lives ripples out of our shifting back and forth between these two seemingly opposite postures easily, wisely, and appropriately.

Conversely, our unhappy, destructive, irrational rigidities, resulting either from our painful childhoods or our current confusions, tie us, bind us, and chain us to inflexible, unbending, inappropriate postures. When we get stuck either leading or following, we get in the way of our own and others' spiritual and relational growth.

Everybody an Elder

"Elders" jumps out at us as Peter's theme in the first verses of chapter 5, "youngers" in the paragraph following. *Elders* hammers into negotiable gold the Trinitarian nugget of "leadership," *youngers* its paradoxical partner, "followership"—both intended everywhere for us all.[14]

First, the old Apostle stresses that his personal leadership, we must understand, remains nothing more than the leadership we have each received, universally, in Christ. He could not be more explicit about the nature of this leadership, its common source, or its high purpose: "Elders among you, I [the co-elder and witness of the sufferings of Christ, the sharer also of the glory about to be revealed] exhort, *shepherd the flock of God among you.*"[15]

This great "shepherding" theme carried, for Simon Peter, really heavy emotional freight. He universalized it naturally for us all, because Jesus had used it, unforgettably, to pinpoint Peter's greatest need—and our own as well. Remember that conversation? After Peter's denial of Christ? After the rooster crowed? After Good Friday? After Easter Sunday? After their seaside resurrection breakfast?

"Simon, son of Jona, do you love me more than these others?"

"Yes, Lord," he replied, "you know that I am your friend."

"Then feed my lambs," returned Jesus. Then he said for the second time,

"Simon, son of Jona, do you love me?"

"Yes, Lord," returned Peter. "You know that I am your friend."

"Then care for my sheep," replied Jesus. Then for the third time Jesus spoke to him and said,

"Simon, son of Jona, *are* you my friend?"

Peter was deeply hurt because Jesus' third question to him was, "Are you my friend?," and he said, "Lord, you know everything. You know I am your friend!"

"Then feed my sheep," Jesus said to him.[16]

Not only did this discussion pivot on Peter's failure to respond to Jesus' deep *agape* "love" question with anything but a weaker, hedging, "friendship" answer; but it also turned on Jesus' consistent demand, whatever Peter's intensity of response: "Feed my sheep."

The paradox of all personality rests in the point-counterpoint of the two *different human functions* Jesus highlights for Peter in that conversation: that of *sheep* and of *shepherd*. Each person is made not only to be a sheep, but also to be a shepherd.

The nineteenth-century German philosopher Hegel said that in all our human self-consciousness there is both a "lord" and a "bond servant."[17] Of course: Each of us is a God-shaped blank, craving the Triune. Jesus, who is both "the Lamb of God who takes away the sin of the world" and "the Good Shepherd [who] gives his own life for the sheep," shepherds us for one irreducible reason: that we may grow up and shepherd others.[18]

Of the fact that this churchwide Christian leadership captures Peter's vision throughout the Epistle there can be no doubt. It stands inherent in his precedent-shattering concept, "the priesthood of all believers."

Here, now, he makes it equally inescapable: "Elders . . . be shepherds of God's flock that is under your care." Four times in four verses Peter uses "shepherd," from Jesus' piercing interrogation, repetitiously hammering at this same root, which recalls his own indelible shepherding commission.[19] And not once does he hint that the least believer is not so called.[20]

Each of us has our own little "flock of God." Lay ministry—to see our secular selves as servant-leaders—in our common, ordinary lives, is *shepherding miniaturized.* So we are to treat people in our circles everywhere—in and out of church—as if they were in the flock, recognizing in each individual under our influence a child of God's staggering potential.

Even Peter's warnings underline his vision's scope and breadth. He urges leaders to "shepherd . . . not by way of compulsion, but willingly, according to God, *not greedy about money* but eager to serve." Leadership, secular or religious, usually carries material rewards. Peter generalizes this cautionary warning about money and motivation, applicable to us all, both clergy and laity. Then he warns us psychologically about our leadership style: "Not lording it over those entrusted to you, but being examples to the flock."

Seeing every group under our servant-leadership as a potential flock, to be touched by our modeling or our example (incarnational evangelism and spiritual formation), Peter states here the apostle Paul's "Follow me as I follow Christ"[21] principle. But he states it as if he were prophetically anticipating—and rebuking, tongue in cheek, ahead of time—our church-history misconceptions. Amusingly, the transliteration alone (rather than the translation) of his combined, condensed counsel could read, "Shepherd . . . the clergy."

I conclude the hilariously obvious. Either this passage doesn't apply to much of anybody in the world except the Pope, or else it applies to us all. And every leader I ever knew, starting with myself, has tendencies to lord it over those we lead. I don't know about the Pope, but I *need* what Peter says here.

This vision is so transforming, so breathtakingly powerful, that we can understand the English poet John Milton's frustrated eruption over this very Scripture during the first blush of the Reformation (1645). Milton fumed, "The title of clergy St. Peter gave to all God's people, till Pope Hyginus and the succeeding Prelates took it away from them."[22]

The Apostle himself here speaks his Trinitarian common sense to us more calmly, as if to say, "Be what you are, a Christlike leader, wherever life takes you." Parents, *parent;* pastors, *pastor;* attorneys and counselors, *counsel;* doctors, *doctor;* accountants, keep good *accounts;* managers, *manage;* executives, *execute;* teachers, *teach;* coaches, *coach;* football players, *play.* Whatever you ordinarily do, do it as a spiritual leader.

Martin Luther's Reformation, in the sixteenth century, penetrated Europe by the same simple strategy: "Every man a pastor to his own family." He described the church decentralized.

The imprisoned German martyr, Dietrich Bonhoeffer, four centuries later, wrote two echoing words. He wrote them in the margin of a letter he had received as he prepared his response to his friend's question about "the world come of age" and modern secularity. During his last days, just before the gallows of Hitler's hangman, Bonhoeffer scribbled on his friend's letter: "Aristocratic Christianity."[23] Bonhoeffer pointed us to universal leadership.

Influence with other people is given to us all. As we each use our inevitable influence, Christ commands us to see ourselves as shepherds.

Functional Freedom: Looking up to People

Every single one of us believers, then, is a reparenting elder—a shepherd called to his or her little flock.

At the same time, every believer is a rechildrening younger. The next paragraph uses our universal age-group categories to address itself to "youngers," telling us to "likewise," or "in the same way," *submit ourselves to elders.* How could "in the same way" make sense, following a paragraph on shepherd leaders and their flocks, unless Peter is combining "leading" and "following" into one, thinking Trinity?

And how do we practice the followership of "youngering"? He says we do it by humility.

Peter the psychologist would not propound submission without squarely facing its enemy: our *pride.* His reasoning is clear: "Clothe yourselves with humility." The rare Greek word translated "clothe" comes from "the white scarf or apron of a slave." Using it, Peter surely remembered the night Jesus wrapped a towel around his waist and washed the disciples' feet.[24]

What is there about submission that makes us always bristle? Why does it keep rubbing us wrong? Its abuse, yes. But isn't there more? What about our lack of humility? Our unreal, self-inflated arrogance? Our empty posing and self-importance? Our hellish vanity?

But if, as Peter says, God "resists the proud," then this puffed-up egotism destroys us. It's the battle we all fight with our own self-destruction. We each have layers of unaware conceits down within us we've never noticed or confronted. We notice pride in others, but not in ourselves. "The 'self-made man,' a horrible example of unskilled labor."[25] But our humble recognition of God as the ultimate reality enables him, fulfilling our unrealized potential, to "exalt us in due time."

You have great things ahead of you.

How do we get this humility? He explains: "Under God's mighty hand." Which means we search for that hand in the unfolding of our everydayness. The ordinary developments of our existence—if we look at them alertly—keep reminding us that we are not in control of the world. God is.

Without recognizing God's hand in the normal—and abnormal—events of our lives, we go downhill spiritually. Frederick Buechner says we start a spiritual decline when we don't "listen to our lives." Trying to be our own god, we start becoming the only other thing, in fact, we humans could possibly be—animals, beasts.

Psychiatry appropriated a name for our sick and lonely pride—"narcissism"—from the Greek myth of Narcissus, the river god's beautiful young son who fell in love with his own reflection. Contrast Narcissus's looking down into the waters for his own proud self-image and our own irrational looking down on God, self, parents, and others; contrast both with Jesus' example. He continually looked up to God, looked up to the Spirit of the Father in himself. Accordingly, he also looked up to others.

Jesus' preferred title for himself was "Son of Man." Our brief Gospels record it from his lips some forty times.[26] We know this name had Messianic implications. But didn't it also have psychological significance? In our preoccupation with Jesus' full and complete deity, have we minimized his equally full human psychology?

Son of Man epitomizes Jesus' humility, his looking up to people. As we now know, he could have called himself Father of Man with equal accuracy. Finally, at the end, he made that fact explicit: "He that has seen me has seen the Father."[27] But instead, he chose this *Son* of Man name to describe *what, who,* and *how* he was and is.

Leading from weakness? You have just described a crucial element in Jesus' management style. Flexing young, he saw a special, unique importance in everyone he met. Jesus was the biggest man who ever lived because he chose to be the smallest—in relative terms. He was humility perfectly incarnate. How else could the mighty Maker of the universe become little and human? On the cross he let himself be lifted up that we might see the humble God to whom we lift our eyes.

The Son of Man designation is, as H. R. Macintosh says, "intrinsically paradox. It binds Jesus to humanity, yet singles him out from other men (in both) supramundane glory and earthly humiliation. Yet this seeming contradiction, far from being fatal to the internal coherence of the idea, is really constitutive of it."[28] *Son* of Man is man the lesser, the weaker, the lowlier, the smaller, *man the younger.*

For our sins, this Son of Man bled away his young life on a Roman torture tree. But that was not the end of the story. Three days later he rose again. Eldered forevermore. If the stone had not rolled back, open and away from that Easter tomb, I wonder if the earth, sun, stars, and solar system might not have split themselves in two? In his Son of Man attitude, role, name, and triumph, Jesus shows us forever that humility is power. Meekness runs the world.

Everyone a Younger: Puncturing Our
Self-Inflation Balloon

Why does the Bible keep warning us that "the works of the (religious) law" cannot bring spiritual success, that our own "works of righteousness" can be worse than useless? Why is the New Testament so cold about our "works"? Well, it isn't. What it's cold about is our thinking these "works" are *our* accomplishments.

Which left to ourselves we invariably think. Left to ourselves, we don't think of Christ's cross as triumph for each of us, or think of "Just as I am I come." Unless we consciously "think gift," our own preoccupation with our achievements (our "works") sets off a chain reaction of inward bragging. Spiritual pride. Self-importance. Strutting. We look down, consciously or unconsciously, on those without our "works." Our "high look," "proud heart," "insolent gaze"[29] thus stares down at people.[30]

Fred Smith says, "Humility is not denying your power. It is realizing that the power comes *through* you and not *from* you." This "thinking gift" reflex helps keep us humble. Only when I realize this truth—that God does the work *through* me by his gift of himself— am I freed from wanting to *be* God. Then I'm free to be a real healing human, continually in the process of being psychologically reborn. The psychology of the new birth is always the psychology of need, helplessness, and poverty. Our bankruptcy gets us in; our moral wealth keeps us out.

My personal hang-ups illustrate. Feeling myself "more spiritual" than Dad, religiously I "looked down" on him. Psychologically I was the "priest," he was not. For me at least, my own consciously earned superspirituality denied him his "priesthood." His running a prosperous business fell beneath my own "richer" spirituality. So, unconsciously, I poisoned my love for him by my son-father rivalry and hate, father-murder festering in me unaware. Our spiritual pride frowns down on others to build ourselves up—in principle the same as any other pride, only more difficult to detect.

Still, ever and again, our unending fascination with Jesus springs from his *simultaneous* power and humility. The combination jars us. We never before saw them together, never conceived the two could be one. Jesus *looked up* to people. He saw their potential.

That's the difference between him and us. He made people feel special and important, while we sharpen our marksmanship to shoot each other down.

Our thirst for our own leadership is so intense, our hunger for significance so ravenous, this God-shaped vacuum of our emptiness so strong, that we inhale riches of every kind to balloon up the void within ourselves: money, looks, muscles, clout, friends, culture, education, travel, race, even helping others (the list is endless)—all to puff ourselves up so we feel tall enough to look down. (And in our loneliness and our fear, we must find someone to look down *on*. That's one reason pets and animals help. Dogs stay humble; Snoopy naturally looks up.)

But in this game of self-inflation to heighten our hollow selves, the most dangerous fumes we breathe are moral, ethical, and religious riches. Smoke. Gas. Carbon monoxide. With these poisonous vapors we inflate the balloon of pride into our ultimate self-delusion.

That's why the Bible's pinprick so continually sticks us with this point: "*not* of works" and *not* by the "works of the law." Because "pride disgusts the Lord."[31] Pride destroys my relationships with others. Only by *not* boasting, *not* bragging, *not* inflating myself, *but trusting the perfect gift*, can I look up to people with Christ's discerning integrity and effortless humility.

It always remains tricky. As the New York socialite Gert Behanna said after her conversion, "Now I look down on people who look down on people!"[32] Acknowledging my poverty and Christ's riches always takes me where? Into his kind of life. Into authoritative submission. Into a continual rediscovery, lifelong and deepening, of the elder-younger principle.

Inflated balloons either stretch themselves to the breaking point or else collapse into limp rubber: popped or pooped. Either way, they self-destruct.

Contrast them with living stones, with Trinitarian relationships' firm flex.

This ancient Epistle's modern psychology stuns me. Its "relationship" language. Its choice of words—its practical application of timeless principles, both between the generations and within all organizations—anticipating twentieth-century behavioral science. It pictures personal conversion only as an enduring growth into familial, vocational, and social harmony. Its decentralized lay perspective gives it both personal practicality and social relevance, and demolishes our hostile, old-fashioned stereotypes.

Could it, today, be more timely?

The Secular Church: Our Own Pastoral Flex

What we have before us, in the decentralized/secular vision of this climactic final chapter of 1 Peter, contains both the Epistle's conceptual crescendo and also its practical application. It sketches for us a scaled-down Trinity.

Following its appeal to arm ourselves—mentally—with Christ's attitude toward suffering, that from his once-for-all crucifixion pain, we may embrace our own necessary pain psychologically, we have at last been shown the here-and-now point of it all.

How are we to function both in the church and in the world, as we continue our growth process? "Elders-Youngers" summarizes it: We learn to flex.

Because our identities in Christ remain rock-solid, we are enabled to be infinitely adaptable in our roles and relationships. Our daily existence becomes a fabric of functional transitions, an intricate interplay of all our psychological and institutional relations.

Most often this divinely inspired flexibility within us is unconscious. Chambers says, "We cannot be conscious of our consciousness and remain sane."[33] Orange trees don't sweat producing oranges; children don't grow taller consciously.

Just so, pastoral flex is the external mark of our interior growth toward Trinitarian maturity. Its therapeutic rhythms soothe away our adolescent business unfinished and our childhood wounds unhealed. Under Christ it reparents and rechildrens others while—simultaneously but discriminatingly—allowing others to reparent and rechildren us. Its curative tempos, fast or slow, fit divinely orchestrated pulsations. Its goal is to make us—each—a happy child in a wise adult.

You cannot make even a *minimal* change in your conduct without causing people around you—also—to change. Every time you alter your attitudes, others near you rethink their attitudes too. Family systems and working-group patterns interconnect so tightly that each person's behavior affects everyone else. No man is an island: Relationships—for better or worse—bind us together intimately.

Flexibility that is pastorlike in character changes the world—one person at a time—by an imperceptible chain reaction.

In his broad-ranging study, *Christ and Culture*, Richard Neibuhr argues our potential for this kind of social change.[34] As he opposes, with discrimination, not only "Christ *against* culture" but also "The Christ *of* culture," Neibuhr observes, "Trinitarianism is by no means as speculative a position and as unimportant for conduct as is often maintained."[35] Through the Trinity, Christ *transforms* culture.[36] Pastoral flex sets out to renew the world.

In its vision of flexing elder/younger relationships, the groups in which we live and work become growing communities of love, support, and therapy. This forms both the idea behind and the goal for the small group movement. This movement has swept the churches and society in the last thirty years. It recognizes that I as an individual cannot change the world. But I *can* change the climate of the more limited gatherings of people where I live and work. This strategy then penetrates, through a broadening and intensifying impact, all our secular home-and-job groupings.

This movement of decentralized church authenticity builds on older and larger church-renewal movements—on the Sunday School movement of the nineteenth century, representing in all its teachers and classes decentralized lay education; Roman Catholicism's various forms of lay awakening from Cursillos to Marriage Encounters to Contemplative Retreats; Alcoholics Anonymous, in its multiplying "sponsors" and "twelve-step" therapy groups that characterize its spiritual vitality; on other organizations such as Lay Witness Mission, Prayer Breakfast Fellowship, Faith Alive, the Salvation Army, Walk to Emmaus, Habitat for Humanity, Medical Missions, The Fellowship of Christian Athletes, Bread for the World, and on and on.

Each of these spiritual programs finds fruition not in the institutional church alone but beyond it, in all the ordinary hungers and secular pains of a hurting world. In all these expressions of faith, and others like them, lay people learn to live triumphantly and joyously, as elders and youngers simultaneously.

Growing in Flexibility

The English essayist, Thomas Carlyle, once observed that *genius is the infinite capacity for attention to detail.*[37] Yet even our folk humor tells us (accurately) that "God is in the details," or "the Devil is in the details."

Can we afford to pray—or expect guidance—about our lives' details? Should we feel silly if we do? Or presumptuous? Would it be *bothering* God? After all, God can always answer our prayers "Yes" or "No" or "Wait." Should we pray about the details of our relationships?

"'Help,' and 'Thanks!' are our basic prayers. But honesty and thoroughness don't come quite as spontaneously," says Eugene Peterson's preface to his contemporary translation of *Psalms*.[38] Thoroughness and honesty—in our Lord's prayer book, the Psalms—both assure us to trust Peter's command/promise here: "Cast all your anxieties on him, for he cares for you."

God's switchboard doesn't go on overload, flash red lights, or blow a fuse. He could handle all six billion of us seeking directions at once—effortlessly, with delight. The One Cosmic Genius—beside whom there is no other—reveals himself to us as the source of all Wisdom.

Authentic spiritual growth always involves our becoming more wisely flexible relationally. Discernment—on when we flex younger and when we flex older—forms the essence of our spiritual wisdom.

How does this wisdom come to us? Four ways:

First, *soaking in the Scripture*. It's not enough to go through the Bible; we need to let the Bible go through us. (Pride—in how much Scripture we know—becomes an obstacle.) We let biblical principle penetrate our thinking about everything—from sex to success, from fun to finances, from time to temperament.

Second, *self-examination*. The cultivation of our conscience—to be sensitive, but not overscrupulous—enables growth in all our relationships. Our faith is a faith of motive. Other people look at our external appearance; God sees our desires and intentions. So we consciously ask Him to search our hearts and our thoughts.[39] And we constantly recognize how far we have to go.

Third, *confidential conversations*. We need spiritually based friendships we can trust—where we can talk openly about our deepest feelings. Marriage offers an ideal option. But if it's not realistic there, other Christ-centered, trustworthy personal affinities will emerge for us. Bonhoeffer said, "The word of God is clearer in my brother."[40] In addition to our confidences, varying other types of relationships can give us differing kinds of help: In a multitude of counselors, there is wisdom.[41] Nothing substitutes for mutual agreements based on common sense.

Finally, *prayer and its inner peace.* Sending up silent appeals for Wisdom's guidance becomes, more and more, a continuing reflex. We pay attention to our inner checks, or hesitancies. Unsureness about what to do tells us to pray. An inner disquiet tells us to wait. In a hurry-up, frantic, helter-skelter world, we slow down and take time—so that the peace of Christ can rule in our hearts.[42] Quietness deep down in our gut gives us green lights about our decisions.

Then our flexibility becomes, more and more, wise, easy, and ongoing. Its Originator called it "peacemaking."

Pastoral Flex

Across history, we in the church have never held onto Peter's elder/ younger message very long at a time. Over and over we've lost it by separating clergy and laity into separate classes spiritually, and by divorcing, in that rift, the sacred from the secular.

So, here are several observations from one who has spent his life in this never-never land, as both a preacher and a businessman. First, we need to face the painful truth. Alexander Chase said, "All generalizations are false, including this one."[43] So I'm going to risk generalizing:

Do the clergy look down on the laity?

Do the laity look down on the clergy?

To both questions, the answer is Yes.

Each vocationally distinct group, alone, tends to feel superior to the other one. This clergy-laity split then, perversely, adds to each group's spiritual pride. The clergy are "more socially and spiritually aware" than the laity. The laity are "more practical and down to earth" than the clergy.

Enough truth rests in each of these two caricatures for both groups to rationalize their superiority. So we each tend to look down on the other. "O Lord, I thank you I am not like this sensual, materialistic layman." Or, "O Lord, I thank you I am not like this sentimental, unrealistic preacher." Our schismatic conceits dehumanize the clergy and despiritualize the laity. Refusing to believe the best about each other, we believe a lie. Refusing to believe the best about God, we miss the Trinity in each other.

Do you wonder that the Apostle, preparing us *in the church* for this awesome vision of institutional oneness, demands that we *begin* with our inside-the-church relationships? "The time has come for judgment to begin; it is beginning with God's own household."[44] Spiritual awakening in society awaits spiritual awakening in the church. Relational growth in the world around us starts with relational growth among God's people.

Only pastoral flex could describe the growth to which we are all called, for it involves healthy submission to one another. It commences from underneath, through our *healthy* lay submission—never knee-jerk or lockstep—to these people, our leaders, who teach us the Word of God. But it only develops through our official church leaders' healthy, voluntary submission to us "ordinary" church members in every way they can—as a part of their pastoral duty.

This back-and-forth flex enables the church to be what she is under our Lord—the model for institutional renewal, transformation, and innovation—for the whole secular world. If the church itself is not changing, can we expect secular institutions to change?

But it's not easy—not for any of us.

For centuries, those of us in the so-called free church tradition—with historical commitments to the separation of church and state—have prided ourselves on emphasizing "the priesthood of all believers." So on this point we have felt spiritually superior to older "established churches"—from state-church traditions—whose commitments to the "lay apostolate" have been more recent.

But the clergy-laity split, unbidden, permeates *all* the institutions in our culture—including evangelical churches. Anyone who has ever heard Baptist pastors argue as vehemently as I have, over the qualitative difference of their "call to preach," will recognize unmistakable echoes of the Roman Catholic or Episcopal clergy's rationale for their "special priesthood."

So we can expect pastoral flex to be painful for the clergy. Just as it is for us of the laity. Because the change I describe—for our churches—is not primarily, or even secondarily, structural. Rather, it is attitudinal, psychological, relational. If structural changes were to follow, they would emerge mutually, out of the relationships.

Pastoring Our Pastors

We *need* clergy-laity distinctions for the church—as an institution—to function effectively and flourish. After all, God's organization is described as a "kingdom"—an organized social entity—not a mob. It's not religious anarchy; it's the historic, orthodox, and forever futuristic Church.

But the pain comes when we try to live together within that structure—especially as we make a conscious commitment to understand the other's point of view—and to respond to anything in it we perceive as valid for us. For that's what hurts—either to change ourselves, or to live with the ongoing tensions yet not break the relationship.

Remember, the laity is responsible for initiating change. The church's enlivening begins from the underside, with us of the laity. So it takes the form of our fresh attention to and deference for our church leadership. Initially that lay adjustment may consist in nothing beyond more than our regular "centralized church" worship attendance. Or it may mean our increased financial support. But those external changes will point us to more intimate changes of attitude for our internal—home and work—secular relationships. We will then really become the "church decentralized." And unless we take those beginning external steps—of time and money for the church as an institution—we will make it doubly hard for those on top, on the clergy side, to change, too.

Describing change in the church as "starting from below" (with the laity) opens me, I realize, to argument. Don't *leaders* have to initiate change? Their *followers* feel powerless. And you could certainly argue from this very text that Peter addresses "elders" first and "youngers" second. I myself spoke initially, you might point out, on "reparenting" and only then, after that, on "rechildrening."

And in all your observations you would be precisely and exactly correct.

But in so arguing you would not destroy my thesis but rather illustrate it. In the Trinitarian model, "leading" and "following" cannot be separated. Forever they remain an indivisible *one*. Splitting them (as I have done to describe our clergy-laity difficulties) can only be limited, incomplete, and to some degree, artificial. For

I describe only our perception of reality, not Reality itself. Rational humans stand awed before the Mystery, however rational we perceive that mystery to be. And the *human* perception of God changed from below when Jesus came. So only servant-leadership-humility in the laity, in response to the Scriptures' revelation borne to us by his messengers, changes our perceptions today to heal the schism and bridge the chasm that separates us.

But the Trinitarian point, please remember, is that those messengers' (the clergy's) Message tells us (the laity) that *we are fully their equals*. We are "a kingdom of priests."[45] Although flexibly below them in the ecclesiastic institution's function, we are absolutely equal with them in our human and pastoral essence.

I believe our clergy today *crave* robust Trinitarian lay equality. Who pastors our pastors? Who tries to understand *their* problems? Who creates, within our congregations and parishes, a climate of sensitivity to, and responsiveness toward, their unique—and lonely—pressures? Who supports them in the distinctive stresses on their families? On their finances? On their time?

No doubt one of the saddest legacies of the clergy-laity split through the centuries has been the "pedestal syndrome." We don't want—or allow—our clergy to be human. Their falls from their pedestals shock us all. But *they* know that our falls are equally tragic, if less widely discussed, and that their unrealistic pedestals—built and raised by our own outdated, unbiblical, frightened lay thinking—cry out for servant-leader change among us all.

Pastoral flex within the church is not easy—but it is essential to our spiritual growth. We grow as we affirm for each other our human and pastoral commonality. The laity becomes the *cheering section* for the clergy; the clergy becomes the *cheering section* for the laity. The laity accepts a backseat role (understood in Trinitarian terms) for the institutional church; the clergy accepts a backseat role (likewise Trinitarian) for secular institutions.

The *people* see themselves as nothing less than pastors; the *pastors* see themselves as nothing more than people. For each group, inescapably today, this means psychological unpleasantness. Our individual vanities, fastened to both the religious and the secular status quo (and to church history's confusions), do not vanish overnight. But let us be clear: Both within the traditional church and outside it, pastoral flex offers us the one route to joy.

On Secular Sacraments: A Portrait of Flex

That remarkable nineteenth-century Scotsman, George MacDonald, touched our era not only through his novels, stories, and other writings, but also through his pivotal influence on C. S. Lewis. MacDonald understood the relational power of the decentralized church. Though a clergyman himself, he grasped the vision that ordinary lay people's everyday tasks could be sacred, too. He portrayed the secular church in the workplace world as quiet—but changing—relationships. He saw how these changes produce small but positive social therapies.

In his 1876 novel, *Thomas Wingfold, Curate* (now reedited and republished as *The Curate's Awakening*), MacDonald makes clear that spiritual awakening in the clergy (Wingfold, the Curate) cannot be separated from—but rather is strengthened by—the spiritual awakening of the laity. In the chapter, "The Common-Place," he depicts this contagious transformation in the thinking and actions of Mr. Drew, a dealer in cloth. This dry-goods merchant thinks "secular church" about his job and his work, following a sermon within the continuing renewal of the local vicar, Reverend Wingfold.

The curate visits Drew's fabric shop one evening just after closing. Drew's spiritual wisdom and vitality once again touch him. Wingfold listens as the layman describes how he came to his latest insights:

> "After the young men had put up the shutters and were gone," Drew said, . . . "leaving me as usual to bolt the door, I fell a-thinking.
>
> There is something solemn in the quiet after business is over. Sometimes it's more so, sometimes less, but this time it came upon me that the shop felt like a chapel—had the very air of one somehow, and I fell a-thinking and *forgot* to close the door. A great awe came upon me.
>
> Could it be—might it not be that God was actually in my shop? I leaned over the counter, with my face in my hands, and went on half thinking, half praying. All at once the desire rose burning in my heart: Would to God my house of business were in truth a holy place, made sacred by his presence! 'And why not?' rejoined

something within me—heart or brain or something deeper. 'Is it, or is it not, of God?'

All of a sudden, I heard a step in the shop and lifting my head, I saw a poor woman with a child in her arms. Annoyed at being found in that posture, like one drunk or in despair; annoyed also with myself for not having shut the door, I had my usual harsh word trembling on my lips. Suddenly something made me look around in a kind of daze. A moment more and I understood: God was waiting to see what truth was in my words.

Then I saw that the poor woman looked frightened—I suppose at my looks and gestures. I made haste and received her, and listened to her errand as if she had been a duchess—say rather an angel of God, for such I felt her in my heart to be. She wanted a bit of dark print with a particular kind of fleck in it, which she had seen in the shop some months before, but had not been able to buy. I turned over everything we had, and was almost ready to give up. At last, however, I found the very piece which had ever since kept haunting her fancy—just enough of it left for a dress! But all the time I sought it, I felt as if I were doing God service—or at least doing something he wanted me to do. It sounds almost ludicrous now, but—"

"God forbid!" said Wingfold.

"I'm glad you don't think so, sir. I was afraid you would."

"Had the thing been a trifle, I should still have said the same," returned the curate. "But who with any heart would call it a trifle to please the fancy of a poor woman, one who is probably far oftener vexed than pleased? She had been longing for this dress—you took trouble to content her with her desire. Who knows what it may do for the growth of the woman? I know what you've done for me by the story of it."

"She did walk out pleased-like," said the merchant,—"and left me more pleased than she—and so grateful to her for coming."

"I begin to suspect," said the curate, after a pause, "that the common transactions of life are the most sacred channels for the spread of the heavenly leaven. There was ten times more of the divine in selling her that dress material as you did, in the name of God, than in taking her into your pew and singing out of the same hymn-book with her."

"I should be glad to do that next though, if I had the chance,"
said Mr. Drew.[46]

The shopkeeper and the woman each underline the churches' capacity for reparenting and rechildrening. Her imperceptible, but
nonetheless real growth, bright amid the dark hurts, bruises, and
wounds of her life, came from the cloth merchant's consciously
seeing his ordinary work as sacred and his "unconscious holiness"
in doing it. He gave her reparenting's needed comfort.

But note her unaware role in his rechildrening. Recounting at
first, for the curate, how in his musing he had forgotten to close
the shop door, the cloth seller revealed another, not insignificant,
personal detail. "My past life came up to me, and I remembered
how, when I was a young man, I used to despise my father's business, to which he was bringing me up."[47]

As priest of the chapel in his shop, Mr. Drew submitted to his
customer's desires. He led pastorally by serving her there. She led
pastorally by deciding to buy. And the gospel infiltrated their mutual world of fabric.

His "pastor principle" (behind the counter, serving her enthusias-
tically), combined with her "church principle" (remembering the
fabric and buying it gratefully). Her "eldering," as an economic
consumer ("The customer signs your paycheck!"), combined with
his "youngering," as the supplier of her demand, making their ex-
change a secular church snapshot.

And Reverend Wingate, the curate, became Mr. Drew's cheering
section: "I know what you've done for me by telling the story."

Functional transitions: In the joy of flex, they each submitted to
the other; "youngers" under Christ, our Elder Brother. A poet would
call it sacramental.

5

Eat or Be Eaten

The Unseen Battle

1 Peter 5:8–9

An idealist is one who, upon observing that a
rose smells better than a cabbage, concludes
that it will also make better soup.
—*H. L. Mencken*

The devil is a liar, and the father of lies.
—*Jesus*

*T*he old-time meat market's gleaming white display case,
with heaping pans of freshly ground red meat, caught the
World War II shopper's eye. As she stopped her cart, she quizzed
the meat cutter behind the refrigerated counter.

"What's that?" she asked, pointing to one dark red, mountain-
ous pan.

"That?" he answered brightly. "Oh, that's blended rabbit,
Ma'am."

"Blended rabbit?" she questioned again. "Rabbit blended with
what?"

"Rabbit blended with horse meat, Ma'am."

"Horse meat?!" she gasped. "Horse meat?!! What's the blend?"

"Fifty-fifty," he smiled. "One rabbit and one horse."

• • •

The old butcher's game of blended rabbit captures, for all of us, our problem relating to each other at home, work, and everywhere else. Left to ourselves, all our love is blended love. Fifty-fifty: You're the rabbit; I'm the horse.

Self-interest, unrecognized but unrestrained, contaminates all our good intentions and noble causes. Idealism deceived, however, remains a deception.

Again and again, misleading and misled, I sell my horse in your rabbit's name. My ambition masquerades as utopia. My selfishness pretends to be sacrifice. My castle building cloaks my need for control; my cloudland camouflages my craving. Unparented and unchildrened, I refuse the joy of relational flex. Instead, whether I realize it or not, I center all my relationships on "me, me, me."

My little problem, therefore, remains this big one: Blindly, I've bought into *the wrong side of the unseen battle between good and evil.* And so have you. As a universal fact, so have we all.[1]

The Battle between Good and Evil

When Archbishop Cranmer put together the *Book of Common Prayer* in 1549, he wrote a litany reflecting the classic explanation of our "little problem" and this bigger war.

> From all the deceits of *the world, the flesh, and the devil,* Good Lord, deliver us.

According to this orthodox view, our sick deceits operate through the world around us, the flesh within us, and the devil, evil personified, who attacks us from without and within.

None of us can overcome any one of these. Christ has, does, and will overcome all three. But if, as the Bible unequivocally puts it, "the world" (our fallen human systems) and "the flesh" (our own self-centered desires) have both been corrupted by "the devil" (evil that is bigger than we are), how do we think, psychologically, about this warfare?

First and foremost, most of us know intuitively that "The devil made me do it!" is unreal because it ignores the other two sources of deceit—the flesh and the world. In addition, we sense that *excess* concern with the devil is irrational, morbidly disproportioned, and unbalanced. "Never paint the devil over your door," said Martin Luther, wisely.

Finally, we know that we can't really sort the three out. It's eternally beyond us, which is why Christ came. So it's not advisable to belabor the problem. As the Proverb says, "Since the Lord is directing our steps, why try to understand everything that happens along the way?"[2] Common sense tells us simply to follow Paul's desire for the Romans: "I want to see you experts in good and not even beginners in evil."[3]

Which does not mean, however, that we are to make the blindly naive mistake of ignoring—or denying—the battle.

Ignoring the Battle

The idea of an ongoing conflict between good and evil has not been in fashion for most of the twentieth century. The popular wisdom of a "scientific" age has been to scoff at the idea of evil as a separate reality, to reduce the arena to one of only the world and the flesh. In 1954, nevertheless, the distinguished Swiss psychiatrist and founder of analytic psychology, Carl Jung, warned us about the psychological consequences of dismissing the battle and the Enemy:

> The devil was . . . abolished, with the result that this metaphysical figure . . . was introjected into man, . . . the wolf in sheep's clothing now goes about whispering in our ear that evil is really nothing but a misunderstanding of good and an effective instrument of progress. We think that the world of darkness has thus been abolished for good and all, and nobody realizes what a poisoning this is of man's soul. In this way he turns himself into the devil, for the devil is half of the archetype whose irresistible power makes even unbelievers ejaculate "Oh God!" on every suitable and unsuitable occasion. . . . One ought never to identify with an archetype, . . . the consequences are terrifying.[4]

Following that blast, Jung entered the then-current battles in theology. He quoted, and ridiculed, a prominent Protestant theolo-

gian who had written in skepticism about our human disintegra-
tion, our sad condition that the Scriptures link to the devil: "We
understand ourselves . . . to be *homogeneous creatures who are not
so peculiarly divided that alien forces can intervene in our inner life,*
as the New Testament supposes."[5] With surprising emotion Jung
ripped into that thinking, which he denounced as being out-of-date:

> The author is evidently unacquainted with the fact that science
> demonstrated the liability [being liable to change, unstable] and
> dissociability of consciousness more than half a century ago and
> proved it by experiment. Our conscious intentions are continually
> disturbed and thwarted . . . by unconscious intrusions. . . . The
> psyche is far from being a homogeneous unit—on the contrary, it
> is a boiling cauldron of contradictory impulses. . . . The unity of
> consciousness . . . is not a reality at all but a desideratum.
>
> I still have a vivid memory of a certain philosopher who also
> raved about this unity and used to consult me about his neurosis:
> he was obsessed by the idea that he was suffering from cancer. I
> do not know how many specialists he had consulted already, and
> how many X-ray pictures he had had made. They all assured him
> that he had no cancer. He himself told me: "I know I have no
> cancer, but I still could have one."

Who, asked Jung, was responsible for this "imaginary" idea?

> He certainly did not make it himself; it was forced on him by
> an "alien" power. There is little to choose between this state and
> that of the man possessed in the New Testament. Now whether
> you believe in a demon of the air or in a factor in the unconscious
> that plays diabolical tricks on you is all one to me. The fact that
> man's imagined unity is menaced by alien powers remains the
> same in either case. Theologians would do better to take account
> for once of these psychological facts than to go on "demythologiz-
> ing" them with rationalistic explanations that are a hundred
> years behind the times.[6]

And yet today, so many years later, the attitude of Jung's raving
philosopher-patient still represents the popular mentality about
evil. Unthinking in our herd heedlessness, we disregard the disci-

plined wisdom of Archbishop Cranmer's liturgy. We may long to be delivered, but we discount the possibility that there is anything to be delivered from.

University of Chicago political scientist Allan Bloom, writing more than thirty years after Jung, underlines the tenacity of such thinking as he relates his college classes' shallow philosophic presuppositions on such central issues as good and evil:

> I began asking a third [question.] "Who do you think is evil?" To this there is an immediate response, "Hitler." (Stalin is hardly mentioned.) "After him, who else?" Up until a couple of years ago, a few students said Nixon, but he has been forgotten and at the same time is being rehabilitated. And there it stops. They have no idea of evil; they doubt its existence.[7]

Speaking into that philosophic vacuity today, Peter does not hesitate, mumble, or stutter in his warning about the reality of evil: "Be self-controlled and alert. Your enemy the devil prowls around like a roaring lion looking for someone to devour. Resist him, standing firm in your faith."[8]

The Bible teaches positive thinking that is realistic, hardheaded, and straightforward, not romantic and sentimental. Therefore, it deals explicitly with Satan, the personification of evil, calling him *the liar, the hater, the accuser, the adversary, the destroyer, the murderer.*[9]

But it also deals with him healthily, never in preoccupation, exaggeration, or superstition. Never does it hint that evil is equal to good nor that Satan is equal to God.

Spelling out this healthy biblical view, the English theologian R. W. Moss writes,

> In regard to the devil's relation to God ... nowhere is there anything like the exact co-ordination of the two. The representation is not that of a dualism, but of the revolt of a subordinate though superhuman power, patiently permitted for a time for wise purposes and then peremptorily put down.[10]

The Bible represents Satan as the ultimate agent of negativity. Against Christ's everlasting, positive "Yes," his enemy throws up an opposite, unaltering "No."[11] But this negation by its very character contains no positive power; Satan makes *nothing whatsoever on his own.*

In its inmost vacuous core, evil contradicts creativity. A self-destroying leech, it mutilates beauty, screws up order, sours harmony, distorts information, and butchers mutuality. Evil can *only* work by negating the good, by thwarting the positive. But it's no match for the definitive, infallible, and overcoming power of the risen Christ.

Evil, in other words, is a formidable enemy, but in Golgotha's crucified Conqueror, good has already triumphed over it. That's the biblical view.

Identifying War Zones

Note the positioning of Peter's explicit reference to the devil here. It *immediately follows* his "elders-youngers" exhortation to flexibility in all our human groupings and organizations. *It all fits together.*

For where do we first encounter the wickedness of tyranny, alienation, and revolt—the demons of accusation, hatred, despair, and destruction? Where but in our structured relationships, starting most intimately with our families, in the battle between parents and children, brothers and sisters? Then the Enemy's conflict escalates into marriage, the war between the sexes making its inroads in excruciating estrangements between husbands and wives. And it doesn't stop there. It continues next down the line of the generations, erupting once again in a replicated war between yet another set of children, parents, and siblings.

From there it spreads to the job, extending these deadly projection transferences further, out into the marketplace—manufacturing, professions, and trades—expanding as noxious firestorms between employers and employees, doctors and patients, teachers and students. And so evil's onslaught stretches wide throughout society, among passive citizens and tyrannical governments alike, and finally brings the nations to war, turning the good green fragrant earth into the dull red stench of hell.

The longest single New Testament description of this spiritual warfare in our families and other institutions comes in the famous fifth and sixth chapters of Ephesians. This passage begins with Paul's soaring explication of the mutual submission principle— Paul and Peter in perfect corroboration on the subject. Ephesians expands and applies its prescriptive therapy to husbands and wives, children and parents, bosses and workers. And then it goes on to portray both the battle itself and the individual's part in it:

> For our fight is not against any physical enemy: it is against organizations and powers that are spiritual. We are up against the unseen power that controls this dark world, and spiritual agents from the very headquarters of evil. Therefore you must wear the whole armor of God that you may be able to resist evil, in its day of power, and that even when you have fought to a standstill you may still stand your ground.[12]

For those recruited in this life-and-death struggle, Paul inventories our military gear, spiritualized from shoes on up to helmet and then on out to shield and sword. What he's describing is the Battle of the Body of Christ: the Battle of the Church in the World. And the battlefield lies in *all* our organizations. Yet, just as surely, the battlefield lies inside each one of us, within ourselves, for what are institutions but groupings of individuals?

Structural Evil: A Parody of Triunity

Many observers today agree that *structural evil* plagues us as qualitatively *worse* than personal, individual evil. Why is this so? Is it not because of evil's derivative, parasitic nature? If evil cannot create—if it can only copy, burlesque, and caricature the good—then structural evil only mimics, misuses, and falsifies *structural good*. It mocks the accord, the oneness, the vital organizational calm of Triunity. Its indifference chills the Trinity's warm comfort; its obstinateness divides Trinitarian teamwork; its estrangement splits Triunity's closeness. Or, more accurately, it chills, divides, and splits us, mocking Triunity's joy, our pastoral flex in human institutions. Evil builds nothing constructive; it only impersonates—and repudiates—the Trinity's offer of structured good.

If a mental image of the Trinity might be three persons living together in healthy, give-and-take union, structural evil can be imagined as three bored, blank, silent people passing the buck.

None of evil's repudiations change ultimate reality, of course. Therefore our search for God, and our amazement as he reveals his personhood to us as Triune, illumines our institutional despairs— about marriage, parents, children, family; vocational despair, departmental politics, office and shop frustration; and especially the twentieth century's Giant Despair, *bureaucracy*.

The impersonal ID-credit-card anonymity of corporate bureaucracies—where the job is more important than the person—combined with our educational, medical, governmental, plus, God help us, philanthropic, psychiatric, and churchly bureaucracies (physician, heal thyself!), locks us into massive institutions, constipatedly computerized, and their data bank facelessness. *The rage we feel at bureaucracy* echoes the impotent anger of the penniless father in a Wolfgang Borchert short story: "He had no face for his fists."[13]

Where in all this is Triunity? Where is our hope? Well, Jesus supplied the face in the facelessness, the face for our fists. That's what Calvary is. He is hurting with us while we parody Triune hope.

Hannah Arendt once said that totalitarianism is rule by nobody. That's bureaucracy, too.

And both are not just "out there." Totalitarianism and bureaucracy—and the evil at the root of both—are in our hearts.

Institutions can only be changed by changed—and changing— individuals. If there had been another way, Jesus would have flipped the switch, snapped his fingers, and pulled the rabbit out of the hat.

Instead, he died alone.

So let me be clear: We'll experience spiritual conflict as long as we live, and the warfare itself will be a means of growth. Imperfect people in imperfect institutions, we'll be on active duty, ever in training for upcoming hostilities, clear up to the very end. Till the day we die we'll be battling, for "the last enemy that shall be destroyed is death."[14]

D-Day and Normandy

Always a fact, perennially true, Christ has won the war already; it's over, finished, accomplished. We share his victory daily, each evening and morning, one step at a time, never in advance. We are the occupying and advancing soldiers in his completed conquest. This shared triumph is the glory of being human.

By a memorable repetition, the Hebrews Epistle describes this glory, twice spelling out the Triune paradox in our relationship with the human Jesus: As our Brother he rechildrens us for serving others; as our Father he reparents us as holy leaders—all to demonstrate the cosmic Purpose in his triumph over evil.

> It was right and proper that in bringing many sons to glory [into *leadership*], God . . . should make the *leader* of their salvation *a perfect leader* through the fact that he *suffered*. For the one who makes men holy and the men who are made holy share a common humanity. So that he is not ashamed to call them *brothers*. . . . Since then "*the children*" have a common physical nature as human beings, he also became a human being, so that by going through death as a man he might *destroy him who had the power of death, that is, the devil.*[15]

Satan has fallen, a defeated foe in that first Easter sunrise. Your disastrously painful battles, however bad, will all turn out consummately good. Decisively and conclusively, evil has been routed. Bethlehem was D-Day. The conquering blood eternally secured the beachhead. Normandy is behind us. Resurrection banners flying, the invasion changed everything. In spite of momentary grimness in battle, long-range now it's just mopping up. Wisdom inevitably beats lunacy. In the Battle of the Bulge, Hitler never really stood a chance.

And yet, though the battle is really over, the fighting still goes on—because none of us is finished yet. The one completely sane man who ever lived was Jesus of Nazareth. The rest of us share, with fluctuating intensities, various degrees of mental and emotional, ethical and spiritual, not to mention physical, infirmity. Compared with his health, we're all sick. The old preachers spoke truth when they talked about "the insanity of sin."

But Jesus didn't come for the well, he said, but for those of us who are ill.[16] He didn't come for the healthy or for those who measure up but rather for those of us who don't. Over the door to the kingdom, as A. J. Russell put it, is posted a sign: "For Sinners Only."[17] And that's the door not only of our entrance, but also of our growth.

That's why, even while my depressive illness leaves me ashamed, I'm glad I got sick enough that I couldn't keep pretending I wasn't. That's no small grace. My ongoing depressive problems keep reminding me: I never have it made. None of us but Christ has arrived. The war has been won, but it still goes on. The Normandy beachhead sits steadfast, everlasting, unshakably established. But Patton's men, puncturing the Bulge, still faced real guns, not water pistols. Hitler defeated remains deadly for a while. We ignore the reality of evil—without and within—to our peril.

Evil Exposed

Perhaps the most insidious form of evil is evil that doesn't recognize itself—the evil of self-deceit and self-inflation.

Born-again life must continue as it begins: out of need, out of poverty, out of helplessness, for *spiritual* riches easily become the most perilous of all. If I think because I'm "filled with the Spirit," or "living a victorious life," or "saved and sanctified" (all gloriously real), if I think that I no longer need Christlike character beyond my current experience, I think irrationally. "If any man says he is without sin, he is a liar and the truth is not in him," says the Epistle of John. "The devil is a liar from the beginning and the father of lies," said Jesus, struggling with the *religionists*.[18] Self-deceit remains deadly serious stuff and evil's most useful tool.

Thinking I have it made means I *look down* on those who don't. If I have *earned* God's favor by my meritorious achievements, of course, that makes sense. But if his approval is an undeserved gift of Christ's grace, looking down on other people is dumb—not only sinful, but also moronic. And as "Telly's Truism" puts it: "A sinner can reform, but stupid is forever."[19]

The psychological difference between "works" and "grace" always remains *pride* versus *humility*. When my eyes are not on Christ, looking down on others gets easier and easier. Locked into pristine self-centeredness, I figure I'm more humble than you. More hardworking. More something. And then I puff up into my own self-righteousness.

This, then, is evil's deadly strategy:

First, through our self-deceit, Satan keeps us from leveling with ourselves. Self-delusion keeps trapping me, you, everybody. Adam blamed Eve . . . and God.[20] And blame keeps going on and on, up to today and beyond. Consider "Johnson's Commentary on Incompatibility in Marriage": "I'm not incompatible—*you're* incompatible."[21] Gert Behanna said that after three divorces she finally realized *she* was the one common denominator, so the problem *might* be hers.

Then Satan deceives us about who Christ is and keeps us from seeing him in each other. Of course, this second deception follows naturally. If I save myself by my own efforts, why look for a Savior? Even if I needed one years ago back when I was "born again" or "got the blessing," I don't need one here in my today. So I don't look for God in ordinary events, don't see him there, *don't recognize a secular Jesus in you.* Unconsciously, of course, I have swallowed the Garden of Eden lie: Eat this fruit, and "you shall be as gods." Like idiots, we keep biting.

Exposing Phony Religion

Our unconscious minds direct our thinking and attitudes so largely that we often remain oblivious to the evil within and around us. The Gospel of Mark, chapter 7, looks closely at a revealing incident in Jesus' ministry, one that occurred out in the countryside, far away from the capital city. He had just, at that time, created a public stir so big that the traditional religious leaders "from Jerusalem" felt compelled to notice it.

These Pharisees—"the name means 'separatist,' . . . distinguishing them from the common people"[22]—were scrupulous extremists, adhering strictly to Jewish regulations about ceremonial cleansing, especially before eating and after coming from the market, where "guilt may have been contracted in both sales and purchases."[23] And it was on the basis of these regulations that they attacked not Jesus himself, but his disciples. Jesus' leadership had intimidated these "spiritual leaders." And so, in the midst of a busy fishing village's lunchtime rush hour, they struck at Jesus' people: "Why don't your disciples live according to the tradition of the elders instead of eating their food with 'unclean' [that is, ceremonially un-washed] hands?"[24]

These "Pharisees" and "scribes" from Jerusalem headquarters had no sooner arrived in the village than they began throwing their weight around, leaning down on the lowly, commonplace disciples. Leaning down from the height of their bigoted, intolerant, fault-finding superiority.[25] Leaning down on the common and the secular.

Their attack infuriated Jesus, and he counterattacked. Why? One reason, surely, was that he was standing up for his disciples against these killjoy clerical bigwigs who were trying to take advantage of his disciples' simple lay weakness.

But I believe he counterattacked for another, even deeper, reason. In the Pharisees' petty legalism he discerned, not a true concern for spiritual purity, but rather an inner contamination, *a guilt aris-ing from their own subconscious.* They were projecting, transferring onto his followers their own inner hidden filth. The heart of their evil, therefore, lay in their self-deceit. ("At whatever point you judge the other, you are condemning yourself."[26])

But what *was* his counterattack? His counterattack that, had they listened, might have exposed their unclean, judgmental minds, their unaware fraudulence, their own inner foulness? Viewed in light of today's scientific intellectual environment, Jesus' conclu-sions still astound us. Two thousand years before Sigmund Freud "discovered" *the Oedipus complex,* Jesus told these Pharisees that their true contamination was father-murder.

Mother-murder.

Parent-hate.

And for this hellish purpose, he said, they were using their reli-gion. Their real fight, their true assault, their actual murder, he said, was against *the Word of God*—"nullifying" it.

"Honor your father and your mother," Jesus quoted to them—the middle commandment, the fifth of the ten, the basic law's pivotal transition from relations with God to relations with people. Then he quoted it a second time, this time from a negative viewpoint—"Anyone who curses his father or mother must be put to death."[27]

Thus Jesus highlighted both the commandment's psychological centrality and the ongoing—and deadly—peril of ignoring it, which is exactly what the Pharisees had done.

The real issue, said Jesus, was the Word of God versus human traditions—the spiritual truth that transforms human interactions in contrast to self-justification's unconscious, hard hypocrisy. And so Jesus exposed the Pharisees by refusing to play their game.

They wanted to talk about others' day-to-day routines. He wanted to talk about their own up-close relationships. They wanted to talk ritual; he wanted to talk reality.[28] They wanted to talk religion; he wanted to talk psychology. And in so doing he pointed unerringly at their own self-deceptive evil.

Exposing a Hungry Hell

In this encounter with the Pharisees, our Lord's holy, healthy human perceptions forced Satan's warfare out into the open—unmasking evil and spotlighting its dark strategies. Twenty centuries later, the well-known Oxford medievalist, writer, and lay theologian C. S. Lewis accomplished a similar feat in his small 1941 classic, *The Screwtape Letters.*

This fictional correspondence from the experienced senior devil Screwtape to his younger tempter-in-training, Wormwood, sprang from Lewis's grasp of our twentieth century psychology—and, prior to that, of biblical psychology as well. Much of *modern* psychology troubled Lewis. But as with all great spiritual writers, he perceived, better than the rest of us, the real issues in all our human relationships, including the nature and reality of evil.

In *Screwtape,* he used a literary device he called "moral inversion—the blacks all white and the whites all black—and the humour which comes of speaking through a totally humourless *personna*" to expose evil's relational processes, which he saw, according to his 1960 preface, as "spiritual cannibalism" . . . a kind of hunger.[29]

> I feign that devils can, in a spiritual sense, eat one another, and us. Even in human life we have seen the passion to dominate, almost to digest, one's fellow; to make his whole intellectual and emotional life merely an extension of one's own. . . . His own little store of passion must be suppressed to make room for ours. If he resists this suppression he is being very selfish.

On earth this desire is often called "love." In Hell I feign that they recognize it as hunger. But there the hunger is more ravenous, and a fuller satisfaction is possible. There, I suggest, the stronger spirit—there are perhaps no bodies to impede the operation—can really and irrevocably suck the weaker into itself and permanently gorge its own being on the weaker's outraged individuality.[30]

And how does such a "hungry hell" work out organizationally? Says Lewis:

My symbol for Hell is something like the bureaucracy of a police state or the offices of a thoroughly nasty business concern . . . an official society held together entirely by fear and greed. . . . "Dog eat dog" is the principle of the whole organization. Everyone wishes everyone else's discrediting, demotion and ruin; everyone is an expert in the confidential report, the pretended alliance, the stab in the back. . . . Every now and then . . . (their hypocritical politeness) gets punctured, and the scalding lava of their hatred spurts out.[31]

Eat or Be Eaten—Eat and Be Fulfilled

Through the voracious Screwtape, Lewis exposes and helps us defeat evil. His portrait of the demonic crackles with realism exactly because it is so psychological—and so biblical. For C. S. Lewis's central metaphor in *Screwtape* is precisely the same one Peter uses in this first Epistle: evil's howling hunger—"looking for someone to *devour.*"[32]

But this "devouring" image was not new with Peter; it is deeply rooted in Hebrew thinking. The famous "forsakenness" Psalm, quoted by Jesus in his dying cry, "My God, my God, why have you forsaken me?" portrays his enemies with similar imagery: "They come at me with open jaws, like roaring lions attacking their prey."[33]

And so does another Psalm, well-known among evangelicals for its inescapable descriptions of our universal fallenness, but less familiar for its graphic portrayal of that fall in all our human relations:

They are corrupt, they do abominable deeds, there is none that does good.

The Lord looks down from heaven upon the children of men, to see if there are any who act wisely, that seek after God.

They have all gone astray, they are all alike corrupt; there is none that does good, no not one. Have they no knowledge, all the evildoers *who eat up my people as they eat bread,* and do not call upon the Lord?[34]

What a picture of evil in relationships: "All alike," chewing on each other and being chewed on ourselves!

And why do people eat people like bread? Because we're starving, empty inside, and we don't know what will fill us up. So we turn on each other.

We consume our best selves—our greatest human potential—by Screwtape's negation reflexes in our minds. As a consequence, we consume others out of this intrinsic hollowness inside our own selves. Evil's negativity sucks out our spiritual core, leaving us starved animals in human shells. This inward-emptying process continually deceives us into believing the lie that other people—particularly our use of or domination over them—can fulfill our inmost cravings.

But within us, the unfilled void only drains deeper. In our self-delusion, Screwtape, through our unreal thinking about how humans can be satisfied, feeds on us. Negativity swallows up negativity: Clutching for the control of others, we abandon our own self-control.

The Sacred Meal

There's no nourishment chewing on others; we simply diminish them and ourselves. Remember, evil carries no real life of its own; it only perverts, parodies, imitates, nullifies, and drains the good. Nothing but good creates, innovates, unifies, reconciles, and overflows. Nothing else fills and satisfies us; nothing else helps us grow.

And where do we find a positive good powerful enough to fill us, to satisfy us, to stop the endless cycle of eat or be eaten? Where but in Jesus himself, who promised us just that:

> Jesus answered them . . . "Do not labor for the food which perishes, but for the food which endures to eternal life." . . . Then they said to him, "What must we do, to be doing the work of God?" Jesus answered them, "This is the work of God, that you believe in him whom he has sent. . . . My Father gives you the true bread from heaven. For the bread of God is that which comes down from heaven, and gives life to the world." They said to him, "Lord, give us this bread always."
>
> Jesus said to them, "I am the bread of life; he who comes to me shall not hunger."[35]

But Jesus gave us more than bread. He also gave us wine. For our starving he gave us not just sustenance, but a party. For our famine he gave us not just a harvest, but a banquet. For our misery he gave us not just comfort, but a celebration.

My inimitable pastor, Buckner Fanning, calls the Lord's Supper "a toast to life!" In that Communion toast, forever dead is devouring evil; forever alive is the bright Resurrection salute to fullness abounding.

Buckner says, "It was *not* the Last Supper. No, we've misnamed it. It was the *First Supper!*"

Remember the Resurrected Jesus on the road to Emmaus, walking along with two of his followers, unrecognized, incognito, unknown? Remember this unrevealed Christ explaining "the scriptures concerning himself," about his suffering, the prelude to his glory? Remember "their hearts burning within them on the way," even before they recognized why?[36]

And remember their unforgettable journey's climax?

> So he went indoors to stay with them. Then it happened! While he was sitting at the table with them he took the loaf, gave thanks, broke it and gave it to them. And their eyes were opened and they recognized him.[37]

Afterwards these two awestruck laymen, one named Cleopas, got up and rushed back to the disciples in Jerusalem:

> Then they gave the account of the events of their journey and how he had been recognized in the breaking of the bread. As they were talking about all this, there he was, standing among them.[38]

Recognized in the breaking of the bread. Did they know him by his hands, by the scars, as he broke the loaf? Cleopas and his friend had not attended the First Supper; perhaps they knew Jesus only at a distance. But Cleopas was enrolled with the *Second Supper.* And afterward came *suppers innumerable.* Twenty centuries later, you and I celebrate that same intimate victory.

The Eucharist, Communion, Lord's Supper, or the Byzantine Rite's presanctified bread and wine: All alike they praise the passion glorious. In music, from the Latin Mass, Eastern Orthodox chants, Swahili rhythms, or Chinese choruses to the homely English of "Let Us Break Bread Together on Our Knees," we focus united on one shattering gift:

> This is my body which is broken for you.

> Then he took a cup and after thanking God he gave it to them with the words, "Drink this, all of you, for it is my blood, the blood of the new agreement."[39]

That First Supper and all it represents changes every other anywhere, anytime supper. Ours is the sacrament of ordinariness: He makes *us also* into broken bread and poured out wine.[40] So, "whether you *eat or drink,* do it all to the glory of God."[41] The Holy Table sanctifies forever every other table.

Observing the Sacred Meal in all our everyday meals points to his real presence everywhere, waiting to be recognized. Christ at the kitchen table. In the breakfast nook. Present in the dining room, the restaurant, the barbecue, nightclub, or picnic. You name it: Any old table will do. We don't have to chew up or feed on each other anymore: "Happy are those who are hungry and thirsty for goodness, for they shall be satisfied."[42]

Devouring me, evil is only emptiness.

Satisfying me, goodness is growing fulfillment.

Controlling Self or Others: Eating up the Wrong Tree

Eating the forbidden fruit "of the knowledge of good and evil" remains the perennial Genesis archetype of my self-centeredness, revolt, and despair.[43] Actually, however, eating the fruit wasn't the first mistake. Most of us forget—as Eve did—that that particular tree was *not* the tree in the middle of the garden. Another—positive—tree entirely stood there, centered in the garden's heart: "the tree of Life."[44]

When Eve conversed with the serpent, letting herself be talked into the primeval disobedience, she misquoted God and believed the worst about him and his Word. She also, therefore in the process, lost her own personal bearings. She saw the *forbidden tree* as the garden's center; she misplaced the garden's middle, its hub, core, pivot, and interior centerpiece. That's when she really lost her way.

Negative thinking about God prepared Eve for the rebellious act. So she ate the forbidden fruit, yes. But in her confusion, she ate more. She also consumed her relationship with her husband. And he, his with her. Bickering, blaming, and marital negativity start that way. We forfeit self-control for the delusion of controlling someone else; negating God, we negate others.

So then Cain consumed his relationship with Abel. Generational negativity, next, chews up sibling relationships. "Am I my brother's keeper?" pictures negation turning violent.[45]

"They eat up my people like they eat bread."

And so on, through our marriages and families, to the bloodsoaked ends of the earth, *ad nauseum infinitum*. We're still "eating up the wrong tree," so we're never filled, satisfied, or content.

Christ was, is, and forever will be the "tree of life" in the garden's middle: "In the place where he was crucified there was a garden," and "on both sides of the river grew the tree of Life, bearing twelve kinds of fruit . . . and the leaves served to heal the nations."[46] Calvary's stark death and luxuriant life bears fruit, today and evermore, as irresistible growth in you and me, healing us first within ourselves, then in our organized relationships, and finally, therefore, satisfying the whole world.

Except for that bare tree on that blossoming hill and its (recognized or unrecognized) development in us, evil absorbs simultaneously our *individuality* and our *community*. Neither of these two essentials survives without the other, for their ultimate source is Triune. Because our childhood experiences remain partial, stunted, or deformed—even under the "best" circumstances, with families, schools, playmates, and adults so often thoughtless or cruel—we yearn for personal distinctiveness and shared solidarity both.

But, since we all stay in various stages and degrees spiritually and psychologically deceived, we don't know what we want. The "great deception" convinces us that we humans alone can fulfill and complete each other. So without realizing why, and with nothing much beyond deformed interpretations of deformed experiences to guide us, predictably we fail to love God, ourselves, or each other.

Given this great deception brutally mauling us and sucking us dry, we find we really *can't* love each other, because of our fears. And our fears seize and hold us because of our experience with devouring evil. First we fear others will devour us; being "youngers" terrifies us. Then, we fear we will devour others; being "elders" frightens us, too. Finally, we fear nobody can change, starting with ourselves.

These fears feed on and compound each other. And so our lives together start to look more than a little like hell.

"Oh well," you say, "you can't change human nature." But that's just the point. Who says you can't change? You can't change *others*, agreed, but what about, through Christ inside you, changing *yourself?*

The very purpose of Christ's coming is to change us. Then through us, little by little, he changes the world. Because, whether we realize it or not, Christ *is* positive thinking in its only healthy sense. Only by his discerning soundness *in* us can we adequately detect negative thinking's fear-filled assaults *on* us.

And then, as Christ's positive-thinking action keeps changing us within, the world around us begins to change, too.

Positive Negativity

One more observation before wrapping up this chapter, with its unrealities so unpleasantly real. God authors positive thinking;

negative thinking emanates from the devil. But positive thinking sometimes *sounds* negative when it stands in a defensive mode.

In Scripture we see this paradox most clearly in our Lord's temptations. These accounts superficially paint him as reacting negatively against negative attacks. But from God's viewpoint—our only true, lasting perspective—he was thinking positively. "Get thee behind me, Satan. For it is written . . ." He thought positively about the positive God's positive words, whatever negativity that produced toward his lonely temptations. Later it gave him a positive negativity toward the macho messianic fantasies of his day.

Such *positive negativism* in the face of evil remains essential to your spiritual-psychological health and mine. Let me illustrate out of my illness.

Writing this chapter, with its specific scriptures and C. S. Lewis language, has helped me recognize again that during my early adult life I consumed my relationship with Dad like bread. I presumed on him, took him for granted. True, I worked hard and contributed a lot to the company, its people, and its growth, across many years of long days and long nights. I feel good about that. But at the same time, I used and exploited Dad and his money in my holier-than-thou, snobbish, false-god ministry, denying that his priesthood was equal to my own.

He offered once to join me and team up together—on some of my speaking trips. And I didn't pick up on his suggestion. I wanted my *own* "thing to do." I regret it to this moment. I guess I thought he wasn't "up" to me spiritually—God have mercy on me and my blended love!

My disloyalty—my relational blindness—was destroying me, even when I didn't realize it. When I presume on others, I presume on God. To get well, to say "yes" to Christ's healing, I had to say "no" to these unconscious attitudes.

My yes demands my no; my no enables my yes.

But there's another twist. The only way I could say no to my human betrayal was to deepen my yes to Christ, which also meant a deepened yes to the psychological truth—as best I understood it—about myself. And the more truthfully I faced my need, the more genuinely I turned to Christ.

For if I hurt Dad, which I did, I hurt myself even more, even while I helped many others. But then I changed, bit by bit, imperceptibly—through my lonely personal battles, through endless talking with my wife, through books that helped and people who cared—by degrees, through the unhurried Christ's systematic Yes. And in the process I grew to love God, my real self, Dad, Mother, my family, associates, and people out beyond, too, far more deeply, intelligently, and broadly.

Only by saying no to my personal temptations can I say yes to unhypocritical love. That positive-negative response may mean I must abandon my use and control of others, but it also gives me an increasingly perceptive, loving self-control. And then, naturally and unselfconsciously, my thought patterns begin to include an awareness of the psychology of others. I begin to put myself in the other person's shoes and respond to what the other person is feeling; my emotional reflexes become more sensitive, loving, and wise.

The Sign of the Prophet Jonah

How does he come to us? To say his everlasting Yes? In his broken body and shed blood—the bread and the wine, the loaf and the cup, our food and our drink. In, together as one, his crucifixion-resurrection life. In *the sign of the prophet Jonah:*

> Then some of the scribes and Pharisees answered Him, saying, "Teacher, we want to see a sign from You." But he answered and said to them, "An evil and adulterous generation craves for a sign; and yet no sign shall be given to it but the sign of Jonah the prophet; for just as Jonah was three days and three nights in the belly of the sea monster, so shall the Son of Man be three days and three nights in the heart of the earth."[47]

In this "dog eat dog" world with its fears of devouring and being devoured, its starvation for simultaneous individuality and community, its insatiable hungers for love's wise acceptance, do we actually realize what Jesus was saying in those familiar "prophet Jonah" words?

They wanted a sign.

Not a triune, relational God; positive, even in pain. They wanted, instead, a military messiah, a political magician, a cheap, fast miracle worker, a spectacular, inexplicable, supernatural push-button showboat.

And he, thank God, said *No*.

His communion, rather, is the communion of the broken and the drained, his fellowship the fellowship of the chewed out and eaten up.

And from that he makes resurrection.

All he would give us: "The sign of the prophet Jonah."

Jonah's name in Hebrew means "Dove." And this first Jewish missionary (from Israel to a Gentile city) pictured, in the long, drawn-out process of his story, Christ's calm, patient Spirit of universal peace.[48] From the ship of his escaping, from the storm of his disobedience, from the self-destruction of his guilt, Jonah was flung into the sea and swallowed by "a great fish." Jonah cried to the Lord from this "belly of death," where he lay "for three days and three nights," praising God in advance for his sure-as-accomplished deliverance: "But from the pit Thou didst lift my life, O Eternal my God."

What happened next? Of course, you know: "Then the Eternal spoke to the fish, and it threw up Jonah on the dry land."[49] Thus, by this unforgettable sign, the prophet Jonah points us, today, to the universal Jesus. Before his story ends, we see Jonah in another dry-land "cross and resurrection" experience that delivers him from an angry temperament and a condemning religion. Jonah dramatically portrays Cross and Resurrection as the long and continuous process of our change and growth, whatever our circumstances, sea-wet or gourd-dry.[50]

When evil swallows good, its digestion always fails.

When death ingests life, from the tomb the gravestone rolls away.

When we kill him in ourselves and in each other, three days later he rises again for us all. Each pain, each defeat, each death produces a new step of growth. Lifetime reparenting. Lifetime rechildrening. The sign of the prophet. . . .

Wait . . . do you recognize the name of Simon Peter's "first birth" Dad? "Jona." The Greek form of the Hebrew Jonah![51] The very name of Simon's human parent prepared him for that cross and resurrection of rebirth!

So has *your* parent's name, whatever it may be. Just call yourself Bar-Jonah.

Today. Bar-Jonah: that's me. Bar-Jonah: that's you.

But, you say, life *is* cutthroat. As they say, "It's eat or be eaten."

"Eat or be eaten?" Oh no, Bar-Jona, wait a minute. You've forgotten the original point.

The third option. *Beyond* "eat or be eaten." Your other choice. *Your* new name: *Peter,* the rock. The solid rock.

You can't eat a rock: The mysterious alchemy of bread, wine, body, blood, and *acknowledged spinelessness.* With time, mixed in tears, it produces living stones, everlasting rocks. Rocks don't eat; rocks can't be eaten. Granite. Flint. Precious stones. Like Simon Peter, from the refining fires of suffering, *a diamond is forever.* "Living stones built up together into a spiritual house."[52]

And the jaws of hell will not prevail against it.

6

Parents Easy to Admire

The Pain, the Process, and the Promise

⌐❧

---
1 Peter 5:9–13

Does the road wind up-hill all the way?
Yes, to the very end.
Will the day's journey take the whole long day?
From morn to night, my friend.
—*Christina Rossetti*

*W*hen I told my wife this chapter's "parents . . . pain"
title, she responded immediately, direct and abrupt:
"*What does THAT mean?* Whose pain? The parent's or the child's?"
"Both," I replied.

. . .

My favorite promise for Peter's psychology comes next. It ties together our pain and our growth: "And after you have suffered a
little while, the God of all grace, who has called you to his eternal
glory in Christ, will himself restore, establish, strengthen and settle you."[1]

When either a bad situation or my old gray-gut glumness pulls
me down, I clutch this sure promise . . . and with numb faith give
thanks. My grip on its reassurance at those sad moments may not
be very strong. And, sometimes for months following, I may not
feel very different. But for all these sixty-eight years its pledge to

me has turned out innumerable times to be true, even though I often become aware of just how it worked out only much later, looking back.

Our hope in this promise springs from its reminder that our sufferings, although real, are neither pointless nor endless. If the word "suffering" sounds too strong for your experience or vocabulary, I urge you to accept it for its ruthless honesty. Biblical language carries our therapy in its plain speaking. Don't deny that "getting your feelings hurt" *hurts*. In Christ our sufferings become the means of our growth, the object of all spiritual psychiatry.

And what does that have to do with parents, and with pain?

Everything.

Our relationship with our parents is where our psychological growth begins. That's where we learn the basics about relationships and, by transference, about God. So that's where we start, relationally, working out our faith.

Which does not mean that faith is something we can invent. Faith is a gift. We can't manufacture it by ourselves; no other human instills it in us, either.

My professor friend says, "Doubt is the occupational hazard of teachers." "No, that's too narrow," I respond. "It's the occupational hazard of us all. Doubts are the growing pains of faith." For, whatever my doubting and my confusions, the unseen battle—between Christ and the Enemy of our faith—is already won. Now faith is available for the asking, the taking, the receiving, the thanking. As Leighton Ford says, "Faith is when I stop saying 'please' and start saying 'thank you.'"

Beyond that primary gift, however, first entrusted to me as a child, my belief's *greatest* boon has come from my parents, who have both been easy to admire. Praiseworthy parents, pointing to God's praiseworthiness, strengthen our faith psychologically and help us grow. Their character reinforces our confidence in God's character. Parental weakness, similarly, undermines our faith's mental and emotional wholeness; our parents' immaturities incline us, unconsciously, toward an immature view of God. Even to begin sorting out these strengths and weaknesses—in them and in us— takes time.

My own Dad was born in poverty, the son of a tubercular father. In 1905 his mother moved her family and her dying husband from western Tennessee to the high, dry Texas Hill Country—at that time the recommended locale for tuberculosis. To survive, with a prayer and fifty dollars' worth of capital stock, she opened a credit-and-delivery grocery store downstairs in the little two-story frame building where they lived. The family slept, crowded, upstairs. Sometimes the boys lived outside, in back, in tents.

In that setting, surrounded by slow, agonizing deaths (both his father and his oldest brother succumbed) and their acute financial need, Dad grew up. At age ten, he started pulling his little red wagon up and down Kerrville's dusty streets, delivering their customers' groceries by hand. Later, after World War I and a stint in the navy, Tivy High's 1914 valedictorian chose to forgo college in the interest of his family's economic existence. Taking advantage of a changeover to cash-and-carry methods, he started stretching and building the business. In those early years, before we became H.E.B., the stores were known as the Piggly Wiggly Butt Company—how's that for a not-taking-yourself-too-seriously corporate name?

My Mother's family, out of deeper South Texas, came from English immigrant stock. Mary Elizabeth Holdsworth must have been her Tivy graduating class's finest, prettiest, and wisest senior, at least to my prejudiced imagination. And, after enough University of Texas to launch her on a teaching career, she must have felt flattered by the continued attentions of the town's rising young businessman. They married in 1924, when he was twenty-nine and she twenty-one. I came along three years later; my sister, Eleanor, and brother, Charles, followed at intervals.

I have always been pleased that by 1933, during Depression years, while the grocery company was still quite small, my mother's Methodist social conscience and my father's strong Baptist roots prompted them to set up the H. E. Butt Foundation, now one of Texas's older charitable foundations. She was the president, he the vice president in charge of funding. As foundations go, it has never been large, but I've seen my mother, through it and other public-service agencies, pour out her life into the lives of others. She used her influence and power to help those who lacked it: she had the gift of helping.

My parents, you see, were not perfect, but they did give me somewhere to start. Something to look up to. Something to admire.

What I have done with those beginnings has been the process of my growth.

Where Admiration Gets Hard

Those qualities that make parents like mine most obviously admirable—their abilities, accomplishments, and recognitions—can become a child's greatest hurdles to genuine generational respect, esteem, and approval. Admiration *competed against* produces grandiosity or despair. As admirable as my own parents are, I've still had lots of pain with them—and they with me.

How then could I say, soberly, that all parents can be admirable?

First, because parenthood itself is admirable. We admire the role, the function, the office; it's humanity's earliest classroom on authority. Next, because—if we want to be healthy—our universal hurts demand that we *think positively* about each other across the generations. If we want to "get it all together," we need this transgenerational unity. And admiration from the bottom up facilitates admiration from the top down.

When the Bible tells us to honor our fathers and our mothers, it prescribes something we all need for growth and healing. If your parents have died, you can honor them in memory. If they still live, you can honor them appropriately now. If you reply that "not all parents are admirable, especially not mine," I can only agree. But I still maintain that positive attitudes toward your parents—within your discovery of God's shared forgiveness—are always available.

Imagine, for argument's sake, that a one-night-stand father leaves the now mother-to-be the morning after conception. The mother decides, nine months later, that nine months has already been too long and checks out immediately after the birth. From both parents, *physical abandonment.** Could such parents possibly be honored or admired?

---

*Another form of parental desertion is emotional abandonment: Parents who are there but not there, physically present but responsively absent, hiding behind newspapers, books, *TV Guides*, travel, work, or sports. Escaping our relationships while bodily in the house.

At a different level, of course, come direct cruelty and child abuse—the cigarette burn, broken bone, or tied-up-in-the-closet type of violence. These do a more extreme

Yes. Yes—though, I admit, not without deep anguish.

The sex act is good in itself, regardless of how either or both our parents degraded it. The gift of sexuality is the gift of creative power. And sexual intercourse—a good gift from a good God—remains our parents' primordial act of creativity.

(For this reason alone, if for no other—that its potential for good is so great—sexuality also represents enormous potential for evil. No area of life pictures evil's character and strategy—to trash, exploit, and pollute the good—more graphically than sex. But however evil may defile sex, it cannot destroy its goodness. In the same way, nothing a parent can do, no matter how evil or irresponsible, can negate parenthood's basic life-giving goodness.)

Friends with whom I discuss parenthood, however, tell me I should water this chapter down. Readers will reject out of hand, they say, my conviction that we should look for—find, and concentrate on—our parents' best traits in order to admire them. These friends argue that bad parenting is now so common—that absentee, abusive, cruel parenting does so much damage and causes so much pain—that it makes this chapter impractical if not impossible.

But, to make my message palatable, do I avoid the unavoidable truth that our psychological health *always depends on love?* Whoever said loving each other would be easy? Or possible, without grace?

The Fifth Commandment, to honor our parents, is the *only* one of the Ten that contains—for us!—a health-related promise ... "that your days may be long." "Admiring" our parents and "honoring" them are one and the same thing. It's for our own welfare.

So is honoring dishonorable parents *ever* hopeless or preposterous? No. Never. Not if we *recognize the honorable* in them, since all parents—including those most despicable—brought honor to themselves giving you birth. There's always something bright and good in them, if we focus our minds on it, for us to regard highly. Maybe the physique we inherited from them. Or the intelligence. Or the playfulness. Or the sensitivity. Or the independence.

---

and more tragic kind of damage, beyond a child's physical or emotional abandonment. Such flagrantly destructive patterns—so often generationally repetitive—underline our central thesis.

Honoring other people *does* demand our deference toward them. Too commonly our century has assaulted the humility each of us needs toward older age. "Don't trust anyone over thirty!" yelled the 1960's firebrand, Jerry Rubin. (But, embarassingly, he grew older too.) Esteem for others flows from the humble recognition of strengths and achievements above and beyond our own. If for no other reason than that they preceded, engendered, and produced our existence, all our parents deserve our humble admiration.

Whatever garbage your parents may have released into your life—however much they may have shamed, abused, or scarred you—the person that the two of them created together is something to shout about. As the bumper sticker puts it, "God Don't Make No Junk," and He used those two people to make you uniquely you. C. S. Lewis said, "You have never talked to a mere mortal,"[2] so I celebrate the two specific parents who made you the one and only— no mere mortal—you.

A beginning, though—however good, twisted, or in-between—is just a beginning. The promise here is that everyone, regardless of how we began, can grow. Even bad starts carry the potential for grand finishes. None of us starts perfect. But any birth makes possible good growth.

Taking Sides between Parents

Whatever parents we've been given, it would have been easier, we figure, with somebody else. Our negative thinking always starts with our parents. So, without the relational healing of a Triune God, we're forever stuck with relational perplexity. None of us finds it easy, always, to admire both our parents. No, from any honest overview, it's not easy. It's hard.

Why is honoring our father and mother so difficult?

First, our tendency toward favoritism makes it hard ever to admire our parents equally. Taking sides between parents—in a fallen world—appears to me *inevitable*. And calamitous.

Balance in society demands our individual balance. We need one basic equilibrium to get the "male principle" and the "female principle" both at full strength: We must love each of our parents. Growth moves us toward equity and balance in our deepest regard for each of them. Tilted parental partisanships block our maximum potential; we rob everybody involved, starting with ourselves.

I've gone through phases where I admired Dad extravagantly, taking his side against Mother on every question in my mind. At times I reveled in Dad's constantly charged-up pace. He kept himself moving ahead—fast forward—against all the odds. Mother, on the other hand, and to our frustration, traveled at her own first fast, then slow—*really* slow—pace. She even drove the car that way—in jerks, with a spastic accelerator. At times, in my mind, his predictable high speed driving seemed infinitely preferable to her unforeseeable starts and stops.

At other times I've felt just the opposite. She was the admirable one of the two, not him, not to me, not then. Fast forward gets tiring, after all. And Mother, amid her stops and starts, always made time for the little items that single-minded folks like Dad sometimes overlooked. She was crippled children's crutches, hospital food-service menus, and reading lessons with a struggling child; he was four-week reports, real-estate deals, and company expense control. She'd check to make sure we had a "picnic" as we traveled Texas's highways; he'd check the number of spaces in a shopping-center parking lot while we drove. She took time to pass out cookies; he took time for one more store.

Maybe that last captures their contrast and my choice: With her, a little boy's hunger; with him, a grown man's discipline. So in my growing up I have had to give his strengths, more deeply, their due. I have had to balance love for her with love for him. And at the same time, in the midst of this forging-ahead process, I have had to learn from her to slow down and "have a picnic" from time to time.

Admiring our parents is hard, then, first because we inescapably take sides between them. Everyone does so unavoidably, not just those reared in single-parent families. (In a single-parent family, the favoritism can be easier to identify.) But a second reason we have trouble admiring our parents is even more basic: Because so often *they're not admirable.*

But we only solve that universal problem by facing the truth that *we're not admirable either.* We, like they, are infected—consciously or unconsciously—not only with imbalance, compulsions, and excesses, but also with distrust, resentment, and vindictiveness. So one part of our generational warfare manifests itself in shame—a reaction deeply rooted in both our individual and familial beginnings.

Admiration Nixed by Shame

Parent-child love starts with the parent's initiative, since the newborn infant's response can only be one of total and helpless dependence. If we think positively and realistically, we value and admire both our parents as the human sources of our life.

As we grow up, though, something happens to that positive attitude toward our parents. It turns—at least in part—negative. It turns into *shame*—sometimes for good reason, but often not: As children we watch well but understand poorly. Shame is different from guilt. Guilt comes from what we have done. Shame comes from what we are.

Adam and Eve, our primordial parents according to the creation story, "were both naked . . . but had no feeling of shame." After the fruit-tree rebellion, however, came the fig-leaf loincloths; self-consciously they covered their nakedness, their embarrassment. This disrespect for themselves—their self-abashed unworthiness—left them feeling forever ashamed.[3]

Each of us today has been formed—physically—out of our own two parents' modern nakedness. And whether we believe in a literal Adam and Eve or not, each of us senses that with our own birth we also inherited "a feeling of shame."

Not all shame is inherently bad, of course; our *good* shame gives us our human boundaries and our need for God. But our *bad* shame gives us feelings of worthlessness, our sense of not ever being good enough. We feel inherently defective; we never totally pass muster; we never completely measure up. As a result, we constantly compare ourselves with others. We feel inferior if they in some way surpass us; we feel superior if we in some way surpass them. But both our inferiority and our superiority mask the unmet needs of an empty self.

Today's "Twelve-Step" programs for addictions (to drinking, eating, gambling, sex, or work), which have grown out of Alcoholics Anonymous (along with the more recent Codependents Anonymous), help us see how often our own self-image has been "shame-based," having sprung from parents whose self-images were shame-based, too. We carry within us our parents' shame, compounded by our own.

As a result, we grow up uncomfortable with ourselves. Something, we feel, is basically wrong with us, not in a healthy "confession of sin" sense, but in an unhealthy inward reproach, a humiliation or deep-rooted embarrassment. And here's the generational rub: We tend to blame our parents for the fact that we feel this way! We fasten negative thinking about ourselves onto some aspect of *our parents'* looks, or work, or reputation.

A poor child feels ashamed of his parents' poverty. An affluent child suffers self-consciousness over his parents' wealth. To us, subjectively, societal acceptance seems tied to people who are our parents' opposites. One teenager feels humiliated by his parents' glaring immoralities; the next by his folks' stuffy uprightness. One feels disgraced over her parents' alcoholism, the next over her parents' bold piosity.

In all these cases, the underlying generational rejection is identical. Left to ourselves, we tend toward a self-destructive shame, and that shame tends—unfairly, if not insanely—to be directed against our parents. We then later project our shame onto our own children; our ashamedness thus perpetuates and multiplies itself. Each generation views the previous one not as the source of its honor, but as its stigma.

During the middle 1930s, I remember vividly sitting on the front seat next to Dad as he drove from our Harlingen headquarters up the Rio Grande Valley visiting grocery stores. On those trips Dad would give me, to read as we drove, white sheets of paper that listed the employees of each store and their weekly pay.

As I recall it, during those Depression years, the wages for the particular people involved ranged from $18 to $37.50 per week. Those were good wages in the Valley for those days, but I felt ashamed. We lived in a two-story brick house on one of Harlingen's better residential streets, and I had plenty of clothes, books, tennis racquets, and baseball gloves. How could our family have so much, I wondered, while other people I knew and liked had so little?

For years, thoughts of those trips and those payrolls troubled me. That memory—and its feeling—triggered innumerable debates inside my mind across decades: socialist versus capitalist, workers versus the bourgeoisie, employees versus management. Finally I recognized the emotion as shame. But please note that, although my shame reflected an inner sense of my own unworthiness, it sprang directly from, and took the form of, condemning *Dad*.

I still acknowledge—and struggle with—the worldwide issues those payrolls involved. Over the years, however, economic realism, psychological insight, and spiritual growth have combined to change my attitude toward them—and toward Dad. Now I know that my shame-based childhood negativism kept me from seeing the other side of the truth—truth that was positive about Dad, and for that matter, positive about all entrepreneurs.

Those payrolls represented both Dad's organizational courage and his willingness, within an employer's limits, to assume a responsibility for others. Deprivation, scarcity, and want in his own childhood—years of monetary weakness—had not kept him from offering gainful, steady employment to many people, and that amid the uncertainty of the Depression. For a man as conscientious as my father, given his value system and economic history, that risk represented no small grace and a very real service to society.

To illustrate his sense of values, in 1945 Dad founded a suburban bank in Corpus Christi, serving as its chairman and controlling stockholder. It grew and prospered. His financial counselor advised him to sell it. The reason? Dad felt that if the bank were ever in trouble, *he personally would be responsible to all the depositors for their deposits.* In 1956 he sold the bank.*

To me, today, my gradual change from an unconsciously reflexive negativism about my father to an emotionally honest admiration—even while we both remained aware of his weaknesses and my own—represents nothing less than Christ's healing of the generations. In our complicated history, Dad's love was the only constant. He, as the leader of our family, absorbed the pain of my negativism. Max DePree, former CEO of the highly acclaimed Herman Miller Co., says, servant-leaders "don't inflict pain; they bear it."[4] As I get older, true to the old saying, Dad gets smarter. Who engineers the transition? Someone Triune. Only in the context of generational healing are any parents—or any children—easy to admire.

---

*Another picture: When I was a young executive in our firm's advertising, I authorized an ad saying, "Our Prices the Lowest," because we thought it was so. Dad

The Generational Promise: Christ's Yoke Is Easy

In those early, crucial days of my psychotherapy, the doctor told me, as I said, "Howard, you've got to talk to your father about how you feel."

You know how I answered him?

"Doc, I can't do it."

I was *scared* to express anything negative, and *unwilling* to express anything positive.

And *that* is counterproductive.

You may feel as I did, too, on identifying your *truly admiring* thoughts about each of your parents. You may feel it's impossibly hard to locate and emphasize positive, constructive things to look up to about *both* your father and mother.

But you really can do it.

And years later you'll look back, as I do now, and say it was easy.

Have you noticed the last verse of the last chapter of the book of Malachi, the last verse of the Hebrew Scriptures, the last verse of the last book of our Old Testament? It finishes the Scriptures that preceded Christ with an amazing psychological flourish—with a prophesy of generational healing. Malachi foretells Christ's coming—its John-the-Baptist preparation, its therapeutic impact, its joyous meaning—with this *family* promise and societal warning: "He will *turn the hearts of the fathers to their children, and the hearts of the children to their fathers;* or else I will come and strike the land with a curse." A great promise and a scary warning for our generational wars.

More than four hundred years later, Malachi's prophesy was fulfilled. Jesus verbalized it: "My yoke is easy and my burden is light."[5] Do Jesus' famous words about an "easy yoke" possibly relate to the battle between the generations? Not only possibly, but direct and intentionally: Look at Matthew's Gospel and the statement's preface.

All things have been delivered to Me by My Father; and no one knows the Son except the Father, and no one knows the Father

---

wouldn't let me run it. "It might not be true on some items," he said. "You can say 'Low Prices,' but I don't want to advertise what *might* not be true."

except the Son and any one to whom the Son chooses to reveal him.

Come to me, all who labor and are heavy laden, and I will give you rest. Take my yoke upon you and learn from me; for I am gentle and lowly in heart, and you will find rest for your souls. For my yoke is easy and my burden is light.[6]

Jesus begins here talking about relationships within the Trinity. Then he promises all who "labor and are heavy laden," "rest for your *souls*": The Greek word is *psyche.*

All humans suffer psychologically, believers and unbelievers alike. Who among us does not *labor* under the weight of family tensions—with parents, with children, with siblings? Who is not *heavy laden* with personal histories—long-developed problems of heredity, temperament, personality, behavior, stressed or broken relationships?

"Heavy laden" surely describes our generational suffering. No parent-child relationship *ever* unfolds without pain. When parents and children try to relate to one another outside this three-in-one God, we end up taking the relationship too seriously (that's idolatry) or not taking it seriously enough (that's loveless indifference). Either way, we hurt each other.

Saving us from both these hellish extremes, God as the Parent in the Child offers us balanced priorities with one another.

Jesus' "yoke" metaphor pictures, literally, a bar of wood connecting two animals working together. Christ's yoke offers, to all of us, parent-child connectedness. The yoke of Christ is the yoke between the generations. But His "yoke" word, in those days, had a secondary meaning too: It meant *balance,* as in the balancing of a scale. Coming to Jesus makes admiring our parents easy because through him we enter the relational balance of the Trinity. His triune yoke *is* easy; his relational burden *is* light.

George Buttrick, speaking of this Scripture, tells "the legend that the birds at first had no wings, and that they rebelled when wings were given because the wings seemed to be a burden; but when accepted, the wings lifted them to the sky. The weight of Christ's yoke is wings to the soul."[7] *Whatever* your parent-child history, He can use it to lift you.

All parents become easy to admire *if* our relationship with them focuses itself in the Trinity. That focus enables us to respond differently to them:

- to see them as an immortally wise gift to us from the perfect divine Parent;

- to see them as fellow participants in the bigger, cosmic battle between good and evil;

- to forgive them for their actions and feelings that have hurt us, hoping that they will forgive us for our actions and feelings that have hurt them;

- to admire them not only for their uniqueness, not only for their gift to us of our own birth, not only for every known or unknown good shaping them and therefore us, but also for their role in our own one-of-a-kind uniqueness. Through the Trinity, our parents—and therefore our children as well—enable us to celebrate parenthood.

Jesus' offer of an "easy yoke" anticipates the promise at the end of Peter's epistle, written forty years afterward. "You will find rest for your souls" says that the Father in the Son *will* "restore, establish, strengthen and settle you."

Of the generational cycle of shame, only the Trinity can keep us broken free. But that freedom comes only through a daily, painful growing process. And it never comes in a short, straight line. Your growth chart—and mine—always zigzags.

The Zigzag Process: The Promise in the Pain

"After you have *suffered* a little while," the Apostle says, good things happen for you. Happiness comes by catching up and staying current on our hurting. Jesus called it being "poor in spirit." We all hurt each other: In families and at work we know each other too well. Spiritual authenticity rides on owning up to the pain. Not necessarily to others: to ourselves. Without our sufferings, we wouldn't be human, we'd be plastic. And we're surrounded by a lot of plastic religion.

Everybody suffers, from the cradle to the grave: it's the human condition. Don't let any persuasive preacher, Pollyanna peddler, or mesmerizing motivator courting you from some split second time frame tell you differently. "Instant happiness" is the gullible's delusion, a psychological fraud, your child-within fleeced by a sideshow con man. But faith gives our suffering a purpose, a limit, and a hope. For faith offers us three explicit promises.

First, *Faith raises our consciousness about our own, often unrecognized suffering.* "Consciousness raising" in any revolutionary movement reflects the faith that something better is available if only we will face what is wrong. *Triune* faith means that we own up to our suffering so it can turn positive. Anger between us—and the emotional pain it means—cannot evaporate until we confront it inwardly.

Second, *Through our sufferings, faith accomplishes good in us— and through us in the lives of others—which would not have been conceivable any other way.* Without our particular suffering, specific and identifiable good things would not have happened. Nothing illustrates this good potential better than forgiveness itself and the community of faith it produces. John Patton's *Is Human Forgiveness Possible?* says that forgiveness is not primarily an act, or even an attitude, but a *discovery:*

> Human forgiveness is not doing something but discovering something—that I am more like those who have hurt me than different from them. I am able to forgive when I discover that I am in no position to forgive. Although the experience of God's forgiveness may involve confession of, and the sense of being forgiven for, specific sins, at its heart it is the recognition of my reception into the community of sinners—those affirmed by God as his children.[8]

Third, *Faith informs us, continually, about suffering's time limits.* Faith is suffering that waits. Faith enables us to accept our suffering, embrace it, and wrest triumphant growth from it. Peter calls us to determined stamina—to perseverance.

That steady endurance within us produces slow-growing but sure-scheduled health. It comes through optimistic grit: optimism for better things ahead; grit to face the pain fearlessly. The absence of either the optimism or the grit hinders our progress. Psychiatrist M. Scott Peck, in *The Road Less Traveled*, says,

> We attempt to skirt around problems rather than meet them head on. We attempt to get out of them rather than suffer through them. This tendency to avoid problems and the emotional suffering inherent in them is the primary basis of all human mental illness. . . . In the succinctly elegant words of Carl Jung, "Neurosis is always a substitute for legitimate suffering."[9]

How does our legitimate suffering, endured in faith, move us forward? My reading of Peter's psychology here suggests three ways. Look at each in progressive depth: (1) The process of faithful suffering lifts and dignifies us—moving us toward the masterpiece God intended. (2) The process of faithful suffering strengthens and stabilizes us, providing us foundational ethics. (3) The process of faithful suffering limbers and unifies us, teaching us flexible wisdom.

The Process Lifts and Dignifies Us

From our universal priesthood to the universal "glory" of this promise, Peter's psychology for you, me, and everyone stands out sharp and clear. In Christ you have already been glorified.[10] Your glory is your servant-leadership. We unwrap this ennobling gift by our patient suffering—for then the gift most intimately becomes our own. We unwrap it *after we have suffered a little while*. How long is "a little while"? It's always longer than we want.

God has set himself the task of making a masterpiece of you. He doesn't care how long it takes; what he starts—and suffers for—he intends to complete. "The God of Patience" is his name.[11] And at this supreme creative task of his, you can be confident, he will endure.

That's hard to believe but crucial to accept: God's timetable is not our own. His timing often seems inscrutably drawn out.

Jean Cocteau asks, "What are the thoughts of the canvas on which a masterpiece is being painted?" What but, "I am being soiled, brutally treated and concealed from view."[12] *Becoming a masterpiece* always, always, hurts the canvas. And it never, never happens overnight.

The name of the game is life eternal. God isn't locked into time like we are—minutes, days, weeks, years, centuries, milleniums. Remember two paradoxical facts about Christ's triumph. First, it happened at one moment in Roman history: "Under Pontius Pilate," as we say in the creed. Second, it happened prior to everything else that ever existed: He is "the Lamb slain from the foundation of the world."[13] Even before God envisioned the universes, said C. S. Lewis, he looked ahead and saw the buzzing flies around the cross.[14]

Your pain has both eternal significance and your own personal progress written all over it—in advance. How can we believe that a God who permits suffering, but never intends it, is *that good?* Because, as Peter reminds us, "He holds dominion forever and ever."[15] Which sounds reasonably reliable, permanent, and trustworthy.

He purposes in this whole enterprise something grander than we dreamed. He purposes a new humanity, and we get to be in on the great adventure.

You have been glorified *at present*—in the midst of the mud, molasses, and misery of the process. If you don't think that fact has anything to do with your present self-image, listen to J. H. Thayer's dictionary definition of "glorified" from the Greek in this very verse: "to make renowned, render illustrious, i.e., to cause the dignity and worth of some person or thing to become manifest and acknowledged."[16]

The process of faithful suffering lifts and dignifies us. As Gerard Manley Hopkins puts it, "He fathers forth whose beauty is past change."[17] Think of yourself as a masterpiece in the making.

The Process Strengthens and Stabilizes Us

Football great Fran Tarkenton calls for our patience within his gridiron practicality. "Beware the big play: the 80-yard drive is better than the 80-yard pass."[18] So the promise that calls us to patience predicts: "After you have suffered a little while, [God] will . . . *re-*

store, establish, strengthen and settle you." Each of these four magnificently sequenced words describes our growth progressively.*

(1) *Restore:* Inwardly we keep discovering our real selves refined, reconciled, and fine-tuned at a deeper level. We focus on God, ourselves, and others more realistically. We get past our parent-child hang-ups more and more. We reassess and shape up our lives, keep maturing within. Our suffering fits into the divine plan; our crosses move us into our resurrections. We go forward into the next step.

(2) *Establish:* Christ unifies, consolidates, solidifies, and organizes us. He sets us up more surely, individually and together, as agents of life, health, reconciliation, change, and newness. *Establishment people* in the best sense, we build up and transform our families, marriages, organizations, and governments.

(3) *Strengthen:* Our sturdier thinking emerges now in the way we act and the moral decisions we make—in other words, in our ethics. Where peer-pressured fears caved us in before, now pain's furnace has forged us a steel backbone. We become more potent in the battle of good against evil. We move beyond personality to character, and that character's "quiet calm sanity" fills us with fresh ethical power.

(4) *Settle:* Our reasoning grounds itself still deeper, away from our fear-filled emotions, down into the one unshakable Rock. By living in the only One who is fully secure in His Identity, we become more composed, more self-controlled, more secure and stabilized in our own identity.

"Oatmeal mush" changes into a "living stone": From "Simon *bar Jona*" all the way to "Simon *the Rock*," it's every bit there for you and me, in a ground-gaining headway of our own.

Reflexive Ethics and the Generations

The ethical climate in society always reflects the generational atmosphere. Inevitably, ethics are relational—positively or negatively. So generational reconciliation produces ethical renewal.

---

*I use the Revised Standard Version's footnoted translation here. It best portrays the forward movement.

For good or ill, we first learn our ethics at home in childhood. I grew up under parents from whom I absorbed the prime importance of truthfulness. They *made sure* I understood.

Once during my Sam Houston Elementary school days, I stood in line at the front steps, waiting with my fellow third-graders to go back into class after recess. As we stood there, from my short pants' right-side pocket bulged—visibly—a brown paper sack. The sack was full of penny candy, bubble gum, and assorted diet delinquencies—junk.

Mother was big on our not eating between meals. But my raging sweet tooth had driven me to steal money from my own bedroom's brass piggy bank and squander the whole take at Mr. Kibbe's school-path store.

Yet for some reason known only to her Foundation projects—heaven help me!—Mother chose to visit Sam Houston Elementary's offices at that very moment.

And I got caught with my pocket open, brown paper sack hanging out.

"What do you have there, son?"

"Oh, just some candy one of my friends asked me to keep for him."

At the moment I thought it was a pretty good lie. But she made me cough up the friend's name! And then she checked with him! So that evening at home I got an especially memorable dose of correction. My wife reminds me it was not for the candy but for the lie.

My parents' discipline was no mild disapproval. No, it was a full-scale, three-of-us-sitting-down in my bedroom, pomp-and-circumstance family conference. Dad presided over the cold-stone-sober big deal. I still remember the discipline from that awesome scene.

Facing America's ethical crisis, we now see a great many University "ethics" courses. But in its midst, a report in the University of Texas's alumni magazine asks, "Can Ethics Be Taught?"

> Recent surveys indicate that at least 60–80 percent of all UT undergraduates have cheated in the classroom. Nor is the problem new. A 1947 article in the *Texas Ranger* showed that two-thirds of the University student body cheated on exams.[19]

I don't claim to be a professional ethicist, but I can't miss the fact that that Sam Houston Elementary candy-store liar and these

University of Texas classroom cheaters—not to mention political fixers, tax swindlers, and con artists—share the same affliction.

Father-murder. Mother-murder. Parent-hate.

It's involuntary. It's universal. And it's hell.

But let's make sure we agree on my analysis. Dishonesty about grade-school candy, just like chiseling university crib sheets, strikes at generational, parent-child relationships—one immediately at hand, one by transference. In a classroom, the teacher is the authority, the parent figure.

My lying about a candy bag struck at my relationship with my parents. The students' cheating on the tests struck at their relationships with the professors. My reflexive lie aimed toward killing my relationship with my parents; their reflexive cheating aimed at killing their relationship with their professors. In both cases, the modus operandi of our social destructiveness was the same. It was hatred of authority. It was relationship destroyed. It was father-murder. And it's all of us every day—without the renewal and strengthening of our ethical reflexes.

Whether I'm in short pants, blue jeans, or a pinstripe suit, my ethical problem depends not nearly so much on knowing there is a right and wrong as it does on having the *wisdom*, the *desire*, the *will*, and the *power* to do what's right.

Nothing works but the royal law of love: to love God completely, and our neighbor as ourselves. Who are our first and primal neighbors? Our parents. For them, us, and our children, Jesus says, "I am the way." He's telling us that without Him, we'll never make it. But He's telling us more. "I am the way" is Jesus telling us that good ends don't justify evil means: Good ends—such as the Father—demand means equally good—the Son. If we want truth at the end, we can't have lies as the path. Little liars can become big crooks.

From our parents, positively or negatively—and from all their successors in all the authority figures of our later lives—most of our ethics are reflexive. Our unconscious value systems put us on automatic pilot. Unless something happens to jolt us—just as my depression has done for me—we cruise along unthinking.

Listening to our lives as seekers for God, we find things every day that jolt us. Conflict with others tells us something, of course, about them. But if we pay attention, these controversies also tell us something about ourselves. Conflicts with others today replicate the conflicts we felt—emotionally—in our family-of-origin as children.

If I'm having trouble with my wife in our marriage—since I can't change her—I must look for ways God may be calling on *me* to change. My own marriage thus demands that I look at Mother and Dad's marriage. Unconsciously I always bring their marriage patterns to my own, either expecting my home to reproduce theirs, or trying to force our home to be different.

If I'm having difficulty at work with my peers, I must reevaluate how my long ago relationships with my brother and sister may affect me today. My early brother-sister relations always hinged on our parents. So I keep getting insights from years gone by that help me today: I can't change my peers, but I can change myself.

Evaluating my present life in light of my inmost history, I'm given directions for prayer, confession, thanksgiving, and change. Confession of sins and praise to God become two matched cylinders in the reciprocating engine that moves me forward. Thomas à Kempis said, "Habit is overcome by habit"[20]: Bad habits overcome by good ones. Growing relationally strengthens and stabilizes our ethics.

The Process Limbers and Unifies Us

Admiring the good in our parents moves us on to wider patterns of admiration elsewhere. We start approving the good we see in others wherever we find it. People we pass every day are withering up, starving for someone's encouragement. They die for attention, affirmation, appreciation—premeditated or casual. They need a pat on the back. Recognizing that need in ourselves, we can become cheerleaders for each other.

The zigzag patient-suffering process constantly grows us *together*. Our growth is never just individual; it is always social.

Peter's social psychology illustrates itself in the Epistle's ending, as it moves from his promise to his practice. In simple relational references, he shows us his vision under a microscope—a small but startling cross-sectional slide: His understanding of a three-personed God has been miniaturized down into his own working relationships. He works every day by pastoral psychology: His flexibility has transformed his relational patterns. To close his Letter, he focuses on three proper names: Silvanus, Babylon, and Mark. Look first at the two individuals, Silvanus and Mark.

Limberness: My Brother and My Son

First, Peter addresses "Silvanus, a faithful brother."[21] Silvanus was very much a *somebody*. He was not only the bearer of the Letter but also Peter's scribe; he transcribed and carried it from Peter to its readers.

But Silvanus is also called, in the New Testament, elsewhere by his shorter name, perhaps a nickname, "Silas."[22] Like the Apostle Paul, Silvanus was both Jewish and a Roman citizen, one of the early church's main leaders, in all likelihood broadly cultured and highly educated—from an old-money, upper-crust family. His Roman citizenship tells us so: Rome represented the country-club set, the first century's political, military, economic and social elite.[23]

Scholars tell us that in this Epistle Silvanus gave both his cultivated polish, and his literary flourish, to Simon Peter's grubby, Galilean fisherman Greek. (Peter grew up speaking Aramaic.)

Next, "Mark, my son."[24] Peter's reparenting of John Mark tells us one of biblical literature's most inspiring between-the-lines stories. As a younger man, John Mark had bitterly disappointed the apostle Paul, on Paul's first missionary journey, by abruptly defecting from their team. As Paul and Barnabas had traveled from Asia Minor's lower coast north into modern Turkey, John Mark had returned south to Jerusalem, driven either by homesickness or disagreements to renege on the trip.

Mark's desertion upset Paul profoundly. So he had split with Barnabas, the young man's cousin, over the issue of whether Mark would accompany them again, on an upcoming trip. Because of that painful disagreement, and team breakup, Silas (Silvanus) had replaced Barnabas as Paul's traveling associate, his second in command, on the apostle's next missionary journey.

All these stormy occurrences took place long before Peter thought of writing this first Epistle. But they cast an intriguing light on Peter's farewell greeting, suggesting how much the big fisherman had subsequently meant to Mark. By the tenderness of his words, "Mark, my son," we know that Peter had built Mark back up and restored him to the inner circle. But we know it, even more memorably, in the ancient tradition that Peter, through his oral memoirs, became the primary (and fearlessly honest) source for Mark's Gospel.

Assuming this tradition is true, we know Mark in the twentieth century chiefly because Peter rehabilitated him: Peter made Mark great. *Paul* and Mark later, many years after their controversy, were reconciled and worked together again.[25] But before that happened, Peter's reparenting had brought about the glorious and historic reclamation of this young man Mark.

Therefore in these two relationships—with "Silvanus, a faithful brother," Peter's working *equal*, and "Mark, my son," Peter's pastoral *protégé*—we see the full development of wisdom's flex in Peter. The Apostle had learned—by the Wisdom within him—to relate to different people differently, perceiving and responding creatively to subtle individual distinctions.

Our patient suffering can build the same relational limberness into us. Divine wisdom demands our adaptability; relationships require appropriateness. *Agape* flexes itself into suitable adjustments and apt accommodations, creating a fit harmony in each individualized relationship, not the dishonest, knee-jerk reactions of hypocrisy's mask, but the intuitively sensitive—"right for the purpose"—response to both our own and the other person's needs.

Undoubtedly Silvanus had helped Peter greatly with this Epistle's Greek. Don't you wish you could have eavesdropped on those literary sessions as they debated, pondered, and prayed over their choice of words? We would freshly appreciate, I am sure, the ongoing mystery of "God-breathed scripture."

In my imagination I hear them arguing with each other about nuances of word choice, grammar, sentence structure, as Peter submits to Silvanus and then vice versa. Obviously, the working relationship between these two men differs dramatically from that of a traditional author dictating to a traditional scribe. Though Peter leads and controls the writing process, he defers repeatedly and humbly to Silvanus's different skills and insights on syntax and semantics.

They work together synergistically: Silvanus, the editor as well as the scribe; Peter, the down-home fisherman serving the uptown intellectual through leadership in a purpose bigger than them both.

As we will soon see, this dynamic working relationship carries within itself a whole new set of implications for human politics. Their enthusiastic unity works exponentially. They are not only one, but also more than two.

And when they finish, I can imagine Peter, satisfied at last with their product and quietly confident, taking the pen himself to write the last three verses. What he wrote with his own hand must have pleased Silvanus:

> I am sending this short letter by Silvanus, whom I know to be a faithful brother, to stimulate your faith and assure you the above words represent the true grace of God.[26]

Triune ethics, relational ethics—applying biblical principles in living and working with others—grow strong through our gradually accumulated psychological limberness. But once again, there is no quick fix or shortcut. We keep on learning after we have suffered a little while; we keep on growing more limber and more united. Relational maturity depends on an inner sense of timing developed through a continuous life of prayer, not rushing in to "do God's work for him," which always backfires, but rather waiting patiently for Him to do the work *through* us—or through someone else. The goal is the process, and the process cannot be rushed.

Relational flexibility, therefore, lifts us beyond legalisms to the law of love. But to love others as we love ourselves calls for internal balance, for psychological equilibrium, for being restored and established and strengthened and settled. Sea-deep inner peace, a Triune wisdom that reaches beyond our lopsided understandings, guides our brief, transitory relational negotiations with everyone around us. We become flexible conduits of unity. We find ourselves working with Silvanus as a brother, while simultaneously working with Mark as a son.

Our Lord prayed, "That they may be one, Father, even as we are one."[27] How are the Father and the Son one? They unite in a perfect individuality that does not violate a perfect community, and vice versa. So the Son says, "I speak only in accordance with what the Father has told me,"[28] yet the Son is resurrected by the Father "on the third day" in accordance with his Son's words.[29] They are (he is) perfect followership in perfect leadership united in the one Spirit of perfectly equal flexibility. So, once again, how does that unifying flexibility—working with Silvanus as a brother, but with Mark as a son—come to us? As conduits of Triunity, how do we learn to flex?

Unity: Male and Female in Babylon

"She who is in Babylon, chosen together with you, sends her greetings."[30] This brief, cryptic, puzzling adieu in Peter's final greetings has fascinated biblical students for centuries. Who is "she"? And what does "Babylon" mean?

On the first question, agreement is near unanimous that *she* means "church." A few diehards might still hold out for Peter's wife, but the "church" consensus has essentially overwhelmed them.

On the second, the "Babylon" question, neither the dimly known Egyptian city of that name nor the ancient city on the Euphrates (by Peter's time in decay) makes much sense. Most interpreters believe Babylon symbolizes imperial Rome.[31] To me, both these interpretations ring true.

Yet, surely since the whole Epistle is so psychological, Peter's closing symbolism here goes deeper and is more daring, higher and is more futuristic than we have yet realized. These few enigmatic words summarize, *in code*, the whole Epistle. They paint a picture of relational unity in the midst of a chaotic world—the relational unity of a secular church penetrating society.

"Babylon" describes all the institutional hells of human society, starting with our marriage problems, on out to nations and civilizations. No wonder Peter picked this word; it is the Bible's word for institutional evil, relational estrangements, and organizational depravity.

Through the whole biblical revelation, "Babylon" encompasses everything evil in human culture, starting with the tower of Babel, that tragic monument to human pride that was destroyed through linguistic disarray—"the confusion of tongues"—so that we can no longer understand each other.[32] Babylon continues with the decaying Roman empire, whose collapse Peter could observe first-hand. It closes with the destroyed city at the end, in Revelation: "Fallen, fallen is Babylon the great."[33]

So "she"—the church—stands "in Babylon," unconfused amid relational chaos and organizational evil, "*in* but not *of* the world."[34] It's no accident that this serene, triumphant relational entity is a "she." For at this point Peter confronts us again not only as pastoral psychologist but also as psychosexual analyzer—and the unity he pictures is that of male and female as well as of parents and children, leaders and followers, clergy and laity.

If the impetuous Peter of old were sexually insecure, he has at last lost all fear of the feminine. He calls men and women alike, in Christ, to virtues we stereotype as *feminine:* vulnerability, kindness, humility, communication, gentleness, feeling, patience, wise weakness, psychological strength, appropriate submissiveness, and service.

The church, he says, is *she.*

Contrast *that* with Babylon. Both *Babylon* and *church,* as biblical word symbols, are feminine. (The Bride of Christ versus the Whore of Babylon: Institutions, in the Bible, are feminine.) Both *she.* But the Scriptures first mention *Babel* as the beginning of the kingdom of Nimrod, "whose name means 'rebelliousness,'"[35]—"the first man on earth to be a despot."[36] And how is this prototype of Babylon, this rebellious tyrant, Nimrod, individually described? It's repeated twice in the same verse: Nimrod was "a mighty hunter."[37]

Hunter! Hunting, now and then, clear back to prehistoric man, says *male.* Macho!

My "buck fever"—when I was twelve and killed my first buck (eight points!)—overrides any other memory I have of that proud occasion. Fear that I'd miss him, that the other grown-up male hunters would laugh, plugs us into our universal male fear—of "not being a *real man.*" Macho games, of course, are the games all we men play, in countless known and unknown ways. Nothing's wrong with the games—nothing's wrong with deer hunting. What's wrong is our male psychology—our fear of the feminine.

But this fear of the feminine is not unique to us males. Female suspicion of men expresses the same fear—just as women's overdefensiveness does about being victimized. Or a stylish mademoiselle smoking a cigar to prove a point. What about female manipulation? Its scheming reflects a dread of submissiveness—of the "feminine principle"—at the motivational level where we truly live. Do women ever insist, relentlessly, on logic? Or fear being caught crying? Or patronize men by treating them like little boys? Has a woman ever devised a plan to keep things under her control? To avoid her vulnerability? To flee the feminine?

And what has this to do with father-murder, mother-murder, parent-hate, shame—where we started? What does it have to do with patient suffering, and with Triunity?

Plenty. Ambivalent feelings toward parents, the unfavorite one or both, rest deep at the core of all our sexual confusion. And sexual confusion leaves all human life confused. Paul's famous first chapter of Romans, in his teaching on sexual confusion and religious confusion, discusses not only the historic problem of perversions, but also indicts, "They show no loyalty to parents."[38]

Our ambiguous feelings about our parents are reflected, ultimately, in our unaware ambiguous feelings about God. He gave us, after all, these two specific humans to parent us. So, all of us—universally, to some degree—stay theologically confused, our emotions exploiting our reason. Religiously puzzled. Spiritually compulsive, or indifferent, all fouled up, lacking healthy faith. If Christ weren't perfect, we'd be sunk.

Every human is *some kind* of a theologian, whether we realize it or not—each of us, with our own individual view of the way things are. We all have value systems, roots for our morals, ultimate loyalties. Atheism is nothing more, consequently, than a theology turned totally negative. Our only choice is good theology or bad. So our theological confusions reflect our sexual confusions universally. And vice versa. And all these confusions interact with our various kinds of religious training. Nobody has it all together.

So, out of the psychology in this explosive Epistle, I come to you as only one togetherless church member and speak from all our tragically togetherless churches. I join my voice with a man called Peter to say, personally: "She . . . salutes you."

The Church's true life of "waiting on the Lord"[39] rises above and discriminates between our sexual stereotypes—tradition's male aggression and female passivity. Our stabilizing perseverance, daily looking for Three-in-One guidance, gives to females healthy assertiveness and to males wholesome adaptability, while each sex retains and enhances its own differentiated (created) essence. The life we live Christ lives within us, beyond our disordered conventional notions, as neither male nor female, but Triune.

This appropriate Trinitarian flexibility, within each person and among us all together, cannot be rushed. It unfolds calmly, persistently and irresistibly, growing—through faithful suffering—into Christlike character. With Paul, each maturing male *or* female can say, "I am what I am by the grace of God."[40] Then God says, through Her, his church, both *viva la difference* and, between the sexes united, exponential strength.

Thus, with specific mention of Silvanus, the church, and Mark, the Apostle draws to his Epistle's close. There's a reason, too, that he winds up his specific, personal greetings on the note of *Mark's spiritual reparenting* ("My son Mark").

Peter hadn't told and retold for Mark those stories about his own spiritual failures for nothing. Nor spent so much time with him. Nor taken his problems so seriously. Peter's listening and talking, his prayers and his stories seemed to help Mark in his problem with Paul—and his problems with everybody else. Many scholars think Mark's mother was a widow.[41] Whether that's true or not, Peter was obviously a father figure for Mark—a parent substitute, an eraser of confusion. Peter was a reparenter, and the old fisherman knew it.

This brings us back where we started. The very zigzag process of reparenting and rechildrening gives us many "parents easy to admire." For God provides not only healing for our generational shame, but also substitutes for those instances where our birth parents, for one reason or another, fail us.

The crucial reparenting truth is that, although we are called to grow through faithful, patient suffering, we are never called to grow alone. When you were born, your parents had helpers—maybe even a hospital—for your delivery. So it is with your growth. The pastors, counselors, teachers, coaches, mentors, and friends we meet across the years—in addition to that original two—will help us all the way through the painful growing process. (And then we'll help them, too.) All of us have, if we will just look for them, *parents to spare*.

And so I don't know about you, but as for me, I have a long way to grow.

For all our reparenting and rechildrening growth, for all our drawn-out sufferings, the one perfect divine Parent has given us an abundance of mothers and fathers. Every confused one of us has "parents easy to admire" aplenty.

PART THREE

❧

Relationships and Democracy

Flex Thinking:
The Citizen as Player-Coach

Happy is the age in which the great listen
to the small, for in such a generation the
small will listen to the great.
—*The Talmud*

When smashing monuments, save the
pedestals—they always come in handy.
—*Stanislaw Lec*

To lift up the hands in prayer gives God glory, but a man
with a dungfork in his hand, a woman with a sloppail, gives
him glory too. He is so great all things give him glory if
you mean they should.
—*Gerard Manley Hopkins*

7

The Politics of Chosenness

Making Democracy Work

---
1 Peter 1:1–2

There never was a democracy yet
that did not commit suicide.
—*John Adams*

*J*ohn Wycliffe, Oxford's fourteenth-century English theologian and reformer, played a heroic role in the story of modern democracy. In 1380–84, he produced the first Bible translation into English—the language of the common people. (Before, it had been available only in Latin.) In his Bible's first edition preface, Wycliffe said, "*This Bible is translated and shall make possible Government of people, by people, for people.*"[1]

In the fourteenth-century's political-religious climate of sacral-state oppression, small wonder that before he died, *all* Wycliffe's writings were banned.

Even that was not enough. Wycliffe's teachings so frightened Church authorities that, thirty-one years after his death, the Council of Constance ordered that his bones be exhumed and burnt. When the Council's order was carried out, his unearthed ashes were cast into a tributary of England's River Avon.

But the people's view of John Wycliffe differed with the Council of Constance. As the popular ditty put it:

The Avon to the Severn runs,
And Severn to the sea;
And Wycliffe's dust shall spread abroad
Wide as the waters be.[2]

For Wycliffe's dust did spread abroad, indeed, across the Atlantic to our American shores. And his idea—his concept, his vision, his "Government of people" phrase—was kicked around, unknowingly, by intellectuals, theologians, and philosophers across almost five hundred years.

The phrase found ultimate lodging in the mind, heart, and thinking of Abraham Lincoln.[3] It became the immortal key for the final, glorious crescendo of Lincoln's Gettysburg Address. He voiced in it a young, uniting country's high resolve, "that this nation, under God, shall have a new birth of freedom—and that *government 'of the people, by the people, for the people,'* shall not perish from the earth."

God and Democracy

Reading the same Bible that kindled Wycliffe's—and Lincoln's—vision, is it too much to call 1 Peter an argument for democracy?

No, it is not, if we make clear that Peter understands democracy as Trinitarian or relational. He goes beyond the oversimplification of one person, one vote, though he affirms the slogan's principle. The picture he paints is that of one person, one vote *in a peaceful structure of organized relationships.*

In this relational sense, Peter portrays the Kingdom of God—in its here and now form—as universal democracy: men and women living together in a system of flexible relationships with leaders serving, servants leading, and change coming from underneath, from the consent of the followers. From these Trinitarian presuppositions, then, he points us toward democratic marriage and democratic working relationships, even—understood from within a Triune organizational structure—democratic churches and democratic families. The natural, obvious next step applies the Trinitarian view of democratic relationships to the larger society.

Trinitarian democracy never fears or condemns the secular; it works best in the everyday, the ordinary, the unnoticed. Religious liberty is its engine, the separation of church and state its chassis, layers of differentiated loyalty its fuel. Pastoral flex overcomes political engine lock. Negotiation and compromise provide us progress—by a transcendent mandate—toward political peace, economic growth, and social health.

When the Bible tells us that we are all now a "kingdom of priests" and that Christ has made us, universally in himself, "kings and priests to God," it announces the most radical political thinking ever to strike the human mind.[4] It announces the *psychological* foundations for a workable democracy, capable of transforming all political systems, even malfunctioning "democratic" ones.

Players on this democratic team act as coaches; coaches keep in shape by playing on the field. Both functions operate simultaneously: the citizen is a player-coach.

All Indians: All Chiefs.

Flexibility unites our followership and our leadership: Without a sense of followership, there is no participation; without a sense of leadership, there is no responsibility.

Universal flex is universal calm; universal leadership is universal glory. In a democracy, said Justice Brandeis, the highest office is the office of citizen.

Greek or Trinitarian Democracy?

Democracy as a political system first appeared, several centuries before Christ, in the city-states of ancient Greece. It didn't last long. As a matter of fact, it disappeared among governments, discarded as unworkable, for two thousand years following its collapse in those Greek states.[5]

A Trinitarian understanding of democracy, however, differs radically from the Greek. It acknowledges leadership, reflecting the Father's role in the Trinity, while simultaneously recognizing equality, reflecting the role of the Son. In the Spirit it offers both roles, united in the divine wisdom of pastoral flex, to all humanity.

Greek democracy offers us no such universal flexibility. It offers only a flat, one-dimensioned, unrealistic and impractical equality. Edmund Burke said, "Those who attempt to level never equalize."[6] So at some point, inevitably, Greek democracy comes to fit H. L.

Mencken's sly denigration as "mobocracy." When that happens, to save the people from disorder and chaos, a tyrant appears.

Even Socrates, the great Christ-figure of Greek philosophy, saw that Greek democracy produces inescapable tyranny. Socrates objected to democracy on the grounds that it subverted justice, offering no respect for authority even between parents and children, and treated any citizen's opinion as equal to any other's.[7]

Socrates argued, in place of democracy, for a wise, virtuous, just philosopher-king.[8] True to his own vision, condemned in a democratic restoration, Socrates died by drinking the hemlock, unaware that his ideal politics, realized in Christ, could offer workable democracy—including appropriate hierarchy or leadership—to us all.

Workable democracy—democracy that could endure—was precisely what the apostles themselves forged, relating to each other, in the early church. It transformed the political psychology of the Apostle Peter, as this Epistle demonstrates, and it offers to transform both our personal and political lives today.[9]

Politics, after all, *is* the human reality. We never escape it. Normally we picture "politics" only in its public forms: city, county, state, national, international. But politics also refers to the total complex of relations between people within a society.

Politics describes what happens in *relationships*. And for this reason, politics is inherently psychological. Politics starts at home: in the bedroom, kitchen, and family room. It starts in our minds, in the close-up intimacy of the kinships where we learned to think. Politics starts between the generations.

Following that, at least physically, it grows up and goes off to work. There our office politics, our company, plant, store, or shop politics, and then our societal politics, take our family politics one step further. One circle larger. One orbit wider.

The Politics of Working Teams

When we take our first job—just as when we get married—we "leave home" in a way different from ever before. We move beyond that original family system out into a fresh employment system. But inside ourselves, psychologically, we take our lifelong family politics along with us as we go off to start with those new people on that new job. We transfer our family patterns onto our first working group. And we keep up this process of transference wherever we go the rest of our lives—most closely in the give-and-take teamwork of our marriages.

Looking at politics this way, and observing political interactions everywhere, we unavoidably conclude that *politics outside the home always begins with working teams:* small groups of people working together on a common task.

This is why the New Testament primarily tells its stories through working teams. And why the New Testament, in one sense, should be called a political document—because the entire New Testament can be seen as *one* story, the story of Jesus' working teams.

It begins with Jesus' initial twelve-person team. We call that original-team portion of the story The Gospels. Following comes the Acts of the Apostles, which is his working-team saga continuing. Only there, in Acts, something completely unexpected happens. The one working team Christ started with in the days of his flesh now multiplies, divides, and explodes in the days of his Spirit, becoming not just one, but *many* working teams, decentralized. Each team separately—and all of them together—incarnates *decentralized unity.*

Clearly, Christ's crucified-resurrected Lordship has started producing and reproducing, under his Spirit, a phenomenon never fully realized before in all human history: innumerable working teams functioning in decentralized unity. Each team is a community of fellowship, reconciliation, truth and love. And *that* is how we got the Epistles, including 1 Peter. We received them from the earliest, most authentic days of the church, the days when decentralized unity was the working model.

And what is decentralized unity?

Once again, it's Trinitarian democracy, the politics of pastoral flex. The story of how this kind of democracy came to us gives us a fascinating glimpse of its astounding power. Because in making democracy work, the Peter-Silvanus-Mark team was only one drama among the others.

The Journey toward Greece

Remember Silvanus, from our last chapter? Fascinating fellow, Silvanus, the Apostle Peter's Number Two man when he wrote this letter. But earlier, Silvanus (Silas) also had been the *Apostle Paul's* Number Two, back before Paul's imprisonment, back when Paul and *his team* had first introduced the Gospel to Greece.

Though he didn't realize it till much later, Paul had been given the perfect (four-man) team for Greece: (1) Paul himself, who was also a Roman citizen, and, like Silvanus, a superbly educated Greek-speaking intellectual; (2) Silvanus; (3) Timothy, the standout Jewish son of a Greek father; and (4) the physician Luke, a Greek scientist.

The way Paul knew that God was telling him to take his team to Greece gives us one of the most dramatic pivot points in all human history.

The drama took place up on the northwest corner of Asia Minor, which is the modern nation of Turkey. Paul had assembled three-fourths of his team deeper down in Asia Minor, much farther to the southeast. As he had traveled north he had tried first to turn sharp west and stay in Turkey, and second to turn back east and move toward the Orient. Both on Turkey and on the Orient, the Book of Acts tells us, God had somehow stopped him. Paul didn't know where to go or what to do next.

Then, up in the northwestern city of Troas, (the ancient name was Troy, the scene of the Trojan War), Paul had a vision that changed his life and ours: "Come over into *Macedonia* and help us."

Paul obeyed his vision, and immediately boarded a ship across the northern Aegean, past the entrance to the Dardanelles (Hellespont) Strait, the waterway that separates Asia from Europe.

"Macedonia" is Greece, the cradle of democracy.

"Macedonia" is Europe, the West, us.

"Macedonia" for Paul turned out to be, twenty centuries later, your history and mine.

When Paul and his decentrally unified team invaded Europe, armed with nothing except the Gospel of Christ's peace, *they came by way of Greece*—Greece, where democracy had been tried centuries before, and discarded.

Greek democracy had been revealed historically then (as it is increasingly today) to be unstable and impractical—a sure route to political failure and tyranny. Paul came to the Greeks preaching Christ, whose Trinitarian offer makes democracy's dream realistic. His working team brought to the Western world the same message

Peter fills in and opens up for us now: Make way for Triune democracy!*[10]

From the Beginning: The Social-Psychological Trinity

The heart of Peter's democratic message is that all healthy individual relationships, healthy institutions, and healthy governments root themselves in the very nature of God. When we work well together, honoring individual worth while eschewing organizational chaos, we are living according to God's disclosed-in-Christ organizational model. The three-personed God is both relational and free. His very nature is pastoral flex. And that relational reality forms the basis for all our organizations and institutions—governments included.

Here's another way of looking at it. Our self-image, our concept of God, and our view of our relationships become radically altered when we come to look at the Trinity not only as divine but also as human, not only transcendent but also immanent, not only theological but also social and psychological. Just as God himself is Triune, so are our thoughts and organizations and relationships when we remain attuned to God's direction. We become, in a sense, miniaturized trinities. The very dynamic of our living becomes the three-personed God, the Social-Psychological Trinity, incarnated in our lives and relationships.

As it turns out in advance, the first two verses of the Epistle announce precisely that. Peter's salutation sketches the Social-Psychological Trinity as both divine and human, and summarizes the wonderful implications for our relational and political health.

These two beginning verses encapsulate, ahead of time, the whole Letter—and more. Up until now, we have been watching as Peter

---

*Looking at these terms and their impact, we can begin to comprehend Pilate's inscription posted over the Cross. Above Christ's crucifixion, Caesar's local governor placarded, "This is Jesus . . . the King." But he wrote it three times: In Hebrew, Greek, and Latin (see John 19:20, KJV). So explaining the Cross, what sign do we read? It says, "This is Jesus the King" in the three *universal* languages: Hebrew, the Jew's language of religion; Greek, the educator's language of culture; and Latin, *the Roman's language of government.* This is Jesus, the relational King, who changes leadership, and changes citizenship, so that the two become one.

extends their inferences and their consequences, more broadly and more detailed, in all that has followed.

Don't miss the simple common sense in Peter's political-psychology lesson plan. First, in these two introductory verses, he tells us what he's going to tell us. Then, in the Letter's body, he tells us. Last, in the Silvanus-Mark-Babylon closing, he tells us what he's told us. He doesn't want us to miss his point.

Throughout his Epistle, Peter's replications of his pastoral-flex theme have constituted its cohesion. From the *macrocosm* laid down in these first verses to chapter 5's final application, the elder-younger-Silvanus-Mark *microcosm*, he is holding before us the transforming potential of Trinitarian thinking.

How does he tell us what he's going to tell us? He does it by deliberately linking three Greek words—words that describe our true self-identities when we think straightest—with the three persons of the Trinity.

Peter starts off by addressing his readers as "chosen," "strangers," and "scattered." The New International Version puts it this way: "To God's elect (chosen), strangers in the world, scattered throughout Pontus . . ."

Then, instantly, he startles us by audaciously plugging these three down-to-earth, ordinary human descriptions into the three persons of the Holy Trinity: ". . . who have been chosen according to the foreknowledge of God the Father, through the sanctifying work of the Spirit, for obedience to Jesus Christ and sprinkling by [of] his blood."

This prologue—Peter's first two verses—previews the whole Epistle and makes its widespread social message unmistakable. It affords us a breathtaking cosmic overview that is simultaneously personal and political.

Verse 1 snapshots the fully human. Verse 2 snapshots the fully divine—and superimposes the divine image on top of the human one. These two little photo verses catch for us the entire Epistle's stereoptic theme. It's all there on these two tiny slices of literary film. To share God's macrocosmic glory as humans is to become—socially and psychologically—microcosmic trinities.

We now see that, throughout the Epistle, Peter's logic has been relentless. The "living hope" to which we are reborn (1 Peter 1:3) is both personal and social, individual and political. Its incipient democracy pivots on the "priesthood of all believers." Democratic social harmony—through "mutual submission's flexibility"—now becomes both possible and practical.

Starting with Chosenness

The whole vision begins with our first self-identity description—the means by which "grace and peace" multiplies itself: chosenness. The indispensable ground of democratic priesthood and universal leadership comes to us in this primary word. *If* together we are to become democracy's flexible player-coaches, we must believe the Good News: You are *chosen*, you *matter*, you are transcendently *important*.

This internalized sense of chosenness produces a particular kind of character—one that begins with love and ends with self-control: "The fruit of the Spirit is . . . self-control."[11] And self-control, translated into political terms, is self-government. Living stones acquire a "weight of glory."[12] In all of your life, including your politics, you progressively take responsibility.

Chosen by Plan, Available to All

In both spiritual psychology and political democracy, the first issue is always self-image. Before you can act responsibly and relate flexibly, you need to know you're loved and welcomed just as you are. You need to know you're important, that you were built to be a leader.

Remember Murphy's Twelfth Law? "You can't lead the cavalry charge if you think you look funny on a horse."[13]

All his life Simon, son of Jona, had wanted to lead the cavalry charge. And all that time, secretly, he thought he looked funny on a horse. But now, mounted and settled, he salutes us. Astride his big steed, he looks spectacularly good. He sits comfortable, confident, poised, in his posture an intangible sense of command. He was made to hold reins! He *feels* chosen, and he shows it. He rides so relaxed, so at home: he seems born to this particular saddle.

That's what a sense of chosenness does for us. Not chosenness misunderstood, which makes our self-esteem sick, but the kind of mature chosenness Peter came to understand and teaches us in his Epistle.

In a sense, of course, Simon Peter *was* "born to the saddle." He was a Jew, one of "God's chosen people." Even then, as we have seen, he still had his growing to do. Yet doubtless his early sense of significance as one of God's *chosen* people contributed to his later, more mature solidity.

Never minimize chosenness, even when it's limited.

Over the centuries since then, what else explains—psychologically—the contribution of the Jews? Their chosenness, their ethnic uniqueness, has given them both psychological and tangible power in vast disproportion to their numbers.

Consider the monstrously perverted witness of one Nazi official who became a principal instrument in the extermination of millions of Jews in Europe during World War II. Before his 1962 execution by hanging, Adolf Eichmann said,

> Now, however, when through the malice of fate a large part of these Jews whom we fought against are alive, I must concede that fate must have wanted it so. I always claimed that we were fighting against a foe who through thousands of years of learning and development had become superior to us.[14]

But it wasn't just the thousands of years of learning and development that Eichmann so reluctantly acknowledged. The Jews also derived their edge from thousands of years of *chosenness internalized.*

Chosenness Internalized

Consider this divinely chosen people's overwhelming contribution to scientific, cultural, and humanitarian progress. From relatively recent times their rich diversity of accomplishment astounds us. In *art*, Camille Pissarro, Marc Chagall; in *ballet*, Alicia Markova; in *economics and philosophy*, David Ricardo, Henri Bergson, Abraham

Heschel, Milton Friedman; in *theater*, Sarah Bernhardt, Moss Hart, Clifford Odets, Arthur Miller, S. N. Behrman, George S. Kaufman, Richard Rodgers, Oscar Hammerstein; in *entertainment*, Goldie Hawn, Edward G. Robinson, Melvyn Douglas, Lauren Bacall, the Warner brothers, Sophie Tucker, Dinah Shore, the Marx brothers, Danny Kaye, George Burns, Eddie Cantor, Samuel Goldwyn, Louis B. Mayer, Woody Allen, Dustin Hoffman, Steven Spielberg, Barbra Streisand; in *music*, Felix Mendelssohn, Gustav Mahler, Arnold Schoenberg, Georges Bizet, Aaron Copland, Jan Peerce, Vladimir Horowitz, Irving Berlin, Leonard Bernstein, George Gershwin, Roberta Peters, Jerome Kern, Benny Goodman, Beverly Sills, Jascha Heifetz, Artur Rubinstein, Mischa Elman, Yehudi Menuhin, Itzhak Perlman, Isaac Stern.

Where would our civilization be without Jews?

In *communications*, think of David Sarnoff, Adolph Ochs, Walter Lippman, David Lawrence, William Paley, Arthur Hays Sulzberger; in *government*, Benjamin Disraeli, Walter Rathenau, Leon Blum, Golda Meir, Henry Kissinger; in *law*, justices Louis Brandeis, Benjamin Cardozo, and Felix Frankfurter; in *literature*, Heinrich Heine, Franz Kafka, Edna Ferber, Gertrude Stein, Joseph Pulitzer, Irving Stone, Franz Werfel, Louis Untermeyer, Max Beerbohm, Emma Lazarus, Isaac Bashevis Singer; in *anthropology*, Franz Boas; in *medical science*, Jonas Salk, Alfred Adler, Sigmund Freud; in *physics*, Niels Bohr, Albert Einstein.

The list could go on and on. History objectively demonstrates, through Jews alone, the psychological *power of feeling chosen.*

Chosenness Universalized

The mature Peter's sense of chosenness—pivotal to his psychology—reached far beyond his Jewish heritage. It hinged on his gradual and growing understanding of the *universal chosenness* announced by Jesus.

This expanded view of chosenness had stood central in Jesus' clash with the Jewish leaders of his time. All four Gospel writers focus on the controversy over universal chosenness.

The Gospel of Matthew's very first verse identifies Jesus as the "son of Abraham" to whom had come the promise of universal blessing: "By your descendants shall all the nations of the earth bless themselves."[15] Next, Matthew offends Judaism's patriarchal chauvinism by including, intrusively, three "irregular" women, all non-Jews, within his listing of our Lord's ancestors.[16]

The Gospel of Mark, observing in Jesus a worldwide authenticity, says, "he taught them as one having authority, and not as the scribes."[17] Then Mark records Jesus' healing the daughter of a Gentile woman—an outsider.[18]

The Gospel of John tells at length of Jesus' impact in Samaria among the Jews' outcasts and rivals, the Samaritans. It also perceives the universal (and political) significance of the fact that Jesus' exclamation, "The hour has come," spoken shortly before his arrest and passion, was triggered by a request to meet with him from *some Greeks*.[19]

Understandably, Luke, who *was* Greek, focused on Jesus' universality most of all. He alone records the "Who is my neighbor?" story with its hero, the good Samaritan (the good stranger, the good foreigner).[20] And only Luke gives us details of Jesus' first sermon to his home synagogue in Nazareth.

You remember the scene: First, Jesus stood up to read the scripture from Isaiah proclaiming Good News for our impoverishments, imprisonments, blindnesses, and bruises. Then, his calm, sitting-down, "Today this scripture is fulfilled in your hearing."[21]

Jesus' hearers' initial response? "All spoke well of him and were amazed at the gracious words that came from his lips."[22]

But Jesus continued. Fearlessly he spelled out his divine strategy, making clear that this Good News was *not* exclusively for the Jews, but for *everybody*. He pointed twice, from the Old Testament deliberately, at non-Jews, outsiders, both times illustrating the universality of God's choosing. First, Elijah's feeding the famished widow outside Jewish territory. Second, Elisha's healing of the leprous enemy general, Naaman the Syrian.[23]

Jesus had more than made his point. He was expanding chosenness worldwide! They responded with murderous fury: "They rose up and put him out of the city, and led him to the brow of the hill on which their city was built that they might throw him down headlong."[24] In Jesus' hometown, it was instant Babylon. And this hellish eruption, this first violent threat on Jesus' life, spewed up, specifically, out of his universalizing chosenness.

What does his doing so mean for us? Quite literally, salvation.

Whoever has abused, demeaned, neglected or ignored you and your feelings, *Jesus* chooses you. However you might have been abandoned, damaged, scarred or hurt, Jesus *chooses* you. Whatever fears—inadequacy, timidity, shyness, or self-doubt—may plague your mind, Jesus chooses *you*.

Healthy, Balanced Chosenness

Our inner sense of chosenness gives us our needed psychological riches. But then we face a different problem. Do those riches make us feel superior, snobbish, or arrogant? Better muscular coordination than other people makes us richer than they are athletically. Better-looking bodies make us physically—aesthetically—richer. Better students are richer academically. All of us have *some* kind of chosenness-riches. So our riches—psychological as well as financial—inevitably imperil us.

Jesus warned us: We can gain the whole world and lose our own souls—through worshiping our wealth, becoming conceited about our chosenness.[25] And yet we can lose everything if we fail to claim it. How can we strike the balance?

Each of us has been chosen differently, each in our personal distinctiveness: Some weaknesses, some strengths. But if we believe that God created us and Christ died for us, our chosenness is undeniable.

So the question is: What do you *do* with your chosenness?

Do you run away from it? Do you use it as a weapon?

Or do you embrace it as a gift, a stewardship, a trust?

If we accept the gift, then the challenge of chosenness becomes to *think about it straight*. But it's no easier for us now than for the Jews in Jesus' time. Which is why, constantly, we need the Social-Psychological Trinity—God's relational flexibility reproduced in our own lives, relationships, and society.

Our individual brand of chosenness may be our psychological riches. But unless simultaneously we turn "poor in spirit," our riches become our hell.

So how can we be both rich and poor at the same time?

That's part of the good news of the Trinity. The Father is riches; the Son is poverty: in the Spirit they are one. To deny my wealth is to deny the Father. To deny my poverty is to deny the Son. To deny that we are both at the same time is to deny the flexible power of the Spirit that unites the heart as one.

The social-psychological Trinity offers us commonsensical wisdom about our own chosenness. C. S. Lewis' calm rationality about his own self-image catches this mental and emotional balance: "I'm as special as anybody else." *As* special, *not more so,* chosen, but not the only one chosen. Chosen to be an ambassador of chosenness, extending "specialness" to others.

The Trinity gives us a rational route to *humble* self-confidence. Balanced, dignified, wholesome self-image grows in Triunity. Its high character is humility.

Chosenness is *not* favoritism: People are chosen only to make others feel chosen. That reality, kept firmly in the center of our self-image, keeps our chosenness balanced. Look at Peter's word parallels: verse 1 gives us the human side, *eklektois,* "elect, chosen;" verse 2, the divine side, *prognosin,* "foreknowledge."[26] Connecting the two is the preposition *kata,* "down from."[27] We are chosen *down from* the Father's foreknowledge. God is *over* us. Humility, before Love's mystery in our lives, forms our only rational response.

The language in and around this "chosen" word gets our specialness exactly right. Peter's mood starts off bold, businesslike, masculine, decisive. You get a clipped, determined feeling here, a sense of firmness, confidence, certitude.

Down from the Father's foreknowledge, we get singled out for our particular leadership, our personal potential. The start of this salvo telling us about our individual significance, *eklektois,* "chosen," is the same word Peter uses again later, twice (2:4, 6), to make us realize our (churchwide) priesthood. He hammers away at it: "You are somebody very important."

Chosenness Makes Democracy Possible

What does chosenness have to do with democracy?

Everything.

A balanced sense of chosenness—the internalized knowledge that I am special, but that everyone else is special, too—makes democracy flexible and therefore workable. Only when we think straight about our chosenness are we able to flex and feel confident enough either to take a leadership role, *or* to follow the leadership of others. Every one of us has been "elected" as a servant-leader and chosen for full citizenship. We best understand true equality and responsible freedom when we most fully understand chosenness's paradoxical nature.

We have seen this balanced, self-confident maturity operating in Silvanus, the pivotal Number-Two on Paul's working team and later on Peter's team. Silvanus realized his leadership by developing the leadership of these two apostles. But if Peter and Paul were team leaders, so, equally, was Silvanus. The interpersonal change between them started with Silvanus, in his deferential humility. But it turned democratic by that same change operating equally within Peter and Paul.

If either Peter or Paul was the "ruler" and Silvanus the "citizen," their mutual servant-leadership made them democratically one. They were equally chosen, equally free. In this new teamwork community Silvanus inhaled a socially Trinitarian atmosphere; he breathed democratic air. It worked because all three sat steady in their saddles, confident both in their own chosenness and the chosenness of the others. Paul and Peter nurtured Silvanus's full equality, in their mutual humility under Christ, without forfeiting their own leadership.

Whether they called it democracy then, we don't know—but that's what it was: a balanced sense of chosenness moving inevitably toward democracy. Democracy, working together in humility and mutual submission, yet perfect servant-leadership equality, is the remarkable power of pastoral flex.*

---

*The history of Biblical Criticism highlights the power of Silvanus's personality and influence. Modern Biblical Criticism started with the German theologian Ferdinand Baur (1790–1860). Influenced by the philosopher Hegel (1770–1831), Baur refused to believe that Peter and Paul ever achieved personal spiritual unity. One "proof" Baur used, for that historic slander, was his denial that this Epistle's sophisticated Greek could possibly have come from an unlearned Galilean fisherman like Peter.

Silvanus played a major role in Peter's restoration to his rightful place as this Epistle's author. Many scholars used, not only the logical inferences from Silvanus's

Peter and Paul

Look at the apostles, Peter and Paul. Psychologically, one of the New Testament's most ignored miracles is the relational unity between these two. Everything argued against it, and many have missed its overwhelming significance.

Both Peter and Paul were dominant males, each backed by differing constituencies that were historically competitive and hostile, each with contrasting leadership gifts that inevitably made them rivals. Paul was small, bookish, scholarly. Peter was big, rugged, outdoorsy. Between these opposites, all the makings of war, amazingly, turned out to be peace.

We cannot ignore their tensions, of course; the Bible reads too real for that. Each one's Epistles refers to the other by name, never in naive, gullible, or blind enthusiasm.[28] But given what happened in the early church, as Jews backed away and Gentiles advanced, and given that Peter stood as the Jews' partisan against Paul, the Gentiles' advocate, the unity within and between their distinct teachings astonishes us.

Their total agreement on Christ's person and accomplishment has long been recognized. Less noticed, but nonetheless crucial, has been their united social policy, bonded to their oneness on relational ethics.

Never forget the agreement between Peter and Paul on something as misunderstood and controversial (then and now) as mutual Christian submission. The balanced sense of chosenness within both men overcame their clashing backgrounds and temperaments; their internal conceptual singleness *illustrated* the social potential in the one truth they each dissimilarly—but unitedly—taught.

A balanced sense of chosenness also triumphed over the sharp, conflicting unlikeness of Peter's and Paul's growth experiences. Peter represents those of us who come along slowly, gradually. Paul stands for sudden breakthroughs and dramatic conversions.

Roman citizenship, but also other abundant New Testament references to Silvanus's (Silas's) prominence in the early church, for that purpose.

The *absence* of any reference to Silvanus in Peter's *Second* Epistle explains that subsequent letter's much poorer Greek. Everything in the story—from the Scriptures and Church History together—argues that Peter and Silvanus's relationship involved both servant-leadership and democracy.

Yet each man stood confident that God had indeed chosen him. And each balanced his initial faith experience with the way he grew. Knocked to the ground by divine lightning at the moment of his conversion, Paul worked through his own human interactions "from his mother's womb"—unhurriedly.[29] And Peter—from Pentecost on—taught us about painstaking, lifelong growth using decisive, first-step, "born-again" language.[30] Flexing to each other, Peter and Paul look different, but equally chosen and transcendently one: unity decentralized.

Peter and John

Look at the way chosenness made democracy work between Peter and one of the original twelve: the Apostle John.

Initially one might think the relationship between these two could not possibly be equal. In all likelihood, Peter was substantially older. John—along with his elder brother, James—often seemed to be accompanied among the disciples by their mother, a telltale hint about his youth.[31] Peter, therefore, held seniority; he had the age advantage.

An even more serious block to a democratic relationship was the clear fact—obvious from the first—that, among that initial twelve, Peter was the natural leader.

By nature, John was quiet; Peter was loud. John was the sensitive contemplative; Peter the blustering activist. John was unobtrusive; he slipped into Jesus' trial—aided by his youthfulness—incognito. Peter drew attention to himself effortlessly; even when wrong, he made things happen.

How could two such contrasting personalities relate democratically?

It looked futile—except for chosenness.

John, in Peter's shadow, understood chosenness. And that understanding produced a giant, every whit Peter's equal.

How did such understanding come to John?

Through his comprehension of the Trinity.

No one in the early church surpassed John's grasp—and communication—of the fact that God, in Jesus, had revealed himself as relational, as Triune. He wrote the most original and sublime of the four Gospels—the one that, more than any other, is shot through with Triune wisdom and political psychology. It alone said of Jesus, "He referred to God as his Father, so putting himself on equal terms with God."[32] It alone gives a personal name to the Holy Spirit or "Paraclete" (*parakletos*, literally, "one who comes alongside to support") and spells out the Spirit's role as helper, comforter, advocate, the one who would be given, in Jesus' place, to encourage, sustain, and guide us into truth.[33] It alone recorded Jesus' words: "You have not chosen me, but I have chosen you."[34]

Compared with Peter—or anyone else—John knew he was equally chosen. He identified himself repeatedly, in fact, as "the disciple whom Jesus loved."

Biblical critics centuries later jumped, perversely, to argue that John meant, by so describing himself, that Jesus loved him *more* than other disciples. In so arguing, they came to an unnecessarily negative conclusion. We see them corrected, especially, in light of John's eloquent statement that "God so loved *the world* that he gave his only begotten Son"—in other words, that we are *all* loved, equally and perfectly. John's self-description as "the disciple whom Jesus loved" simply meant he could *discern* himself as perfectly loved by Jesus—chosen just as surely as Peter or anyone else. John saw chosenness democratically.

For some reason, John seems to have been temperamentally attuned to human politics. None of the other Gospel writers, in fact, *thought* politics quite like John. The evidence is that his father, Zebedee, was wealthy—a successful fisherman—and therefore could maintain homes both in the north, Galilee, and the south, Jerusalem.[35] While Matthew, Mark, and Luke, authors of the "synoptic" accounts of Jesus' life, centered their Gospels in the north around Galilee, John alone centered his in the south around Jerusalem, the seat of government.

Is it surprising to you, then, that Greece, "the cradle of democracy," so fascinated John? Perhaps it explains both his Gospel's prologue (1:1–18) and its epilogue (21:1–23). The prologue describes a Triune deity; the epilogue a Triune humanity.

John's prologue pivots on a famous term from the Greek philosophers: *o logos*, "the Word." He picked this Greek metaphysical term—meaning "mind," "expressed idea," "divine reason . . . the rational principle of the universe"—and applied it fearlessly to

Jesus. And then he made it clear that *o logos* was relationally one with God. Though John didn't spell out "Father, Son, and Holy Spirit" at that point, his assertion that "the Word was *with* God, and the Word *was* God" is unmistakably Triune.

For centuries, Greek philosophers such as Heraclitus, Plato, Aristotle, and Zeno had grappled, in their treatises on logic, with the idea that language (*logos*) alone is "the specific distinctive of the human species"—in contrast with the animals.[36] Now in Jesus, *o logos* made flesh, John recognized Triunity's supernal logic. Divine equality—within the hierarchy of the Father and the Son— is the pattern for healthy human equality. Divine politics shapes psychological politics. Triune reality therefore changes all our social-psychological realities—for instance, the social-psychological interaction between John and Peter.

The *epilogue* of John's Gospel—twenty chapters after the prologue's logic—narrates a story that teaches us just that. Universal chosenness makes democracy work: John's leadership is one, the same, and equal with the leadership of Peter.

You remember the scene. A small band of post-Resurrection disciples follow Peter into a boat to fish and fail miserably at it. They fish all night and catch nothing. Jesus appears on the shore and redirects the fishermen so that, in their first haul, they bring in 153 big ones. The fact that their nets do not tear amazes them.

After breakfast on the beach, Jesus walks with Peter and talks with him once again on the subject of leadership. What is it? To love him truly, feeding his lambs, pastorally flexing, leading as a servant, nourishing his sheep so they grow. Following Jesus, in other words, is leadership's essence.

Distracted during this painful conversation, Peter turns, sees John walking behind them, and wonders out loud about *John's* leadership. "Lord, what about this man?" he asks.

And Jesus answers, in so many words, "Old buddy, it's *none of your business! You* follow me!"[37]

On this prickly, too-human church politics note, John's Gospel ends. Having opened his Gospel with the Trinity in *macrocosm*, he closed it with the Trinity in *microcosm*—with Jesus' down-to-earth admonition to Peter (and to John) always to consider each other, under God, as equals.

Subsequent church history has more than confirmed that they did just that. The early chapters of the Book of Acts show Peter and John working closely together—healing a blind beggar, appearing before the Sanhedrin, praying together, traveling to Samaria to preach.[38] And although the two of them subsequently carved out different ministries—working in decentralized unity—each took his equal place as an eloquent interpreter of Triunity.

Among the early church Fathers, the Book of Revelation, John's apocalyptic vision, became the single most quoted New Testament book.[39] In our own time, devotionally, the Gospel of John has become the most quoted, most loved Gospel.

And so, in the pages of the New Testament, we see three unrepeatable individual rarities—Peter, Paul, and John—fuse into an unbreakable unanimity. Miniaturized Triunity like that between these three men bases itself in two paradoxical perspectives:

(1) A Triune God had chosen each one of them individually.

(2) That same essential chosenness was available to everyone else equally.

Triunity operating in the lives of those early apostles offered the world exactly what Greek democracy lacked—balanced, healthy chosenness. It offered to everyone flexible power—socially, psychologically, and politically.

Choosing to Choose Our Chosenness

To be chosen means to be outstanding, remarkable, noteworthy, inimitable, unique. It means that we have been given democratic capabilities—the self-esteem we need to live in freedom and equality. And, as the New Testament makes abundantly clear, each one of us has been chosen.

But the Bible makes *another* point painstakingly clear as well: We have a choice about our chosenness.

Chosenness is God's gift of who we are and who we can become: In Christ that gift is extended to us and everyone. But we must then *choose to choose our chosenness* by humbly accepting the gift.

What happens if we don't? Well, we've seen the social and psychological consequences throughout this book.

Our chosenness is the gift of the Father. In Christ's crucifixion we all rejected the Father in him: *All* of us are Christ killers, primordial Father-murderers. Rejecting our chosenness today is, therefore, still essentially father-murder—and its implications echo from our families of origin to worldwide politics.

Choosing to Choose Our Parents

How did we get chosen in the first place?

Genetically speaking, it happened through our parents, the two people—mother and father—whose union, physically, produced each one of us.

The mathematical odds, after all, against that one specific sperm's penetrating that one specific ovum at that one specific time to produce the one specific you, are overwhelming.

So at the beginning point, the chosenness concept demands that we grow psychologically as well as spiritually—that we come to terms with our own parents. Fully accepting my chosenness means consciously choosing to accept the particular mother and father whose physiques united to produce and/or nurture me.

Accepting God's love, goodness, and wisdom in selecting our two specific parents is where our psychology and our spirituality collide. Can I, as a human, accept my own chosenness if I disagree with God's choice of my own original family? Is the God of creation and the God of redemption not one and the same God? With my own distinct family's generations, my theology and my psychology inevitably intersect.

Emotionally, it is in our families of origin that we either do, or do not, accept the down-to-earth consequences of God's practical plan of chosenness for us. Theologians call our basic gift of human creation "common grace." And it's hard to grow in "special grace" (our salvation) if we have rejected "common grace" first.

The Creator formed each of us, especial and particular, through our individuated two parents. My family of origin remains the one place where my real personal existence cannot run away from Divine sovereignty. We did not, any of us, pick our parents or our brothers or our sisters. About that unique family system, we had no choice. We are stuck with each other.

If I neglect to "choose to choose" my parents, if I harbor anger toward either of the two, if I decline to think positively about both of them (as hard as that may be), in my heart of hearts I have rejected my own chosenness. I have negated God's selection of the two human instruments through which he chose, and chooses, my existence. I have committed father-murder, and in so doing I have disconnected myself from the self-esteem I need to be healthy.

Our inability to love our parents is the ultimate human limitation. To love them, equitably, appropriately, equally—as we need to—takes Triune help.

Father-Murder Writ Large

Rejection of chosenness starts with psychological father-murder— our relational refusal to accept our physical chosenness through our parents. Unfortunately, however, our psychology has social consequences. Our misery is contagious and can infect all the parts of our lives.

Culturally nothing reveals father-murder quite like *anti-Semitism*. Does that seem like a big leap from accepting our parents? It isn't if we realize that the values we cherish in our Western civilization come largely from our Jewish roots. We speak, now more frequently, of our *Judeo*-Christian traditions and ideals. Finally we're beginning to get it right. The "rule of law" we hallow in Western civilization grew from Moses, and his Ten Commandments, long before it came from Socrates, Plato, and Aristotle. However much we may abuse our ethical heritage, few of us can doubt its Hebrew base.

Any objective observer of history must surely regard our ongoing anti-Semitism—hostility toward the Jews—as more than a curious blip. What else—besides father-murder—explains this familiar old phenomenon made all too modern today? What else explains Western civilization's record of prejudice, hatred, and murder toward the Jews? Or Islam's ongoing hostility toward the Jews and hatred of modern-day Israel?

The irrationality and perversion of Western anti-Semitism reached its crescendo at Auschwitz, Dachau, Treblinka, and Buchenwald. Those cruel Nazi concentrations of gas-oven, death-camp inhumanity distilled into the stench of burning flesh our own spiritual and psychological disorder. Russia's anti-Jewish pogroms say that Germany itself was not the problem. Anti-Jewish humor, snide epithets, and country-club discrimination still remind us of it, here in our very own American hearts.

"Jewish conspiracy" slanders; "skinhead" spray-paint vandalism, or Ku Klux Klan synagogue attacks pinpoint for us, grotesquely, Western history's deeper corruption. Cultural conceit in the Christian majority has turned our accusing anti-Semitic depravity upside down: For many long centuries, relationally, *Christians have crucified Jews*. The Holocaust's slaughter of six million records and underlines the obvious. Nazi genocide—the attempted extermination of the Jews—lays bare Western civilization's blatant, if unconscious, father-murder.

That grisly Christian history makes the Arab-Israeli conflict today—in complexities, so far beyond our understanding—doubly arresting. When we study the common roots of Judaism, Christianity, and Islam, we see that Islamic hostility toward Israel echoes with father-murder, too.

Each of the world's three great monotheistic faiths—Judaism, Christianity, and Islam—agree on the primacy of one ancestral personality: Abraham. Monotheism itself—the worship of one God—traces itself back to this same individual. We know this originating patriarch first through the Hebrew Scriptures, which tell how God singled out the man Abraham to leave his native Mesopotamia and migrate to the land of Canaan, and second through a variety of recent archaeological discoveries.*[40] The whole story, for each of us, started with Abraham.

Arabs today, following the prophet Muhammad, claim their descent from this same father, Abraham. They trace their lineage back

---

*In 1909, archaeologist Arthur Ungnad published cuneiform texts from Dilbat, south of Babylon, containing references to Abraham. In these texts, dating from Babylon's First Dynasty (around 1867–47 B.C.), the name is spelled A-ba-am-ra-ma three times, A-ba-ra-ma three times, and A-ba-am-ra-am once.

More recently, Johns Hopkins archaeologist and longtime director of the American School of Oriental Research, F. W. Albright, pointed out that the specific *meaning* of Abraham's name in these texts is "problematic" since the original language of the texts may be either Accadian or West Semitic. In Accadian, the name means "to be high"; in West Semitic, it means "to love." Together, curiously, the two translations describe *servant-leadership*—"high love."

through Abraham's oldest son, Ishmael.[41] Following Ishmael, all Arab males undergo circumcision, the Abrahamic sign.† The holiest Muslim city, Mecca, is not only Muhammad's birthplace but also, according to Islamic tradition, the site of Ishmael's pilgrimage with his father, Abraham. Ishmael and Abraham together, the Koran says, "raised the foundations" of the Ka'bah, the cube-shaped building that is the center of Islamic worship in Mecca. Thus the significance of Islam's holiest shrine springs directly from its connection with father Abraham.

In the beginning Islam did not reject its connection with Judaism. In fact, during the earliest period following Muhammad's initial visions—about A.D. 610—he taught his followers to pray *toward Jerusalem*. Some students maintain that in those initiating years Muhammad himself was close to being a Jewish convert. Only after his break with the Jews in A.D. 624 did he assert "the specifically Arabian character of the Islamic religion" and instruct Muslims to pray not toward Jerusalem, but toward the Ka'bah in Mecca.[42]

Even then, the connection between Islam and the Jews remained relatively close. The Koran in places speaks favorably of the Jews (as well as the Christians) as "people of the Word." So the Jews were to be considered more favorably than those who completely denied the revelation of the One God to father Abraham. Even today, *Allah*, the Arabic word for God, is used by Arabic-speaking Jews and Christian Arabs as well as by Muslims.[43]

Scholars of present-day Islamic attitudes toward Israel agree: Anti-Semitism does *not* run, completely or consistently, back to a seventh-century hatred of Jews by Muhammad; it is *not* systemic to Islam's whole history.[44] Its recent worsening roots itself in the unfolding of nineteenth- and twentieth-century colonial politics, the formation of new nations and geographical borders, and the ensuing plight of the Palestinians.

A spiritual and psychological reality operates here. Implacable Islamic hostility toward the Jews is father-murder writ large: *It attacks the historic ties between Islam and Abraham.* Islam and Israel

---

†You will recall Ishmael as Abraham's son by Hagar, the bondmaid of his wife, Sarah. Sarah had been frustrated by her longtime inability to get pregnant—a pregnancy God had originally promised. Finally, in her doubt and despair, she gave Abraham her slave girl, Hagar, to bear him a child. Thus, by Hagar, he sired his first son, Ishmael. Later Sarah did in fact bear Isaac, the son of promise (Gen. 16–21).

claim common parentage in Abraham, and Muhammad recognized the Hebrew Scriptures, which include the promises of Abrahamic land. Older brothers like Ishmael will learn: You can murder your father and reject your own chosenness by rejecting your father's younger son.

Choosing and the Paradox of Freedom

Choosing our chosenness, of course, does not end with choosing our physical parents and accepting our cultural heritage. For as Jesus taught so clearly and Peter confirmed, we choose to accept our *spiritual* chosenness when we believe and thus are born again, when we are spiritually reparented.

The Triune God is *El Shaddai*—the Father-Mother God—the name he announced *after* the birth of the slave-girl Hagar's son Ishmael but *before* the birth of the son of promise, Sarah's son, Isaac; the name he announced to their father Abraham.[45] In Himself he offers us a morally transcendent Parent—and the freedom either to choose or reject that divine parenting.

All freedom—political, psychological, spiritual—has its origin in the Triune heart of God. Coercion, threat, compulsion, and force *negate* the relational liberty of that perfect love.

But relational freedom, too, is a choice. God grants us the liberty of choosing bondage. As our religious history shows us, we often do just that. State-church expansion by military might—Christendom's evangelism at the point of the sword—violates our Triune freedom as surely as Ottoman conquest or Communist repression. The "sacral state"—government buttressed by an official religion—always violates religious liberty, denies relational freedom, and polarizes democratic flexibility.

Humbly choosing our chosenness—by contrast—day after day gives democracy's aircraft its engine and its fuel. It powers the wings of freedom and gives them their flexible lift.

There's an implied contradiction, of course, in choosing liberty and, especially, choosing to be chosen. It's the paradox of "election" (or "predestination") versus "free will." It has perplexed thinking Christians over the centuries. We have frequently tilted from one unbalanced understanding of it to the other—from chosen conceit to father-murder.

If we are chosen, can we really be free to choose? If God has already "elected" us, are we really free to accept or reject the gift?

The answer to both questions, according to biblical faith and Triune reality, is *yes*.

Throughout history, many have argued against the doctrine of election because they said it fostered inconsistency. They contended that free will and election are mutually exclusive. But free will is actually the flip side of election; ultimately, you can't have one without the other.

God never tramples the sacred human will, which he created inviolable; to do so would transgress his own character by plundering our integrity. We must always elect to accept our election—to choose our chosenness. Simultaneously, however, we are chosen "down from the father's foreknowledge," granted the rich treasury of who we are and who we are becoming physically, spiritually, psychologically. And most of the time, we recognize the divine planning behind our choice only in retrospect. Usually it is only in looking *back* that we can honestly pray, with *The Book of Common Prayer*,[46] "O God . . . whose service is perfect freedom."

In *advance*, his service often looks dreadful, like slavery, and it's hard to make the choice. But once we choose, that's when we know we're chosen.

If I want to make "election" and "free will" enemies, I can do so only in theory. In practice they are one. Psychiatrist James Mallory describes their unity in our experience this way:

In heavy traffic, surrounded by every imaginable kind of car, you drive down a crowded, fast freeway. Far up ahead, before your straining eyes, appears a big high green expressway sign: PEACE, LOVE, JOY, LIFE, FORGIVENESS—EXIT 2 MILES.

You question your friend on the front seat, consulting your instructions and a highway map. The exit number fits. You bulldoze your way across into the right-hand lane. Soon overhead you see the exit sign, its white arrow pointing: PEACE, LOVE, JOY . . . EXIT ONLY. You think deliberately again, then confirm your decision to yourself. "Yes. . . . This is what I want to do; this is where I want to go."

You drive off the freeway, slowing down now. You continue onto the Access Road. Less traffic now, quieter. Suddenly you realize: You have passed through a beautiful gate. Startled, you look up into your rearview mirror. You stop the car. Twisting in your seat, you look back. There, above the gate's splendid arch, *visible only from inside*, you read the letters: CONGRATULATIONS! YOU HAVE BEEN CHOSEN!

This mystery—"uncoerced freedom" joined perfectly with "predestination"—escapes us when we think theoretically. To each of us, philosophically, these two conceptual poles are set against each other, antithetical, hopelessly opposed. Particularly today, in psychological circles, "determinism" is usually thought to preclude "free choice of action." Our age three to five experiences, plus our genetics, have supposedly set us in concrete.

So in abstraction, our liberty balks, frightened by "the father's foreknowledge." But we do not live in abstractions, nor in conceptually sterilized, intellectually germ-free laboratories. Ideas have legs.[47] Thinking has consequences. We live daily in realities of blood, tears, and sweat. We are creatures of the dirt with an irresistible longing for the stars, predestined for eternal love, forever willing to be made willing.

The commonplace experiences of life—not only our alternative options, but also our intractable destinies—reflect innumerable instances, large and small, of the "absolute free will/predestination" paradox. This paradox, itself, is our torture. Atheistic existentialists such as Jean-Paul Sartre describe its unavoidable agony as that of being "condemned to be free."[48]

And that painful paradox is precisely what Christ took for us. Christ's crucifixion for all our sins, according to the Scripture, was his ultimate free choice. His Resurrection on the third day, according to the Scripture, was his ultimate predestination. These two events were one. And this oneness reconciles paradoxes, unites the generations, and out of warfare brings forth peace.

Chosen to Be Free

Once again, there are no shortcuts. To open the blocked way into that unity's peace, Christ had to bleed. He had suffered for our paradoxical confusions, psychologically, long before that physical Good Friday: Triumphant Suffering is his character from before the beginning. You remember, therefore, that he told us—the implications extending to our own psychology, our families, our working teams and their extended politics:

> Do not think that I have come to bring peace on earth; I have not come to bring peace but a sword. For I have come to set a man against his father, and a daughter against her mother, and a daughter-in-law against her mother-in-law, and a man's foes will be those of his own household. He that loves father or mother more than me is not worthy of me, and he who loves son or daughter more than me is not worthy of me; and he who does not take his cross and follow me is not worthy of me. He who finds his life will lose it, and he who loses his life for my sake will find it.[49]

The sword Christ brings to mature us, in these subtle, hidden, and ambiguous intimacies of our families and working relationships, is the painful sword of psychological suffering in his Cross. It alone brings socially Trinitarian peace. Jesus said, "If the Son sets you free, you will be free indeed."[50] His freedom is not cheap.

Chosen—and choosing—to be reconcilers, peacemakers, and unifiers, we start practicing the life of the cross—first in our homes, and afterward in the ever-widening circles of our world. But then something wonderful happens. Whenever we freely choose the cross, we also get chosen for the Resurrection. Our morally transcendent Parent grows us up, personally and politically, into self-control. Into freedom and equality. We have been chosen for servant-leadership, for teams of decentralized unity. We have been chosen to be free.

Love's mystery in our experience, once explained the late Corrie ten Boom, is like a door. When you enter, you see these words printed on the door's outside: "Whosoever Will May Come." Inside the same door, on its back, we read—only after entering—"You Have Not Chosen Me, But I Have Chosen You."[51]

The good news of personal, social, and political salvation, all day every day and forever, gives us the door's two opposite sides—together. The Triune Christ says, "I am the door": If Christ has been chosen, so have you.[52]

8

Strangers to Our Estrangements

The Journey toward Sanity and Wholeness

∼❧

---
1 Peter 1:1–2

I, a stranger and afraid
In a world I never made.
—*A. E. Housman*

*R*ock icon Jim Morrison of The Doors captured not only the mood of the sixties but also the perennial human condition when he wrote the lyric,

> *People are strange when you're a stranger,*
> *Faces look ugly when you're alone.*[1]

He caught the same note Thomas Wolfe had struck in the twenties with his prologue to *Look Homeward, Angel:*

> Naked and alone we came into exile. In her dark womb we did not know our mother's face.... Which of us has known his brother? Which of us has looked into his father's heart? ... Which of us is not forever a stranger and alone?[2]

Amid our cities' suffocating density—layered billboards, stacked freeways, space-starved parking, squeezed-up sidewalks, tintinnabulated eardrums—none of us escapes our own inner isolation.

"America's greatest problem today," said Billy Graham in his 1991 New York Crusade, "is loneliness."[3] Loneliness hatches our neighborhood gangs with their turf-war violence. Loneliness explains our escapist drugs, addiction festering into crime. Gut-level loneliness breeds pornography, dragging sex to the animal level. Stalking the famous, choking crowded subways, plaguing plush boardrooms, splitting marriage beds, haunting crushed stadiums, loneliness makes us—one and all—strangers.

"Which of us is not forever a stranger and alone?"

But, to teach us spiritually positive thinking, the second word Peter dares apply to us, in this capsule prologue to his psychology, is this negative one. He calls us *strangers*—describing our universal alienation—but doubled back on itself, redeemed, turned positive!

What does it mean, finally, for me to feel at home in God?

It means to be a stranger, yes—but a *chosen* stranger.

And what does it mean to be a chosen stranger?

It means that, once we have "chosen our chosenness," we have started on the road to becoming *strangers to our estrangements*. It's a lifelong journey toward sanity and wholeness as we gradually separate ourselves from the rifts and polarizations that rend our souls and isolate us from love and responsibility. And two basic changes occur on this journey, changes that renew us as citizens and as persons.

First, we start becoming strangers to ourselves.

And then, as a result, we become strangers to the others around us.

Strangers to Ourselves: Health for Our Personal Insanities

The overeager young journalist was interviewing the famous writer-humorist Mark Twain.

"Mr. Twain, do you believe in rational life on other planets?"

"Yes, son, I surely do."

"You *do?* Why?"

"Because they're using earth as their insane asylum!"[4]

. . .

Twain's joke strikes us as funny because—not only *in* but also *around* ourselves—we cannot avoid its punchline conclusion. The evidence for our composite crackedness overwhelms us. We've even picked a biblical term for it: "The Fall." And we've known from the very beginning that at the core of this human madness lies our deep (and natural) selfishness—our soul-deep estrangement from God, ourselves, and everyone else.

Whether you prefer "universal insanity" or "universal neurosis," the gist is the same. Describing our self-centered human derangement, John Wesley said, "Myself am hell." Fluctuating, relative, and diverse—our lunacies, our destructive immaturities pivot on our self-centeredness. *To love others as we love ourselves is balanced; everything else is unbalanced*—and, more often than not, our self-centeredness teeters into some kind of imbalance.

But growing as *chosen* strangers, we gradually internalize the gift of being "chosen down from the Father" and more consistently recognize that this chosenness is universal, designed for everyone. As that growth takes place, we find that we have embarked on a lifetime of contemplative rethinking. We turn farther and farther away from our old monolithic, inflexible, and egotistical thought patterns, replacing imbalance with balance, self-centeredness with love.

Progressively—to our dead, locked-in, hopelessly determined attitudinal sins; to our twisted thoughts, our irrationalities—we become exiles, aliens, foreigners. In a deep sense, we become strangers to our own selves.

We are now living as chosen *strangers*, new citizens of another kingdom.[5] And no sooner have we begun to find our way around in this new country—the land of the Trinity, this nation of Three-in-One—than we find we have been appointed ambassadors—diplomats of Trinitarian graciousness representing our new nationhood to a foreign land.

More and more we absorb this new kingdom's fresh thinking, sponging up its centered mentality, learning to focus in new, positive, morally original ways. We grow in reflection, in meditation, in responding relationally. Every day we start all over again, growing in heaven-on-earth's peacemaking politics. We are learning flex and balance, learning to lead and to follow, learning to love others as ourselves.

We're not there yet, of course, and we know it.

Spiritual wholeness, perfected forever by God within us, is our true destination, our ultimate home. But before that perfect heaven—during this *intervening* period, this *interim*, this *meanwhile* here on earth—we're not home yet.

We're flawed ambassadors, therefore, of an unflawed wholeness.

Acknowledging that fact makes us strangers not only to our everlastingly true selves ahead, toward which we're moving, but also to the egocentric false selves we're slowly leaving behind. Ordinary living, as we travel along in this in-between, turns out to be a pilgrimage, a trek in a foreign land. We continually live, in the words of the old folk-song hymn, as "wayfaring strangers."

Strangers to Others: "Beside, but Not Beside, the People"

If we become strangers to ourselves, strangers to our own strangeness, then, we inevitably *become strangers to others*. And our brief relational prologue teaches us just that.

Peter uses a complex Greek word for his "stranger" idea:[6] It's built on *demos*, "people," from which we get our English word *democracy*. But it prefaces its *demos* core with two short Greek prefixes that stand *over against* each other: In context, they're obviously, transparently paradoxical. The first of these two prefixes conveys the idea of "along with,"[7] the second, the idea of "over above."[8] "Beside, but not beside": It's the trinitarian, servant-leadership idea of democracy.

It echoes Jesus' description of his followers as being "in, but not of, the world."[9] We're visitors here on earth, outsiders, temporary strangers passing through.

And where is our permanent homeland? Our real citizenship is in Christ, in his Triune territory, his Trinitarian kingdom. As "no longer strangers, but as fellow citizens with God's people and members of God's own household,"[10] we become preoccupied with "along with and over above," engrossed with "beside, but not beside" and wisdom's balance between the two.[11]

We could almost anticipate in Peter's prologue, therefore, which of the members of the Triune Godhead parallels "strangers." What, in the social-psychological Trinity, corresponds to "outsider"? And what makes us "outsiders" to an unbelieving world?

Sanctification in the *Spirit*.

The very dynamic that unifies us with one another in Christ also sanctifies us—and *sanctify* conveys exactly the same concept as *strangers!* The Greek word we translate *sanctification*, describes "a separation, a consecration, a dedication, a setting apart."[12] It actually *means* "beside, but not beside, the people." It describes an unself-conscious holiness—a Triune healthiness. It portrays the creativity of Trinitarian politics in everyday relationships—Trinitarian politics as social therapy. We grow toward sanity together, slowly becoming strangers to our rebellious, self-centered selves and to the rebellious, self-centered world around us: That's sanctification.

Holiness and *sanctification*, and our ideas about them, get so colored by our religious presuppositions that they need this secular word *strangers*. For to be a chosen stranger always means a flexible willingness to become strangers to our own *religious* cultures, traditions, or mind-sets, as well as to our *secular* ones.

That willingness, personally, has cost me a lot of misunderstanding among Baptists. And among businessmen, too. Many people, knowing both of my faith and my financial circumstances, consider me on the face of it, not only "strange," but even phony. From my own experience, I can assure you: A chosen stranger's life wins no popularity contests.

Both our secular and our religious cultures turn out deadly; the neuroses within and around us—both major and minor—prove numberless. Growing in maturity means growing progressively estranged from those neuroses. Inevitably, that means growing increasingly estranged from others.

And that hurts. Like the sick old Simon Bar-Jona, we want to be at home with everybody, settling in with the crowd at hand, forgetting we're spiritual foreigners. But in our eagerness to feel at home in the world we forget a vital reality: Only as chosen *strangers* can we become as wise as possible relating to people around us. Only as chosen strangers can we distance ourselves enough from our own pain and others' collective neuroses to be available helpfully to their own sad strangenesses, too.

Admitting my own self-centeredness—and growing away from it—enables me, paradoxically, to identify with the self-centeredness of everybody else. Facing *my* insecurities, I get wiser about yours. Together, we both begin to grow. Sanctification in the Spirit is a contagious sanity.

Growing in this Triune political hope, then, means that our former hopeless ways of thinking, both about ourselves and about each other, start appearing foreign to us. They seem like ancient relics of our unchosen past, tired remembrances not only of our rejections and hatreds, but also of our conceits, despisings, and superiorities.

We increasingly recognize these old, frightened thought patterns for what they are—dead. For only as we grow within, becoming more and more our old self's stranger, can we also grow without, relating to each other not out of desperate need or competitive selfishness, but as friends and brothers. Sanctification, "beside but not beside the people," enables us to practice mental health progressively with each other.

That secular view of sanctification permeates the New Testament. When Christ died, the massive veil in the Temple, the curtain that hid its most religious, "sanctified" space, suddenly split in two from top to bottom.[13] The separation between sacred and secular got ripped apart—torn to pieces—from above.

Until that crucial event, sanctification had soured and spoiled; it had turned stuffy, dank, musty, and ceremonial—involving special routines for special people in special places on special days. Now, however, the holy place is open. Everyone can be a special priest, a chosen stranger. The secular ground you walk on is sacred every day, and your physical body the Spirit's natural temple.[14] Secular sanctification smells clean, free, and fresh. It's the essence of pastoral flex; it shapes both our relational and political lives. And it separates us from our negative neuroses.

Such positive thinking makes flexibility rational and peacemaking possible. *Adaptation to each other*—through the One who is Community within Himself—*breaks down our polarized isolations* and our entrenched estrangements.

That fact can be seen first in human sexuality, as all of us cope with its ever-present strife.

Strangers to the Estrangement between the Sexes

The battle of the sexes is nothing new. For centuries, it has provided material for novelists, playwrights, essayists, cartoonists. It undergirds the plots of soap operas, provides material for debates, ruefully underlies gossip sessions in coffee shops and locker rooms. What man or woman has not wondered, from time to time, whether people of the opposite sex came from a different planet? Often maddening. Certainly strange.

Still more painful, perhaps, is our ongoing struggle against the nuances of our own sexuality. Our struggles to "be a man," to be a "real woman"—or, conversely, our spouting anger at the sexual typecasting society imposes upon us. Most especially, our ongoing suspicion—on the part of both men and women—of the stereotypically "feminine" role of submission.

Sexual estrangement, in one of its forms, turns into homosexuality, which rejects the replication—generationally—of the sexual union between the parents from which it came. But warfare between the sexes assumes a myriad of other forms as well—some scarcely noticed, some stark and dramatic. Lust—men seeing women as things and not as persons—harassment, fornication, adultery, patriarchy, matriarchy, machismo, even sadism, masochism, spousal abuse, incest, and rape. Our more subtle personality traits like shyness, pushiness, or temper tantrums may also constitute a few of sexual warfare's manifestations.

Sexual polarization is all-pervasive—transmitted to each of us across the generations both by dysfunctional families and dysfunctional societies. From psychology's point of view, strife between the sexes represents our core estrangement.

We need to see ourselves as strangers to it.

That need, of course, is what makes marriage a sacred gift. Marriage—"this is a great mystery: but I speak concerning Christ and the church"[15]—is secular sanctification's most popular training ground. But whether we marry or remain single, we can enjoy the Spirit's reconciling growth beyond our polarized sexual antagonisms. We can increasingly become strangers to our sexual estrangement.

Redefining Maleness

In the biblical view, spirituality and sexuality are inextricably intertwined.[16] God created our sexuality as an artist creates a picture. The artist is in the picture but the artist is more than the picture: he *transcends* it.

So with God and sexuality: He created it; it is good. He is, to use the theologian's term again, "immanent" within our sexuality; therefore, regardless of how humans debase it, we can always see sex as a good gift of a good God.

But not only is God in our sexuality, he is simultaneously above it: he transcends sex. If we do not focus on God's transcendence, we miss completely what the Bible is telling us not only about God but also about ourselves.

The reality that God is both in and above our sexuality must especially inform our reading of the scriptural accounts of our own sexual identity. And so must the reality that, from the beginning, God has related to us as free beings, at liberty to accept or reject him.

According to the Genesis story, for instance, God first created the male: first Adam, then Eve.[17] And this order of creation tells us something, as long as we don't take it to an extreme. Adam's priority in the order of creation indicates that maleness pictures leadership, authority, and responsibility. So, in a limited sense, does the fact of creation—that males tend to be physically stronger, with a larger bone and muscle structure, compared to the average female's. Males also have a higher level of the hormone testosterone, which affects human assertiveness and aggressiveness.

If the Genesis story and the evidence of creation were all we had, therefore, we might conclude, citing God's words after the Fall to Eve about Adam, "He shall rule over you," that God has ordained male authoritarianism—patriarchy. (Clearly, many have come to such a conclusion over the centuries.)

But the Genesis story and the evidence of creation are not all that we have.

We have Christ.

In fact, the whole point of God's self-revelation was the coming of Christ. And Christ's coming as the second Adam points us toward healing for our sexual estrangements.

The Triune God came to earth in person, in flesh, as a male. Why? Because only as a male could Jesus confront our crazy, irrational, insane ideas—developed in the Fall—of what it means to be a man. Only in Jesus' maleness could we finally see the second Adam, the corrected version, the original idea of what leadership, authority, and responsibility are really and truly about. Jesus is maleness complete.

If we—as Christians—don't think through the Old Testament's incompleteness, we get all hung up and confused, particularly about patriarchy. The one indispensable principle for us clearly should be—given our faith—the simplest: We interpret the Hebrew Scripture in terms of Christ.

Of course, the Jewish Bible is chock-full, literally from first to last, of prophesies about him. It breathes, over and over, intimations of Triunity. It gives us Triune concepts of sexuality, in powerful hints.

But unless we start with Christ, the progressive nature of God's self-revelation leaves us at some midpoint perplexed and distraught, reading about an "irascible, capricious, volatile deity, mischievous at best and downright murderous at worst, 'not to be conceived as holiness or righteousness but as vitality.'"[18] Such a false, punitive view of the Hebrew God may become faddish from time to time, but a relational understanding of revelation's progressive nature frees us from having to form our doctrine of God or sexuality either one before we get to Christ and the Trinity.

Maleness redefined in Christ explains how God could choose to depict himself for us all—men and women—in "male" language: Father, Son, and Holy Spirit.

Redefining Femaleness

One reason patriarchy has so characterized society at large is that matriarchy has so often characterized its homes. Both these perversions of sexual organization fight Trinitarian democracy.

From this book's beginning, I have argued that we transfer our family-of-origin organizational experience into our entire later lives. In chapter 3, I began arguing also that the Apostle Peter turned our sexual stereotypes—of male dominance and female subservience—on their heads by teaching that "submission isn't just for women but for all Christians." Simon had gleaned this dramatic insight personally from human history's one completely authentic male, Jesus. From Jesus he learned servant-leadership. The one true male, Jesus, incarnated both the "male" principle of authority and the "female" principle of submission.

God revealed himself as Triune in "male" terms because he wants everyone, men and women alike, to live with a personal sense of individual spiritual authority.

Just so, he came in the flesh as Jesus *the Son* because he wants everyone, men and women alike, to get over our fear of the "female" principle of submission—which "sonship" equally teaches.

Why do I say submission is female?

First, because the female anatomy suggests it. The woman's bodily sexual structure is one of receptivity, acceptance, and yielding. The female's generally smaller bone structure and her lower levels of testosterone point in the same direction.

Even more important, submission is a female principle because the biblical revelation portrays the people of God in female terms. Christ is the bridegroom, the church is his bride.[19] Wayward Israel is pictured as a fickle wife, having fallen into prostitution.[20] All human history comes to consummation in "the marriage supper of the Lamb."[21] Submission to God and obedience to his will make the spiritual and psychological implications plain: As G. K. Chesterton put it, "Men are men but Man is a woman."[22]

The mystery of the Trinity, then, begins to shed light on the mystery of human sexuality. When Genesis tells us, "'Let us make man in our image, after our likeness.' . . . So God created man in his own image, in the *image of God* created he him, *male and female* created he them," it not only gives us intimations of the authority-submission flexibility within the One God, but also gives us a new psychological basis for human unity, starting in our marriages.

The political dynamite in the Trinity is that the Father and the Son—male authority and female submission—are equals. Both the Scriptures and church history unite, confirming that crucial equality. Under the Trinity, marriage can never be patriarchal or matriarchal; it can only be a union of two fully equal partners. Equality demands flexibility, and the Trinity makes flexibility both possible and rational, as we will see.

Islamic veils and Western porno flicks—though in obvious visual contrast—represent the same kind of confused thinking. They each take sex too seriously. Such confusion easily results from our being closed to the truth of sexuality transcended. By contrast, the servant-leadership of the Triune God, who transcends our narrow views of sexuality, takes us beyond all our slavery and domination derangements.

Sex is the primal unity—the original human creativity. The central schematic of the human race is maleness and femaleness; their differentiated, united interaction produced us each. The sexual context subsequently permeates all our mental and emotional processes. Growing health in our attitudes about sex, therefore, contributes to growing health in our attitudes about government. That political payoff comes from the marriage of two otherwise polarized kinds of thinking.

To summarize so far, then, for each of us chosen strangers, married or single, the goal is sex-specific authoritative submission—not some bisexual, androgynized confusion. Triune love makes males male, females female, and both—in authoritatively submissive flexibility—Christlike in character. The psychological-social goal now includes allowing Triunity to permeate all our divergent, disconnected thought patterns.

Strangers to a Historic Rift in the Way We Think

In the summer of 1961, on the banks of the Frio River in the Texas hill country, the Butt Foundation opened the Laity Lodge Retreat Center. As our featured speaker for our two initial retreats, we had invited the distinguished Quaker philosopher, Elton Trueblood.

I felt good about having Dr. Trueblood as our opening speaker. His long advocacy of "the ministry of common life" made him perfect for the launching of a retreat center for the laity. And yet, as construction on the Lodge was being finished, I began to feel uneasy, sensing that our planned introductory program was incomplete. We needed something or someone else.

Dr. Trueblood was basically a conceptual speaker. His approach was logical, cerebral, based on reason. But as we prepared for the meeting, I began to think we needed someone in addition who would speak from experience. Someone who would be more personal.

My Oklahoma oilman friend, Keith Miller, agreed then to come and share his spiritual story. The impact of the two men teaming up together was electric.

Ever since—for over thirty years now, and through innumerable program formats—we have continued to follow that basic formula. One speaker—usually the featured one—teaches by the mental formulation of ideas, images, and concepts. Another speaker—or often a couple—shares his or her personal faith story, recounting some portion of his or her own individual journey.

Contemplating those events today, as I analyze the way I came to that pivotal decision, I realize that my own thought processes reflected those two kinds of presentations—and that my growing maturity of judgment demonstrated the power inherent in merging the two approaches.

My decision to invite Dr. Trueblood was a rational one. My reading had told me that, broadly speaking, Hendrik Kraemer and Elton Trueblood were the two great lay-ministry scholar-spokespersons on the contemporary church scene. I happened to know Elton Trueblood, so inviting him seemed a logical choice.

In contrast, I invited Keith Miller by intuition. While I could have come up with some sort of reasoned explanations for asking Keith, the real reason I invited him was that I felt drawn to do so. I sensed that we needed him.

In those decisions—and in their consequences across thirty-plus years—I believe the Triune God was teaching me how my thinking processes could mature. As I grew in sanctification, I was becoming more and more a stranger to the centuries-old split between two different—though complementary—methods of thought and problem solving.

Estranged Thinking

That different people approach reality differently is no secret; it's a fundamental dynamic in all our relationships. And just as fundamental, usually, is our deep-seated conviction that our approach is the right one and another person's approach is wrong. We are usually sure that our way of thinking is the only workable approach.

These polarizations in our thought processes tend to push us into one of two camps. These camps have been explained, over the years, with a variety of terms: rational/intuitive, analytical/creative, objective/subjective, hard science/soft science, thinking/feeling, Athens/Jerusalem, left brain/right brain—even cold and unfeeling/flaky and overemotional. I find it helpful to think of these two approaches as "cognitive" and "narrative."

For a variety of reasons, the polarized rift between these two general thinking styles has become connected to the estrangement between the sexes. Rational, objective, abstract thinking has been considered essentially male, while intuitive, feelingful, subjective thinking has been considered female. And anyone who has ever lived knows that these distinctions have been a source of friction between men and women.

Males have typically been taught to fear and distrust the subjective, intuitive, personal, female approach to reality that I call the narrative approach. Women have scorned and distrusted the abstract, objective, analytic male way of thinking that I call the cognitive. The battle of the thought processes undoubtedly forms a frontline skirmish in the battle of the sexes.

I remember recognizing for the first time during 1961—as I thought about turning my religious work over to God—that surrender or yielding or giving in is fundamentally feminine. Which may be basic to why, as a man, it frightened me.

But I'm a stronger man today than I was then—more responsible, more secure, and more self-controlled. That added strength has come in part through a growing awareness—and appreciation, and experience—of these two different ways that all of us, male and female, can think and communicate.

The Case for the Cognitive

Cognitive thinking enables us—indispensably—to *think in principles.*

Cognitive thinking clarifies, codifies, and classifies reality. It brings informational content; it sets standards; it makes organization possible; it keeps our thoughts from flying out in all directions. It is essentially objective. We need cognitive thinking to keep our life coherent.

But at this point we run into a further estrangement in the way we think. Over the past few centuries—ever since the so-called Age of Reason and the development of the modern scientific method, God has gradually been excluded from the cognitive realm. In the popular mind, science and mathematics have come to epitomize rational, objective, hard thinking, while religion epitomizes irrational, mystical, soft thinking—and the two are considered to be mutually exclusive. To many, cognitive thinking has been ruled out as a way to encounter God.

Years ago, in the 1950s, I conducted a Layman's Crusade in Boston under the chairmanship of my long-time friend, the late Harold Ockenga, who then was pastor of Boston's historic Park Street Church. One day in his study, while we were discussing evangelism, I approvingly quoted the theologian Nels Ferré, who wrote, "Modernism failed because of its low birthrate"—that is, it lacked evangelistic reproduction.

Harold replied, "That's good, but I don't agree with it." Today I understand his reservations. Modernism failed, not because of its low birthrate, but, more basically, because it wasn't true. It put itself above the mind of God; it claimed sole title to the cognitive and denied the biblical revelation as objective and rational. In so doing, it became estranged from its own roots.

To say that God is Triune, as orthodox believers affirm, is to believe that God is Mystery. But Triune mystery is not gaseous, undefined, irrational, great-god-as-pious-gush mystery—not a riddle without clues or solutions. Triune mystery, rather, is open, revealed, sensible mystery. It is conceptual, reasoned, and principled—self-named, self-defined, and self-explanatory.

This concept of God as cognitive reality, of course, is the classic view of the church. As Robert L. Wilken, Professor of the History of Christianity at the University of Virginia, writes in *The Christian Intellectual Tradition*,

> Credulity is no virtue. A necessary component of faith is reason. The phrase "reasonable faith" was first used in the fourth century by Hilary of Poitiers, sometimes called the Latin Athanasius be-

cause of his fine book on the Trinity. In his view, "Faith is akin to reason and accepts its aid." When the mind lays hold of God in faith it knows it can "rest with assurance, as on some peaceful watchtower." No leap of faith into the unknown for Hilary. In his view, as in the view of all early Christian thinkers, faith was not a subjective attitude or feeling, but a reasoned conviction.[23]

Modern Christian thinkers, as well, have effectively punctured the shallow assumption that only science and math can claim objectivity. The British novelist and essayist, Dorothy Sayers, of Lord Peter Wimsey fame, quizzes us,

> Why do you complain about the proposition that God is three-in-one is obscure and mystical, and yet acquiesce meekly in the physicist's formula, "QP-PQ equals IH over 2 Pi where I equals the square of minus 1," when you know quite well that the square root of minus 1 is paradoxical and Pi is incalculable?[24]

In his seminal work, *The Doctrine of the Trinity*, the Regius Professor of Theology at Oxford, Leonard Hodgson, argues that Trinitarian thought represents a rationality that is more advanced—and more closely tied to reality—than most "objective" modernist thinking. Hodgson describes the social system of the Trinity as "not mathematical but organic."

He calls it a mistake to "identify the mysterious with the irrational." What we miss in doing so is the obvious truth that between the two—the "organic" versus the "mathematical" type of unity—*mathematical* unity is more likely to be proved ultimately "a figment of the human imagination."[25]

Ironically, says Hodgson, it is twentieth-century science, with its understanding of organic and dynamic unity—Einstein's theory of relativity provides a well-known example—that has prepared us to see this reality: "By the labours of post-Renaissance scientists, [God] has familiarized our minds with the idea of *internally constitutive unities*."[26] And he adds, "To the internal unity of God the unities of the self and the atom are more nearly analogous than that of mathematics."[27] This is the idea of unity revised—from a simple "mathematical" unity to an internally constitutive "differentiated" one.[28] Differentiated unities are *organic and complex.*

Hodgson calls the Trinity a "rational mystery." He points out the dramatic difference between "a mystery . . . alleged to exist in spite of admitted irrationality, and a mystery . . . acknowledged because it is believed to embody a *rationality* which we are not yet sufficiently experienced and educated to comprehend."[29]

Internally constitutive unities—in physics, chemistry, biology, neurology, psychology, or sociology—now help us understand more about the reasonableness of the Trinity. Hodgson puts it: "So far from it being irrational to hold that a single personality may include and unify other personalities, *reason* now shows that this relationship lies at the heart of all existence!"[30] Accordingly, Hodgson concludes:

> It is not through trust in our reason that we go wrong, but because through our sinfulness our reason is so imperfectly rational. The remedy is not the substitution of some other form of acquiring knowledge for rational apprehension; it is the education of our reason to be its true self.[31]

We require cognitive thinking to mature spiritually because God is a rational being. To be created and renewed "in his image," therefore, is to become more and more capable of thinking things through—and to do so from Trinitarian presuppositions. As our godliness develops, we grow more and more logical and organized—but flexibly so, never rigid nor dogmatic. We set our priorities by a rational network of interconnected principles—trustworthy axioms.

Jesus taught from that logical premise. When he said, "By their fruits you shall know them,"[32] he spoke from his analytic thinking—he taught a cognitive principle.

But then with His enemies, as now, inflexible minds insisted on limiting God's higher reason to a rigid, one-dimensional level. With no conception of the one God as Triune—and without a cognitive awareness of the personal, social, and political benefit that has flowed from that realism in history—the Jews were understandably astonished when Jesus said to them not only that he predated their father Abraham, but that "If the Son shall make you free, you will be free indeed."[33] They couldn't grasp God's unity as "internally constitutive," nor that it offers us our freedom.

Jesus didn't seem surprised at their reaction. He and his Father must have anticipated beforehand, both objectively and intuitively, not only the Jews' rejection of him and then the emergence of Islam, but also our universal modern longing for democracy. He knew that their dogmatic unitarian logic couldn't handle—at that time—the advanced notion of a democratic flexibility based on cognitive thinking, a differentiated political unity.

It's a cognitive truth all of us have yet to address fully: The Triune God—that rational, relational Reality—is the organizing Principle underlying all of life as we know it.

The Cognitive Made Narrative

But we need more than cognitive thinking to live healthy and integrated lives. We also need narrative thinking.

Narrative thinking is thinking as *story*. It differs from cognitive thinking as the *action* differs from the *idea*. It humanizes the concept; it enfleshes the proposition; it puts the thought into practice. Its chosenness goes on the road; its beliefs wear walking shoes.

Narrative thinking provides the plot, the drama, the laughter, the tears. Narrative thinking turns the thesis into an adventure, a headline, a romance. Narrative thinking proceeds not by logical progression, but by leaps of faith, by yielding to the flow of experience, by finding truth encapsulated in specific experiences and concrete objects rather than abstract principles.

We need narrative thinking to keep us growing, to keep us moving, even to keep us in touch with that rational Reality beyond the reach of our limited intellects. And that, no doubt, is the reason why the eternal Intelligence behind the universe, Triune Thinking, became human—became story, became biography.

Incarnation is, in essence, the cognitive made narrative.

Look once more, for my rationale, at John's famous prologue to his Gospel. Its viewpoint predates Genesis as the storyteller predates the story:

> In the beginning was the Word, and the Word was with God and the Word *was* God. He was in the beginning with God; all things were made through him, and without him was not anything made

that was made. . . . And the word became flesh, and dwelt [liter-
ally "pitched his tent"—John's choice of words graphically illustrating the "chosen stranger scattered" idea here too] among us,
full of grace and truth; we have beheld his glory, glory as of the
only Son from the Father.[34]

The Word—thinking, conceptualizing—becomes flesh, news item,
physical history. In Jesus, cognitive thinking became explicitly narrative, without ceasing, simultaneously, to remain cognitive.

Please recognize that each incarnational component retains its
own unique integrity. The Word remains the Word; God remains,
to use Rudolf Otto's term, the "Wholly Other." And the flesh remains
the flesh; Jesus remains, in G. K. Chesterton's phrase, the "Everlasting Man." Yet in the eternal flexibility of Triunity, the two remain
one entity—one "Word made flesh."

This everlasting unity of Word made flesh, of cognitive made narrative, also offers the answer to the battle of the thought processes.
For the incarnation happened through the soft, warm, young female
flesh of Jesus' mother, Mary.

In Mary's historic yielding to that divine impregnation—"let it
be to me according to your word"[35]—the feminine in us all found
its healthy, tangible expression. In her Magnificat she captured the
cognitive, rational, male implications for herself and all of us when
she asserted, anticipating a bedrock concept of modern behavioral-
science research: "His name is Holy; his mercy sure *from generation
to generation.*"[36] She thrust forth, for us all then, the principle of
generational healing.

Mary's surrender, to the Father's impregnation of her womb by
the Holy Spirit, previewed our unforgettable male breakthrough
into the principle of feminine submission made rational and universal. Mary's female surrender anticipated Christ's male surrender,
making worldwide reconciliation between the sexes possible.

It happened historically some thirty years later, when Jesus the
Son, the fruit of Mary's womb, prayed in Gethsemane, "Not my
will, but thine, be done." The next day he submitted to the cross;
the male principle for our maturing had forever been changed, and
all our discontinuous, unhinged human thinking—sexual and political—had been reunited. The internally constitutive power of that

reunification appeared—to be seen, watched, and objectively handled—the morning of the Third Day.

The Cognitive-Narrative Cadence

We need cognitive thinking, then, to order and inspire us, for reaching above the muck of physical existence into the world of ideas and concepts. We need narrative thinking for keeping reality down to earth, for keeping us chosen strangers on the move, and for accessing the reality our cognitive minds can't reach. But more important, we need the living flex of Word-made-flesh, cognitive-made-narrative, in our lives, relationships, and societies.

This cognitive-narrative cadence characterized Jesus' teaching. His educational techniques revealed how his mind functioned. Some of his teaching, like the Sermon on the Mount, was cognitive; some of it, like the parables, was obviously narrative.

The first Beatitude, for instance, is quite clearly a cognitive, conceptual idea: "Blessed are the poor in spirit, for theirs is the kingdom of heaven."[37] But later Jesus conveyed this same thought through the parable of the proud Pharisee ("I thank thee that I am not like other men") and humble publican ("God be merciful to me a sinner").[38] By telling a story, he taught that pride condemns us while humility brings us forgiveness. In other words, Jesus used both the cognitive and the narrative in rhythm to teach that poverty of spirit blesses us.

Is it coincidence or Providence that the full, Trinitarian, relational revelation, our New Testament, combined the Greek language—the language of reason, philosophy, cognitive thought—with an age-old Hebrew story about a betrothed people, given in bold matrimony to their one true God? The New Testament completed the Hebrew action narrative in aggressive, assertive, cognitive language—the language of evangelism, language to convince the mind. Its very existence demonstrates the cognitive-narrative rhythm.

Cognitive-narrative flex permeates the actual text of the New Testament as well. Generally speaking, the Gospels, the Acts, and the Revelation are narrative in character, while all the various Epistles are cognitive. Each, however, contains elements of the other, in alternation and flex.

The balance between concept and story, which I stumbled into while starting Laity Lodge, contained the same incarnational rhythm—of doctrine plus experience—as the New Testament. Humans always need teaching and experience tied together; each one is incomplete without the other. What happens when we split them? The evidence surrounds us, both religious and secular. The Word become the word turns dull and lifeless. The Flesh become the flesh declines and decays.

Incarnational living—the Word made vital in our human flesh—demands wise flexibility between cognitive and narrative thinking. It is the whole point of becoming strangers to the estrangements in the ways we think. Its paradoxical rhythm has enormous consequences—positive if it's present, negative if it's absent—for human government.

Strangers to the Denial of Democratic Government's Essential Paradox

"Heresy," says one spiritually thoughtful person, "is *always* the denial of paradox." Nowhere does that principle apply more truly than in our thinking about government. Peter's psychology—out of his theology—demands that we think about government paradoxically. These two prologue words that describe us stand in jarring juxtaposition—when you think deeply about them: *"Chosen strangers" means paradox.*

Most people consider it an honor to be chosen. Those we consider chosen transfix us, even if we don't feel chosen ourselves. We often use the word *elegant* to describe them: "The chosen few, the beautiful people." *Elegant* means chosen: It comes from the French and Latin "to choose out." It's Peter's idea calling us the chosen, the "elect."[39] That's the paradoxical point: Not snobbish elegance, not stuck-up elegance, but the elegance of a *stranger*.

For if *chosen* is a term of power, *stranger* is one of weakness. *Chosen* denotes a polished sense of belonging; *stranger* implies humility before the unknown. *Strangers* are seekers, searching out the way. The chosen are insiders; strangers are outsiders.

So we have here the stunning paradox of "elegance" tied to sanctification or holiness. The Mystery of this triune paradox brought down-to-earth can help you and your citizenship. Never fool yourself: "Paradox" is supremely practical.

"Elegant holiness" violates all our old, preconceived images of sanctification. The two words sound like oil and water: They don't, won't, can't mix. We've used Francis of Assisi, or Mother Teresa, or underpaid pastors, or impoverished missionaries as our models of being saintly. "Holy elegance" sounds secular and materialistic.

But the Incarnation itself—from the gifts of the Three Wise Men at the manger, to the luxuriance of the Seamless Robe for which they gambled at the cross—was just that: "materialistic." The Apostles—themselves later—constituted for the infant church a clear-cut leadership elite.

"Elite" and "elegant"—and the ideas behind those words—come from the very same root as Peter's Greek word, "elect." Which helps me, as an executive, decide—to live "holy"—that I don't have to become a second-rate St. Francis, penniless in the woods. Nor do other professionals—stockbrokers, journalists, actors, bankers, doctors, entertainers, lawyers, politicians, educators, artists, athletes—have to forsake their eliteness.

We choose, rather, to choose our chosenness as a gift, a stewardship, a trust—to accept our eliteness and use it responsibly, as best we can, as a Christlike stranger in our relationships.

Chosenness saves us from our meaninglessness; *sanctification* does something even harder: It saves us from our do-goodism. We no longer have to rescue the world: Jesus did that. We only have to walk wisely in the personalized steps of our one-and-only set-apartness. Elite holiness produces flexibly therapeutic citizenship.

This flex, required for healthy democracy, is the *player-coach* paradox. The *coach* is the "elect"; he has the power of team control: He can put on the football field whichever players he chooses; directly or indirectly, he calls the plays.

The *player*, by contrast, can play only that position on the team that his coach chooses. The center cannot play quarterback, unless the coach has put him, at the snap, under, not over, the ball. The coach is the insider administering his team, the player is a follower-of-the-signals outsider. In relative power—which is what politics and government are all about—the coach is the chosen, the player is the stranger.

Combining into one person these coach and player roles, uniting the psychology of both the chosen and the stranger, gives us the kind of citizenship democracy demands. Sanctification is cooperative, constructive, hope-filled politics.

Whether you consider yourself more a player or a coach, all we *players* in life, at times, must serve as *coaches* too. And all we *coaches*, on occasion, must *submit* to coaching. We live out our daily life in the humdrum flux of such unconscious leader-follower alternations. Our only choice is to do so positively or negatively—as either therapeutic or destructive—as either servant-leaders or rebel-tyrants.

Learning to make the positive choice is the essence of our sanctification in the Spirit. Our discernment of the Truth we follow always involves paradox, flex, and balance. Truth comes to us in the give-and-take of our relationships with God and others: Thinking straight means, inherently, flex thinking.

Built-in Political Flex

In the U.S.A., presidents come and presidents go, but something *spiritual* accounts—both from our nation's constitutional process and from our presidents' personal adaptability—for our decisive, dramatic, but tranquil and orderly transitions of government. Such spectacular administrative power shifts—whenever they are peaceful—come from some explanation beyond the simply physical. They require an explanation that's more than earthly. Wild, untamed animals may fight to their grisly death over command, dominance, or leadership succession. The issue of who controls among them gets settled by blood and gore. That's the primitive human solution, all too often, also.

Peaceful, quiet transfers of human power, by contrast, come from flexibility—structural, personal, relational flexibility: Jimmy Carter steps down, Ronald Reagan steps up; Ronald Reagan steps down, George Bush steps up; George Bush steps down, Bill Clinton steps up. Adolf Hitler or Joseph Stalin never considered such flexibility an option.

Whatever we may think of Carter, Reagan, Bush, or Clinton personally, Trinitarians reflect that the ultimate source of such calm, quiet, composed leadership transitions rests in the Triune Spirit. Yet, especially when you compare it to older and more violent forms of human government, the whole flexible democratic process certainly seems strange—unusual, peculiar. One day, in the voting booth, the citizen governs. The next day, back home, the citizen is governed. And it's the same citizen, both places.

Let's face it—Trinitarian thinking *is* strange. But it has been a proven path to political peace. Never forget that our American forebears' minds were surrounded by, and often saturated in, Trinitarian theology. The intellectuals of that era took Christianity seriously, even while they were also influenced by skeptical Enlightenment thought.

The "consent of the governed" idea grew out of subconscious Trinitarian thinking. Remember, our Founding Fathers came from an era when literate English-speaking people signed their letters, *"Your obedient servant."* This closing for their correspondence with each other became so common that it was often abbreviated to *"Yr obdt svt."* Remember also that the people who used this phrase to conclude their communications, just as we use the word "Sincerely" today, were society's leaders. The educated elite: fixated on servanthood.*[40]

James Madison, the chief architect of our United States Constitution, had studied the Scriptures for himself in both the original Hebrew and the original Greek.[41] Thomas Jefferson, despite a deep distrust of institutional religion, devoted long hours of his retirement to compiling—in four languages—the basic teachings of Jesus.

---

*This servanthood legacy came from the faith of our English and European forebears. Dealing with "European Civilizations" in his *A History of Civilizations*, the twentieth-century French historian, Fernand Braudel, says: "Western Christianity was and remains the main constituent element in European thought—including rationalist thought, which although it attacked Christianity was also derivative from it. Throughout the history of the West, Christianity has been at the heart of the civilization it inspires, even when it has allowed itself to be captured or deformed by it, and which it contains, even when efforts are made to escape. To direct one's thoughts against someone is to remain in his orbit. A European, even if he is an atheist, is still the prisoner of an ethic and a mentality which are deeply rooted in the Christian tradition. He remains, one might say, 'of Christian descent' in the same way Motherlant used to say that he was 'of Catholic descent' although he had lost his faith."

Other founders such as Benjamin Franklin and John Adams professed their fundamental belief while decrying any form of enforced faith.[42]

University of California historian Edwin S. Gaustad says of that period, "The Bible provided a common core of ethical teaching, of cosmic understanding, of historical unfolding, of metaphysical or theological underpinning."[43] Triunity—unity decentralized—however secularized and acculturated, had permeated these pivotal Americans' political values. Their deep reaction against the clergy's historic dogmatism and domination produced our separation of church and state; they expressed, vis-á-vis the clergy, their full equality.

Trinitarian beliefs about Ultimate Authority provide us a rational base—perhaps unaware, unconscious, and unacknowledged—for the secular concepts that underlie the United States's healthiest political principles. You can see it in the emphasis on the supreme value of the individual, in the protection of minorities from majority despotism, in the precept of federalism uniting the individual states, in the separation of functions among executive, legislative, and judicial bodies, in the sharing of powers between federal, state, and local governments. When it works right, its wholeness flows from flex to flex to flex, from autonomy united to mutual submission to balance in the system. Its true foundation is Trinitarian servant-leadership.

The Horror of Our Twentieth-Century Half-Truth Splits

What happens—governmentally—when we split into two the Trinitarian paradox with hostile, "rationalistic" half-truths? The twentieth century tells us: Each half-truth, attempting to pull apart Reality's unbreakable whole, turns into a cleaving blade bloodying itself and the world.

Half-truths give us Fascism and Communism.

Remember that the Trinity—alone—gives us two essential virtues united—*hierarchy and equality*.

Fascism gives us the half-truth of hierarchy.

Communism gives us the half-truth of equality.

The English poet, Alfred Lord Tennyson, said, "A lie which is half a truth is ever the blackest of lies."[44] Our American anthropologist, Margaret Mead, observed long ago that Communism and Fascism are both *Christian heresies*. The Polish novelist, Stanislaw Lec, said, "In a war of ideas, it is people who get killed."[45]

Communism's revolt against economic hierarchy (capitalism) ignores the wisdom of the French writer and social philosopher Simone Weil. She said, "It is not religion that is the opiate of the people, but revolution."[46]

The target for Communist revolution—in the name of pure *equality*—was, of course, the Trinitarian paradox's other half, *hierarchy*.

Yet—in tribute to Triune indivisibility—the Communist pursuit of equality demanded ruthless hierarchies, from Stalin to Castro to Ceausescu. From control of the media to the Gulag Archipelago, its tactics exposed its lie: one totalitarian, *unequal* ruling party. The "dictatorship of the proletariat," the "working class" dream, turned out to be the dictatorship of the party, which in turn showed itself as the nightmare of naked dictatorship—reverting in demonic irony to the other half-truth of hierarchy.

Ten verses from the very first chapter of Proverbs could have spared the twentieth century incalculable bloodshed. These Scriptures tell us that Marxism's half-truth of equality, which is in essence an appeal to social, political, and economic father-murder, is not new. Centuries ago, the Bible's wisdom literature had warned us against materialist egalitarian revolutionary violence.

> How does a man become wise? The first step is to trust and reverence the Lord! Only fools refuse to be taught. Listen to your father and mother. What you learn from them will stand you in good stead; it will gain you many honors. If young toughs tell you, "Come and join us"—turn your back on them. "We'll hide and rob and kill," they say; "Good or bad, we'll treat them all alike! And the loot we'll get! All kinds of stuff! Come on, throw in your lot with us; we'll split with you in equal shares." Don't do it, son! Stay far from men like that, for crime is their way of life, and murder is their specialty.[47]

The appeal of the young toughs sounds so modern—rejection of the older generation, appeal to human community, revolt against the establishment, redistribution of wealth. "We'll split with you in equal shares." Stalin's purges, however, belatedly convince us to listen to Wisdom: "Murder is their specialty."

More than two hundred years ago, as Western intellectuals began buying wholesale into a skepticism toward our theological roots, the famous thinker, Samuel Johnson, perceived the temper of the times and where it was headed. He ridiculed the cynics: "Truth, Sir, is a cow, which will yield such people [the skeptics] no more milk, and so they are gone to milk the bull."[48]

Samuel Johnson's humor anticipated these last two centuries. He described revolution-based government: Overthrowing our faith, our forebears, and our past to establish an impractical equality, is as foolish as rejecting the cow and milking a bull. The problem is, bulls give no political nourishment. Bulls may be indispensable, but only cows give us milk. The half-truth of equality is an empty pail.

Christ, who "is our wisdom," incarnates the truth of the Proverbs: "Cling to wisdom, *she* will protect you. Love her, *she* will guard you." For two hundred years the world has made an idolatry of revolution. Our paradigms—in human and political relations— have all been adversarial rather than cooperative. Now we must learn to flex, or die.

The Half-Truth of Hierarchy

Long-term health in a democracy depends on widespread psychological maturity. Ralph Waldo Emerson said, "A man in the wrong may be more easily convinced than one half right."[49] Half-truths by definition are never entire. And Victor Hugo said, "Right is right *only* when entire."[50]

Learning mature flexibility comes slowly, but it never was more crucial for our nation than today.

Many years ago, shortly after Laity Lodge opened, some right-wing political activists tried to infiltrate—and use for their purposes—our Laymen's Leadership Institutes. (These were larger meetings around the country that Billy Graham, Duke McCall, and I, for a time, sponsored together. These Institutes were precursors to Laity Lodge.)

Beyond my own hesitancies about what these conservative extremists were trying to use our Institutes to accomplish, however, counsel from two older men whom I esteemed highly brought me the reassurance and conviction I needed to steer clear.

First, my Dad, a political conservative, said to me, "Howard, they're trying to argue that liberals can't be Christians, and you know that isn't true."

Second, an older businessman who had moved to America after World War II said, "Howard, I'm ashamed to tell you that, as a young man in Germany between the wars, I organized youth groups like these they're talking about. My groups, later, were taken over by Hitler."

Pastoral flex, above all else, is *pastoral*. Its whole purpose is the healthy use of leadership. The vigor making us flexible is the strength that stands up to challenges. Resurrection power in you doesn't wilt; sometimes, to move forward, the only thing you can do is take a stand.

Fascism, by contrast with Communism, is the half-truth of hierarchy. Just like its twin, it is completely negative. Whereas Communists negate capitalism, however, Fascists negate the Communist vision of pure equality itself. Fascism is anticommunism. Since Christ is God's eternal Yes, forever beware of any "anti" movement—and its negativism—as potentially demonic.

If Communism is this century's dominant half-truth on the left, Fascism is its half-truth on the right. The word *Fascism* comes from *fasces*, the bundle of rods bound together to symbolize Rome's imperial authority. *Führer*, the name Nazi Germany used to address Hitler, literally means "leader." Such tyrannical leadership—without a view of the people who are led as equals—turns out to be naked dictatorship, *which is the murder of the son* (as in the murder of the Son)—which is hell.

I oversimplify, of course, if I leave the impression that Fascism arises primarily, or even secondarily, from anticommunism. Fascism arises primarily from the unquenchable thirst for order and stability. Crime, violence, and social unrest, therefore, breed Fascist governments. A strong leader who promises law and order brings quick and easy answers to our desire for social tranquility . . . quick, easy, and catastrophic.

Wildfire Democracy

Our true alternative to the hellish half-truths of Communism and Fascism, to their governmentalized matriarchy or patriarchy, is the Trinity. The social-psychological Trinity tells us simply that God, within himself, is the perfect government. He is perfect individuality in perfect community, perfect unity in perfect diversity, perfect coordination in perfect decentralization, perfect order in perfect freedom, perfect organization in an envelope of *agape* love. We function best when we base our organization on that Trinitarian model.

Nothing brings us face-to-face with this truth quite like *the first-century church's decentralized unity*. Examined with political objectivity, her dissimilar oneness becomes as persuasive to us now as the man Jesus had been then to them in person. This church disperses Triunity through its multitude of social solidarities, its deployments of unlike people wedded in joint cooperation. (Upper-class Silvanus, here in only one example, serves lower-class Simon Peter.)

This united diversity, expressed in the varied unity of the New Testament documents, wins our minds today, just as it won their minds in the first few centuries after Christ. It proved so convincing that the early church roared across the dried tinder of the Roman Empire like a prairie fire of health.

The disillusioned disciples, first, had been convinced by the Resurrection. Now the disillusioned Empire became convinced, too, by a new quality in human relationships. Within Rome's cold tangle of human isolation—cynical, harsh, mean, and often bestial—a self-fueling conflagration of servant-leadership community broke out. Across the sprawling Empire, on the breezes of regular daily secular contacts, it spread in unnoticed, humdrum, day-to-day affairs. Gradually it grew, as if sparks of human kindness were igniting the piled dry animalistic chips of Roman brutality.

Soon it exploded, in bewildering multiplications: improved manners, changing dispositions, forgiven hostilities, rare conversations, unprecedented communication, unforeseen apologies, family reconciliations, softened temperaments. Surprise triggered surprise: startling empathy, stunning adaptability, astounding agreeableness started appearing broadly, in normal human flesh and blood.

Uncounted legions of ordinary early Christians lived out a new psychological creativity. Enfleshed Triunity remade their personalities, changed their thought patterns, integrated, matured, and socialized their association of ideas. Their impact together compounded. Attitudinal chain reactions, growing among, through, and beyond these inconspicuous lay people, merged into a molten river of love and community. Flooding the Empire with warmth, it became, every day, a healing, cascading torrent of relational resurrections.

At the center of this firestorm of progressing wholeness stood a small group—a small group composed of small groups. Its integrity, mutual support, and sensitivity—its small-group friendships' depths—to this very hour keep warming our cold estrangements. These people pattern human authenticity for us, both singly and en masse. Through the Scripture, their story trains us for living together as individuals in community. These apostles, along with their wives, families, and close associates, forever pioneered new thinking—Triune thinking—about human interactions.

At the heart of this thinking was a changed view of leadership. Jesus himself, alone, was the Triune model, our ideal human authority. But he was more. Through his Spirit, he breathed Triunity into the very lives of those who trusted him. Through them he announced to a divorced, disconnected, and divided world: With Christ, master-slave governance has died; resurrection leadership means appropriate flexibility between equals. In Trinitarian democracy, leadership and equality are no longer opposites, but one.

The Primal Flex of Religious Liberty

The sacral state, as I said earlier, buttresses governmental power with an official religion. Trinitarian democracy doesn't depend on such enforced spirituality.

Jesus' teaching—"Render to Caesar the things that are Caesar's and to God the things that are God's"[51]—has often been regarded as his primary lesson on the separation of church and state. But this "layers of loyalty" teaching is not Jesus' only instruction to us on religious liberty. He taught it far more broadly—and more repeatedly—throughout his whole ministry. (Jesus was crucified, remember, by the sacralists of his day.)

Religious liberty lies at the heart of Jesus' teaching on heaven and hell.

God's eternal, unbeatable, always available love gave us Jesus' doctrine of heaven. If you will only take it and say thanks—through accepting Christ's death and resurrection—heaven is in your hand. But no one will be forced to take it; God never jerks our strings as he would a puppet; he doesn't cram heaven down our throats. God never violates our human will. He wants relationships, not robots. As C. S. Lewis reminds us, there are only two kinds of people: first, there are those who say to God, "Thy will be done"; and then there are those to whom God says—with a sigh—"Very well, then, *thy* will be done."

Hell is the absence of love, of light, of life, of others, of God: utter aloneness, "outer darkness." And if you don't want heaven, you can—in total freedom—reject it.

Jesus' doctrine of heaven and hell gave us—for all time, including our twentieth-century purgatories—absolute and complete religious liberty.

Ideologies of both the left and right lack this essential religious-freedom flex. Both, therefore—the right, attempting to turn America legislatively into a Christian nation, and the left, trying to push through their own version of socialistic Christian liberation—share equally the same flaw. They miss the chosen strangers paradox—of inner autonomy and inner self-control—which alone makes democratic societies realistic long term.

·   ·   ·

Unfortunately, Western history itself is not strong on religious liberty, so we must practice discernment. Only in America has the separation of church and state flourished.[52] The famous Emperor, Constantine, following his Christian conversion in the fourth century A.D., bound the Christian church and the Roman state together. In doing so he destroyed Jesus' religious-liberty vision, and returned us to a pre-Trinitarian, pre-democratic, patriarchal Jewish concept—a sacral state.

Now we've a long way to go to get over it.

So "special priesthoods" remain a big part of the problem, as we will see in our final chapter. Oxford's Anglo-Catholic teacher Charles Williams, in his helpful church history, *The Descent of the Dove*, wrote:

> It is doubtful whether Christendom has ever quite recovered from the mass-conversion of the fashionable classes inside Rome and of the barbaric races outside Rome. Those conversions prepared the way for the *Church of all the after ages*. It is at least arguable that the Christian Church will have to return to a pre-Constantine state before she can properly recover the ground she too quickly won.[53]

This book is, in part, an appeal for the church to return to its pre-Constantine state. For that to happen, for spiritual awakening to come, we must be willing to become strangers—strangers to our religious and our secular cultures, strangers to the war between the sexes, strangers to our inflexible thinking, and, perhaps most obviously difficult today, strangers to all our over-simplified, half-truth, polarized politics.

9

Triumph Scattered

The Forward Potential in Our Pain

---

1 Peter 1:1–2

Freedom is a system based on courage.
—*Charles Péguy*

The love of liberty is the love of
others.
—*William Hazlitt*

*O*n the white limestone fascia of the University of Texas's
main building and library tower, you read a famous
text, appropriate for all the disciplines of education in a democracy:

Ye Shall Know the Truth,
And the Truth Shall Make You Free.

But this well-known text carries no reference. No author is credited.
And that omission—the blank space beneath the tower's quotation—clearly expresses our intellectual, cultural, and governmental
crisis. That blank limestone emptiness explains a society now legalistically rigid, yet coming apart (with its overcrowded prisons and
log-jammed courts). A society desperate for constructive, positive
flexibility in ordinary human relationships. A society in deep need
of Triunity.

Who uttered those famous words, about Truth making us Free?
Jesus spoke them, of course.

The tower's forgotten reference is John 8:32. It is the conclusion
to Jesus' saying, "If you continue in my word"—his words about
our continuing growth, our onward spiritual movement. Its full
context gives us one of Jesus' most complete explanations of the
relational flex within the Trinity. Those very words—"the truth
shall make you free"—triggered a horrific controversy with his inflexible Jewish opponents, climaxed by his devastating claim, "Before Abraham was, I am."[1]

The inflexible legalists of Jesus' day simply could not accept the
paradoxical idea—and the political dynamite—of his unique Triune
personhood. As a result they remained stuck, imprisoned by their
own preconceptions, unable to grow and move forward in freedom.

The essence of Trinitarian reality is life-changing movement—
flexing movement, outward movement, forward movement; advancing relational growth and ongoing spiritual progress. Which
brings us to the final self-identification word in Peter's prologue,
"scattered"—the movement word that brings Peter's prologue-
summary to its completion. The apostle—encapsulating his argument in advance—now ties our healthiness into the *final* member
of the Trinity. We are:

"Chosen" down from the foreknowledge of God the Father,
"Strangers" in the sanctification of the Holy Spirit,
"Scattered" for obedience and sprinkling of the blood of
    Jesus Christ.

Our "chosenness" (since God takes the initiative) puts the Father's
foreknowledge on the move.

Our beside-but-not-beside-the-people "strangeness" places the
Spirit's *sanctification* (setting us apart) into motion.

Now our "scatteredness" sends into action the good news of Jesus
Christ's conquering *blood sprinkled*. Chosen strangers scattered are
people stepping forth, people on a journey, people growing toward
full relational health. Through us, the Trinity moves out and on,
advancing through history and permeating the common fabric of
daily life.

That permeation, of course, transmits the very essence of the Social-Psychological Trinity into the world. What Peter's psychology—from start to finish—has been saying now becomes very clear: *The whole Trinity is in you.*

God does not give himself to us in parts. The democratic flexibility and spiritual growth we need is always the Trinity within us: In our troubles, the one thing God offers us is himself. The Divine Unity gives himself—entire—to us for our own human unity. And that unified center—the Trinity in us—describes the essence of our relational mobility. Visualize, therefore, the unstoppable movement of chosen strangers scattered.

Scattered People, Sprinkled Pain

Scattered. The very word brings movement to mind.

Think of God—a crucified, resurrected, Triune God—standing at the center (as well as the circumference) of the universe. Think of him scattering his people out from that center as a sower scatters seed, in ever-widening arcs, ever-broadening circles of influence.

That image, of course, reminds us of the true identity of chosen strangers scattered.

They are the secular church. The laity.

The church assembled for Sunday congregational worship is called "the church gathered." The church dispersed for its everywhere-else-relationships is "the church scattered." The church *scattered* is the ordinary you—maybe churchy or religious, maybe not—that Christ calls to change the world.

We can now rejoice in our down-to-earth, nuts-and-bolts, everyday ordinariness. What offended the Jews about Jesus was just that—his ordinariness. He came from nowhere; he worked in a family business; he refused to perform miracles on demand. He wasn't spectacular enough, religious enough, or macho enough to suit them.

Now God offers us, through him, our own commonplace glory, which is precisely what democracy demands.

The scattered idea summarizes the democratic ideal—authority and responsibility scattered among all the people. It also includes our potential for changing each other's lives for good—reparenting and rechildrening each other—scattering good news through our ordinary daily interactions in ever-widening circles.

In a word, "scattered" means us—all of us.

Clergy and laity alike, we're all—democratically—the people of God, scattered.

Years ago, when I was a very young lay preacher, people disturbed me by saying, "Poor Howard. He can't decide whether he wants to be a preacher or a groceryman."

So I began telling them that, after my deepened teenage commitment, there was *never* any question whether or not I'd preach. The only question was *how.* Since I'd been reared in the business, I had to decide: would I speak as a grocer or not?

That reply helped, but still the talk bothered me. Then one day I read, in Acts 7–8, the story of Stephen, who was the first deacon (that is, layman) killed for preaching. Persecution followed his death. Reading about it I ran across the line, "Now those who were scattered abroad went everywhere preaching the word."[2]

With glee I pointed this out to my critics. This would fix them: Laymen preaching! Back came their reply: "Oh yeah? Those were the clergy, the pastors, the apostles."

Then I noticed a few verses earlier: "And they were all scattered abroad . . . *except* the apostles!"[3]

Boy, did I have fun with that! I started telling people, "I bootleg the Gospel; I preach without a license." Later, because I didn't accept money for my preaching, I accused them of inviting me because I was the cheapest person available! But I felt comfortable that I had an answer for my critics. "Chosen strangers" was never meant to be limited to religious professionals.

Well, that word, translated "scattered" in the Acts' story, comes from the same term Peter uses here describing us all.

Through chosen strangers scattered the Triune God keeps Christ's kingdom on the move. Following our Lord's example, we are—each and all—called to take our player-coach newness into the many circles of our ordinary lives. We "preach" there by the newness of our relational dependability. That newness—spreading through our secular circles' relationships—scatters itself out in sublime coordinations.

Envision the CEO of the Airline, his pilot, plane, crew, and their terminal, working *in flawless sync* with the skycap checking your bags. Then picture a storybook flight, with perfect weather and scrumptious food. Imagine gentle-as-a-baby's-touch baggage handling, moving your luggage along without a hitch, followed by a car-rental service so prompt, efficient, and friendly it startles and delights you: *envision for yourself a glorious trip.*

If this air-travel example disappoints you—making the Almighty God sound like holy teamwork—I have no choice but to risk it. Trinitarian teamwork is the only way husbands, wives, fathers, mothers, sons, daughters, employers, employees, clergy, laity, governors, and citizens can live together positively. That teamwork happens when chosen strangers scatter Triunity into all the circles of their influence.

Divine Suffering Sprinkled

But as we have seen over and over, Trinitarian teamwork—player-coach flexibility—*hurts.*

Being chosen strangers *scattered* means participating in divine suffering *sprinkled.* The goal of our *scattering* is the "*sprinkling* of the blood of Jesus Christ."

The *Oxford English Dictionary*'s first definition of *sprinkle* reads, "to scatter in drops; to let fall in small particles here and there; to strew thinly or lightly" or, figuratively, "to disperse, distribute, or scatter."[4] The image of *blood* sprinkled brings with it an unavoidable sense of suffering.

And that is the heart of our difficulty with the Apostle's Triune message.

We don't really have trouble with his "scattered" idea; we like the idea of spreading authority around in teamwork and democracy. No, what troubles us is the *content* that Peter—echoing Jesus—put into his "scattered" concept, by linking it with "obedience to Jesus Christ and sprinkling of his blood."

Peter calls us here to scattered suffering. Democratic pain.

Which, as I told you early in this book, I *hate:* I hate suffering.

So do all of us.

Which is probably why Peter feels compelled to reiterate the theme throughout his Epistle (and I to reiterate it in my reflections on its psychology). It takes awhile for the truth about suffering to sink in.

The Purpose in Our Pain

When I sat down to complete this study I still had not realized what I see now as self-evident: *All politics involves suffering.* Pain-free politics does not exist. In practice we begin learning that lesson in childhood, but, emotionally and rationally, we learn it at a snail's pace.

The ruptured circles of our relationships—the breaches of our estrangements—surround our lives like a jagged circumference of psychological spikes: A broken wedding ring, beside bringing relief, can become a crown of thorns. The politics of sex, home, office, club, city, state, nation and world—in each political layer we hurt. And nothing can change that fact.

What can change, however, is our attitude about it. We can always change our refusal to recognize our pain and thus change the meaning and significance we see in it. We can always change the way we respond to it personally. Healthy faith offers us purpose in our pain—however mysterious—and spiritual triumph over it. We share Christ's victory over Satan by becoming more Christlike ourselves. Our pain with each other offers us the therapeutic possibility of practicing forgiveness, which has the power to take us beyond the past into new relational beginnings.

Forgiveness—up-close, intimate, unconditional forgiveness of our parents, children, spouses, siblings, friends, bosses, and employees—hurts so deeply because in it we enter the mystery of the divine sacrifice. "The sprinkling of the blood of Jesus Christ" requires the acceptance of suffering in all these scattered relationships, suffering faced and acknowledged, suffering understood as obedience, suffering overcome in the grace of our daily human reconciliations. If we love others, we make peace with them; if we do not recognize our own hardness of heart and wipe the slate clean with each other, we do not really love.

The sprinkling of the blood of Jesus Christ is the scattering of human forgiveness. He scatters his healing mercy through you.

If we don't accept our psychological pain, and triumph over it by pardoning each other, we jump out of the frying pan into the fire of pain that is worse. We become, as Karl Menninger's book title—on suicide and the psychology of self-destruction—puts it, *Man against Himself.*[5]

Healthy faith offers us much more than a chance to reach past our pain through forgiveness; it offers self-government, the self-control that walks away from unnecessary hurting. We can step back from chemical addiction's agonized futility. We can forsake the diseases of matriarchal or patriarchal marriage. Governmentally, we can turn away from Communist or Fascist state-authorized dominations.

All these unnecessary hurtings—our self-destructive habits like overeating, overdrinking, overloafing, overworking, overplaying, overleading, overfollowing, overdependence—stem from the neurotic motivation of *oversuffering.* Our oversuffering is the *under-sprinkling* of Christ's blood—underforgiving of others, under-accepting of Christ's forgiveness of us. Since nothing was superfluous—nothing unnecessary, nothing wasted—in Christ's death, he offers us freedom from suffering that is not therapeutic.

Instead of our old self-fighting, self-demolishing patterns, spiritual growth's by-product is our growing self-control. Because Christ is *for us first,* we gradually become *people for ourselves,* capable of then turning away from uncalled-for pain and becoming *people for others.* "Man against himself" changes into man *for* everyone.

If you don't believe that change spells practical politics, look at the places where democratic self-government has emerged in the world. You see it where Trinitarian spiritual growth has been most widespread. It springs up where the priesthood of all believers is taken seriously, where each and all the people of God see themselves as equally called, equally responsible, equally important.

This ministry of common life, expressing itself as we "submit to one another in the fear of God" and as we "serve one another in love" gives to the clergy not diminished, but enhanced respect, admiration, and love. The "secular church" strengthens the "institutional church." And both, through the circles of interconnected human relationships, strengthen democratic constitutional secular self-government.

Secrets of Therapeutic Suffering

How does hell-on-earth—Satan's demonic maneuvering—produce our psychological pain? By fouling up—in us—the Trinity's political core: equality and hierarchy as one.

That foul-up obviously explains all our Hitlers and Stalins (including our petty tyrants at home and on the job): Their hierarchy gone berserk mass-produces suffering. It also explains the havoc of father-murder large and small: Equality gone berserk spawns suffering just as surely. Suffering in human life is an inevitable consequence of our conceits about who's in control, who's on top.

Look back briefly at this steady theme in our study. In the first chapter we observed that one of the tragedies of church history is that Peter's Great Confession has not, in tradition, been interpreted psychologically. Here is another similar tragedy: The "suffering" in this 1 Peter Epistle has been too often interpreted as physical rather than psychological, persecution rather than relationships.

Which gets it precisely reversed. If the early Christians had not recognized their suffering as first psychological (Gethsemane), and only second physical (Calvary), they would not have made enough impact on the Roman Empire to make killing them worthwhile.

So to debate whether Peter, in this Epistle on suffering, is preparing his readers for persecutions under Nero (who ruled Rome A.D. 54–68), or Vespasian (A.D. 69–79), or any other Roman emperor, is ultimately pointless for us lay people. It helps the scholars, but it stumbles before the central point—that Peter prepares people to die in faith only secondarily. His first purpose is to give us the courage to live—by showing us how to transform our inevitable suffering into scattered therapy.

His psychology's first extended discussion of Christian suffering, the 2:18–25 section, describes suffering in our everyday tasks through the ranking order in our jobs. Peter (and Silvanus) write in master-servant language, first-century management's terms, their most familiar language relating to regular, common, daily work.

How does a believing slave, realizing in Christ he is his master's equal now, handle himself? Does he kill the master, revolt, escape, or run away? Old political psychology, on whatever timetable, left him no equality options other than these.

Peter teaches him a new, Triune way to think—unheard of, bewildering, tough, but healing. Love the master. Do what he wants you to do. Make yourself the best worker you possibly can. Adapt to his goals, adjust to his aims, so long as it does not violate your higher loyalty to Christ. Show the master, by the quality of your work, that you care for him. Serve him in love like a pastor: You are a leader, too, every whit his equal. Out of your new dignity in Christ, you willingly do his bidding.

In your work you will exhibit Christ's freedom to suffer, his stretched elasticity, his resurrection snapback. And you will need it, for this plan is achingly specific: You follow this poised adaptiveness not only toward "kind and gentle" masters, but also toward the "overbearing."[6]

"Overbearing" is the Revised Standard Version's translation. The King James Version translated the same word as "froward," which means "disposed to go counter to what is demanded . . . perverse, difficult to deal with, hard to please, adverse." We forget this outdated froward word, but we embrace its old deadly mentality: "habitually inclined to disobedience and opposition, contrary, unfavorable, not easily managed, stubbornly willful, pigheaded, obstinate."[7]

Triune psychology reveals overbearing masters and froward slaves as identically negative, twin tokens of Satan's disorganization. But it also reveals the transforming potential of servant-leadership. Masters and slaves who turn to servant-leadership inevitably experience a constructive hurting, a wholesome, positive, and therapeutic suffering.

Heaven on Wheels

We started this chapter with the image of Christ as a sower, scattering his people, the laity, out into the many circles of their influence. If you think that way, of our lives as scattered in progressively broadened circles, from family to work to society to government to world, and if you admit that all our relational lives involve suffering—then it becomes natural to think of suffering in terms of scattered circles, too.

By choosing to approach their suffering positively, chosen strangers scattered disperse Divine Blood sprinkled in all the circles of their lives. They also implement the flexibility of positive thinking; they implement democracy.

But they do more than that. Chosen strangers scattered also distribute resurrection. And resurrection makes suffering therapeutic.

The scattered circles of our suffering are resurrection bursts from a rounded cave sealed with a massive circular stone: For you the circle *moves*.*[8]

The open circle of that empty tomb stands as the most validly authenticated fact of ancient history—absolutely dependable for all our histories today. If Christ is not risen, what else explains the Church? What but that vacant sepulcher explains the transformation after Jesus' death of those frightened, fleeing, demoralized disciples? What else explains their message's conviction that, in a few short centuries, split history into B.C. and A.D.? What but those hollowed-out, empty grave clothes could explain their transparent, confidence-building integrity about eating with, talking with, touching the resurrected Jesus? What else explains, finally, the martyrdom of these apostles?

People do not die for what they know to be false: The anguish of Christ's death had turned full circle—into life.

Here's the crucial point for us all: Jesus' circle of suffering rolled forward! Your life in Christ is not an endless cycle of suffering, but a rolling, growing, advancing movement toward ultimate joy. Resurrection power is what gives the circles of our lives their forward motion.

You can be sure that when Peter wrote "the sprinkling of the blood of Jesus Christ," he had in mind human pain turned fully triumphant. He had in mind your pain, and mine. There's a monumental difference, of course; our pain is pint-sized, and Christ's is cosmic. But when the stone moved—cracking open the grave that

---

*All three synoptic gospels specifically note that a rounded stone was "rolled away" from Jesus' grave. For important, spacious tombs like that of Joseph of Arimathea's, in which Jesus' body had been laid, explains Hastings, "The opening to the central chamber was guarded by a large and heavy disc of rock which could roll along a groove slightly depressed at the center, in front of the tomb entrance." "The door to such a grave," according to Douglas and Tenney, "weighed from one to three tons."

first Easter morning—billions of spectacular sunrises across billions of years broke wide open for you, too.

Today your suffering is a moving circle, rolling even now—if you will believe it and give thanks in advance for its good to come—into your sunshine of victory, full-orbed.

I think of it as heaven on wheels.

What, after all, is a wheel but a forward-moving circle?

Triunity is our Exodus travel's centering hub, our bound for the Promised Land radial, the unstoppable Kingdom's axle. You don't reinvent the wheel; it whirls, turning to further our forward progress. Eternally speaking, when you're a chosen stranger scattered, you're on a roll.

Moving in Rhythm: The Dance of Obedience

Experientially, of course, it's hard to feel that inexorable forward movement. In the scattered circles of our everyday lives, it sometimes feels more like being stuck, or sliding backward, or spinning sideways out of control. More often, in our intimate relationships and in the wider circles of commerce and government, the movement in our lives feels like back and forth, push and shove.

To use another movement metaphor, it sometimes feels like dancing a jerky two-step in which both partners are determined to lead and someone is always stepping on your toes. It gets you nowhere, and it's definitely no fun.

And this brings us to our last pivotal prologue word: obedience. It literally means "hearing under." And that implies listening to a heavenly sound system—three dimensional sound, Triphonic music. It's hearing the beat and moving our dancing feet to its rhythm. And that kind of attentive movement is the whole point of being scattered out into the world. It's the key to relational suffering turned therapeutic, the impetus of our onward movement and growth, the secret that turns our clumsy clogging into a graceful dance: We are "scattered . . . *for obedience.*"

This final summary phrase not only takes us to the heart of everything we've studied, but also takes us to the center—whether we recognize the name of that Center or not—of all psychological, behavioral, and relational therapy. It takes us to the core of flexible, workable, healthy democracy, because it adds an eternal dimension to the perennial nagging question of who's in charge.

Pastoral flex produces peace, order, and freedom in all our relationships—from family to society—*only* because we move in obedience to the One who invented relationships in the first place.

For many modern Americans, nothing illustrates where Peter is going in this final phrase better than the Twelve Steps of Alcoholics Anonymous and all its related programs. The first three steps—the initial, direction-changing ones—point directly to the question of obedience:

> 1. We admitted . . . that our lives had become unmanageable.
> 2. We came to believe that a Power greater than ourselves could restore us to sanity.
> 3. We made a decision to turn our will and our lives over to the care of God as we understood Him.[9]

To use Peter's psychology, healing begins when we admit our need for management by—or *obedience to*—a Higher Power. We start to dance forward—to make sense of our suffering—only when we begin tuning our ears and our steps to the Triune rhythm.

Assertiveness or Acquiescence: Dancing to the Right Beat

Reinhold Niebuhr's "Serenity Prayer," which AA made famous, helps people so much because it plugs into this prologue's Trinitarian principles. It sums up how the dance of obedience fits in with the overall choreography.

> *God, grant us serenity*
> *To accept the things we cannot change,*
> *Courage to change the things we can,*
> *And wisdom to know the difference.*[10]

The serenity to accept those things we cannot change, in the Epistle's language, is obedience to the sprinkling of the blood of Jesus Christ. It is suffering *accepted*. It encapsulates the feminine principle of *submission*, of acquiescence, of the inevitability, for each of us, of the cross. Some things we cannot change. Jesus could not change his cross; we cannot change ours: We accept our obedient suffering with serenity.*[11]

Courage to change those things we can comes to us out of our chosenness from the Father's foreknowledge, out of the masculine principle of *authority*, of assertiveness—out of the potential, for each of us, of the resurrection. New, resurrected life within us provides the courage to change the things we can.

Wisdom to know the difference comes by sanctification in the Spirit. As strangers to ourselves and others, we have been set apart for wholeness. Cognitive-narrative thinking brings us discrimination between *obedient suffering* and our addictions, our martyr-complex codependencies, the suffering of our *disobedience*. The Spirit's wisdom teaches us which way—authority or submission—to flex. To help us follow that heavenly music that we cannot hear fully yet, the Triphonic symphony's Composer-Conductor gives us our cues.

Catching the Beat

How do we begin to perceive the Triune rhythm?

The same way the early church came to perceive it: by recognizing Christ's crucifixion and resurrection as *one event*. Splitting them apart, thinking of them as two events, disrupts our dancing as surely as a high-school gang breaking up the senior prom.

No wonder Jesus, after prophesying his united death-and-rising-ahead, erupted after hearing Simon Bar-Jona's dense-like-us response, "No, Lord, this should never happen to you!" Simon had divided the one united episode into two. He revealed our hellish self-pity, as if Jesus' cross contained no third day. And at Simon's split of the indivisible—to teach us all—Jesus exploded, "Get behind me, Satan!"

---

*Elsewhere Scripture describes such relationally unavoidable suffering as "making up what is left behind of the suffering of Christ for the sake of his body, the church." When, as we relate to others, our clear duty involves pain, resurrection life in us will use that pain to build up the strength of his therapeutic body both in us and in the broader world.

Unbelief blinds me to the resurrection, both in Jesus' cross and in my own—and stops me dead in my tracks. But hearing the cross-resurrection beat gets my feet moving again.

So these first disciples found Christ's cross and resurrection *two connected stages of only one occurrence,* a timed double-phasing within a single happening. They recognized the crucified and resurrected Jesus to be identical, unquestionably one and the same man. Since they had touched him with their own hands, they now acknowledged him; they knew him. By this sure identification, they comprehended his dying and rising the third day as one irreducible, inseparable occasion, his mighty indivisible deed. They grasped it as *the rhythm within his one completed action.*

Thus, just like it happens today for us, they began to hear, really hear, what Jesus says about the Trinity.

First, they started putting it all together through his cross-resurrection prophesies followed by the one historic phenomenon—first his words and then his accomplishment.

Then, after Pentecost, while they were proclaiming this news—his cross and resurrection as one achievement, one operation, one victory—their own thinking kept changing about God's Oneness. As Jesus both described and revealed it, they increasingly saw God as the Three-in-One. As they did, they began to see solutions to the insoluble riddles of all humanity.

Watching, we get the idea of just how they did it, just how it happened through them. Keeping the church itself united and spreading its adaptable peace out into the world through its members, the cross-resurrection rhythm moved them forward together.

They spent the rest of their lives learning to follow the Triune relational rhythm:

The Father is conservative, the Son is liberal; in the Spirit they both support the past and claim the future.

The Father is age, the Son is youth; their Spirit is mature wisdom, forever young.

The Father is tradition, the Son is innovation; the Spirit judiciously constructive change.

The Father is propositional, the Son existential; their Spirit brings intellectual truth relationally alive.

The Father is concept, the Son is action; their living Spirit makes insight break out in healthy perspiration.

The Father doctrinal, the Son incarnational, the Spirit forms the Word made flesh in you.

The Father is universal, the Son is particular, their Spirit shapes global love into family ties.

The Father is the goal, the Son is the process, the Spirit is clarity—one step, one day at a time—in the task.

The Father is responsibility leading, the Son accountability serving, the Spirit builds collaboration into productivity.

The Father is individuality, the Son is community; in the Spirit they interact as distinctly three yet indivisibly one.

Within himself God remains forever the generational process, the perfect family system, clear-headedness at work, social-interpersonal love united in joy. This contagious joy moves out from within each of us into our broadening human circles. In us, either acquiescent or assertive, Triunity's pastoral flex is internal-external, cross-resurrection, one-event rhythm.

Learning to Dance

For every one of us the dance of obedience is different; for every one of us, its rhythm is the same. Our human environment is Christ's cross; our Father's purpose, His resurrection; love's triumph for us remains their everlasting cotillion's indivisibility.

Christ communicates this beat to us continually if we will listen. How? Under Triphonic music, first we listen for what others want us to do, then we listen for what we want to do ourselves, and finally we listen for God's harmony inside us, by his peace uniting and directing our actions, as we take our next measured, obedient step. Triphonic music includes in its everlasting rhythm the fact that God speaks to us through others, just as he broadcasts directly to our souls.

To improve my hearing—my attentiveness to cross-resurrection rhythms within and around me—and to help me learn democracy's dance, I often pray a fourfold prayer, the first two parts of which come from C. S. Lewis:

> Lord, help me to pray to you, not as I think you are, but as You know yourself to be.

Grant that the me who prays to You will be the real me, and
not imaginary.

Grant that the word by which I pray to you will be your true
Word, and not my understanding of it.

Grant that the church for which I pray will be the Church in
your mind, and not the one in our own.

That prayer is especially important to me because, as a Baptist,
I grew up—rigidly—not dancing. Did that fact contribute to my
suffering, to my pain in learning *psychological* flexibility? Physically, I'm inclined even today to be stiff, creaky, musclebound,
about as limber as a two-by-four. Yet I've been trying to learn the
flexibility of obedience for years.

I read recently that *women tend to be more supple than men*, which,
at least physically, confirms my feminine-flexible argument.[12] This
gets very close to home: Before she married a Baptist, my wife danced
superbly. She's also more supple than I am psychologically!

Dancing to a One-Two-Three Beat

The Associate Director of our Laity Lodge retreat center, the Roman
Catholic layman Eddie Sears, teaches country-and-western dancing. When the Bolshoi Ballet performed in San Antonio, Eddie and
his wife Gail were recruited to teach them some Texas steps.

Gail and Eddie explained to me a few things about dance that I
find intriguing. When you dance, you can move to several different
kinds of beat. Perhaps the most common in ballroom-type dancing
is a two-step, in which the partners move back and forth to a one-
two, one-two beat. A waltz, on the other hand, is a *three*-step dance.
And when the music switches to that one-two-three beat, the dance
really takes off. In the grander type of waltz (visualize a period-
piece movie from the golden age of cinema) the partners glide in
forward-moving circles.

To paint the picture of how spiritual growth produces a balanced
flow in human relationships—essential to democracy—think of
your own life as a kind of dance.

All our relationships, consciously or unconsciously, involve authority and submission: We exercise authority or we submit to it.

Beginning as infants in a crib, ending up in some nursing-home hospital bed—and everywhere else between—we give or take orders. We call signals or follow them. We live every day, whether we realize it or not, by the authority-submission two-step: give or take, win or lose, assert or submit, rule or be ruled. Ordinary human politics can offer you nothing more: no unity, no freedom, no flex, no forward movement.

But what the Trinity growing within you does is make that two-step into a three-step waltz: give-take-flex, win-lose-flex, assert-sub-mit-flex. We then begin moving to a relational rhythm; our relationships become a gliding promenade to heavenly music. Authority and submission gradually cease to be two different experiences, but rather one Triune experience, interconnected.

Strauss waltzes can only intimate audibly the spiritual sense of harmonious flow, the ordered cadence, this tempo in tune with the freedom of the universe. You can waltz through hell because the Triune beat brings you, as the first accent in the coming measure, heaven next. It makes for upbeat living: Progressively our lives dance along in concert with the music of the spheres.

Suffering—because of evil—remains our human condition. But our everlasting destiny is *not* suffering, but rejoicing. The dance of Triune democratic relationships—in marriage, family, work, and government—choreographs celebration right in with our discomfort. And the "one-two-three" dance of pastoral flex always ends on the upbeat, ready to move on. Obedience and sprinkling of the blood of Jesus Christ means we each scatter, through our pain, resurrection joy.

Moving Steadily On: A Destiny of Rejoicing

When I was a little boy, gyroscopes fascinated me. A gyroscope looked to me like a dancing circle: spinning freely, yet perfectly balanced and steady, held upright by some mysterious inner power.

So, as I thought of suffering scattered through the circles of our lives, and of the Trinitarian rhythm that turns our obedient suffering into a dance, my childhood fascination with gyroscopes conjured up those dancing circles once again.

Then I looked up *gyroscope* in my *Encyclopedia Britannica*. Imagine my delight in reading that a gyroscope consists of "a spinning wheel mounted in such a way that it is free to turn about any of *three possible axes!*" I was reminded then, as well, that gyroscopes are more than dancing scientific toys. They stabilize our planes in turbulent weather, steady our ships as they sail through raging seas, and guide them automatically by their compasses.

So they sound to me like circles dancing to Triphonic music and, at the same time, providing steady balance in our forward motion.

The little boy in me still says: that looks like fun!

And the open-eyed adult in me, looking around, whispers, "We've never needed it more!"

When Things Fly Apart

The twentieth century, we know all too well, has not thought in Triune categories. We have therefore massively compounded our suffering. Perhaps the most memorable description of the anguish and torture of modern politics and modern relationships came from the Irish poet, William Butler Yeats. In 1921, during the decade between Communism's rise in Russia and Fascism's in Germany, Yeats wrote these famous lines, anticipating from the left and right rulers like Stalin and Hitler:

> *Turning and turning in the widening gyre*
> *The falcon cannot hear the falconer;*
> *Things fall apart; the center cannot hold;*
> *Mere anarchy is loosed upon the world.*[13]

History happened, of course, as Yeats predicted. Things *did* fall apart. The center did *not* hold. Mere anarchy *was* loosed and, with it, World War II's blood-soaked terror.

And today, it seems, the falcon still spirals high above our heads, flying wide and out of earshot. The macho huntsman falconer cannot hold together the dizzying arcs of our spread-out politics and relationships. Our families, our institutions, our society, the world—all seem poised to fall apart. National and international circles have flung themselves asunder, out of their orbit. The center, it seems, cannot hold.

Yet in the midst of our shattered world—revolutions hurled apart and ripped to shreds—Peter speaks to us the message of Triune hope. The Trinitarian essence is life, motion, movement—but *stable* movement. Gyroscopic movement: circles dancing but kept steadily on course. As Scripture says about Christ (through his individual obedience), "By him all things *hold together*."[14.]

For that's the substance of our hope, the rationale for every advancing, forward-looking step.

Expecting Beauty Ahead

To me, Ray Stevens's future-affirming pop ballad vocalizes forward-looking hope.

> *Everything is beautiful . . . in its own way.*
> *Under God's heaven, the world's gonna find a way.*[15]

But, of course, the song is pure sentiment, shallow, positive/wishful thinking, unless you make two prior assumptions:

(1) The cross and resurrection make up *one event.*

(2) The purpose of suffering is *joy.*

And both these assumptions are true. "*Under* God's heaven" implies humble obedience to that sprinkling which alone makes everything beautiful.

Isn't this the Apostle's keynote? Listen again:

> By his great mercy we have been born again to a *living hope* through the resurrection of Jesus Christ from the dead. . . . In this you *rejoice*, though now for a little while you may have to suffer various trials. . . . Without having seen him you love him; though you do not now see him you believe in him and *rejoice* with unutterable and exalted *joy*.[16]

Everything *is* beautiful if we believe the cross is beautiful. That's why, of that ugly, disgraced instrument of Roman torture—of that "emblem of suffering and shame"—we sing, "I'll *cherish* the old rugged cross." Centered in that cross we become courageous. We see beyond our personality problems, our damaged self-image troubles, our inner feelings of shame. We see beyond our loneliness, estrangements, our isolations.

Centered in that cross, we expect beauty ahead.

"Beauty is only skin-deep," says Kelch's Observation, "but ugly goes all the way to the bone."[17] In our study we have repeatedly seen that without help, our deepest self-image is bone-ugly despondency, our bone-ugliness bottom-buried. God takes these deep uglies within us *as they are* and from them fashions an internal beauty that is *distinctively ours.*

We only *saw* ourselves as ugly because of our blindness to God's wisdom in the circumstances of our chosenness. "Who sinned, this man or his parents, that he was born blind?" the disciples asked Jesus. Who's to blame? Genetics? Environment? Is it his own fault? "Neither this man sinned nor his parents," Jesus replied (Quit trying, negatively, to distribute blame!), "but that the works of God might be made manifest in him, we must work the works of him that sent me." *Then he helped the man to see.*[18]

Isn't *that* our human condition *and* our forward potential? In a sense, all of us were "born blind," but it's useless accusing our heredity. All of us have chosen to be blind, but unraveling our self-centeredness is impossible. Understanding all the explanations *why* we choose darkness rather than light is futile. The point is: *We can start opening our eyes.* Beauty is there for us to enjoy. As we start seeing, and enjoying more and more, someday someone will tell us that our ugly blindness *itself* has made us a good-looking sight to behold.

Expecting good results from bad events takes courage. But all pain becomes obedient pain whenever we give thanks for its potential. ("Thank you, God—in advance—for the good you can bring out of this trouble!") And then, once we've given thanks, the "courage to change the things I can" turns our pain positive. In bad times, it sings. In every cross it finds resurrection possibilities. Bravely accepting "in three days," as good-out-of-bad's unpredictable timing, your fearless serenity waits. The beauty your endurance expects is Christ. He always has the last word.

The Now and Coming Kingdom

For all our courageous, fearless waiting for Him, our steadying expectation of beauty and joy, theologians hatched up the big word *eschatology*, "the study of last things."

In 1 Peter we have studied what these theologians call *realized eschatology*. In common language, "realized eschatology" means "the kingdom of God is *now*." This Letter gives us the single most concise *realized* eschatology in the post-Pentecost Scriptures.

For this reason among others, the church also canonized 1 Peter's counterpart, 2 Peter, which presents a *future* eschatology. "Future eschatology" means "the kingdom of God is *coming*."

Balance between eschatology *present* and eschatology *future* remains essential for our psychological and spiritual health. The unbalanced emphasis on the "now kingdom" takes ourselves, and our ideas of the kingdom here, too seriously. In its extreme forms, secular or religious, it decays into utopianism, theocracy, or dictatorship. The unbalanced "coming kingdom," by contrast, "so heavenly minded we're no earthly good," turns us toward "pie in the sky by and by" instead of cornbread on the table here and now.

Beware: The *now* kingdom and the *coming* kingdom can never be authentic if divorced. Today and forever they abide as one. Social impact, therefore, part and parcel, springs from eschatological hope.

How we need that Hope to look positively at humanity's insoluble travails, to see our giant tribulations as labor pains. Our intractable anguishes assault us without and within:

- world hunger,
- crime, violence, threat of nuclear war,
- racial prejudice,
- sexual harassment; discrimination against women,
- poverty, illiteracy, economic despair,
- totalitarianism,
- bureaucracies.

To even *start* such a list smirks at our torments: child abuse, drug addictions, pornography, violations of the environment, family collapse, alcoholism, money madness. The endless register of our insanities rattles on.

But we dare not quit and give up, overwhelmed by these problems' enormities. Hope within this world grows with hope beyond it. The second coming of Christ offers us the ultimate hope, a final purposive vision to motivate, prioritize, and inform our actions today. No one of us can wage effective battle at all these ramparts of evil alone. Each one of us must pick, choose, and specialize, joining hands with like-minded others at work on our specific, common concerns. Waiting for the real Messiah's return, we can forsake our messianic temptations and embrace our individual, life-sized here-and-now tasks.

This freedom of private obedience belongs to each of us exclusively but also merges into the collective universal good. We can be freed from our political utopias' delusions, believing more wisely than ever in practical, realistic social change.

Holy boldness for down-to-earth human betterment gets nourished by clear-thinking expectation of a kingdom to come. We never give up. There *is* something we can do. We *don't* have to whip the universal problem to attack it. We can accept not only our human limitation, but also His divine potential. Courage for the cross is resurrection hope. The ultimate victory comes from beyond us, but glorious and immediate victories await us here at hand.

Thinking to the Beat

Evermore the cadence pulses: First, groans; then, gladness. But not for flabby wills or undisciplined minds: "To bring every thought into captivity to Christ" starts with our thinking patterns now.

"Watch, for in such an hour as you *think not*, the Son of Man comes."[19] This psychological command calls for our twofold time frame, *Eschatology both present and future.* Christ's coming again ultimately lies out ahead, in that final, great, unknown tomorrow. But he comes again also, here at this very moment, in the *good* around and within us.

He comes to you now in your breathing, digestion, eyesight, hearing, aliveness. He comes to you in sparkling whitecaps on a green bay under a clear blue sky; in cold Coca-Cola on a scorching August afternoon; in good music, food, friends, conversation, ideas, smiles, and laughter. He comes in breath-catching serendipities, happy co-incidences, "it's a small world" pleasures, warm hospitality. He comes in hoped-for, prayed-for reconciliations between people, just as our Hill Country's leafless, death-of-winter trees bud every year into those bright April peach-blossom bouquets.

He comes to each one of us, too, in the personal eschatology of death. Beside the candle on their writing desks, old-time medieval saints used to work at their daily task with a *skull* sitting in front of them.

Personal eschatology for today; death before your face: It *does* focus the mind. "Come quickly, Lord Jesus!" you pray.[20] And he responds to you, "Behold, I come quickly!"[21] He's been coming all along. "Count your many blessings, name them one by one . . . and it will surprise you what the Lord has done!" The old gospel song is not the world's greatest music, but its counsel is unexcelled. The Christ who is coming is the one we've known all along: Realized eschatology issues constantly in our positive-thinking *gratitude* and our forward-thinking *anticipation*.

Are we immobilized, made ineffectual, or demeaned by the implication that we have been put here on earth to learn how to think? Not if how to think means growing in the mind of Christ, thinking God's thoughts after him. Not if it means mature—male/female, cognitive/narrative, authority/submission flexibility—Triune thinking. Such thinking would not demean but exalt us. It would not only explain, but also ennoble and energize us.

Since God is rational, our Trinitarian thinking is, inherently, rational courage. Its assertive acquiescence sees the resurrection beyond the cross. In that wise confidence it braves itself to embrace the pain and overcome it. "Despising the shame,"[22] it accepts "the shape of its own obedience."[23] It dares to think and act unflinchingly through to the gladness ahead.

St. Peter's Therapeutic Dance

Your pain only precedes your joy. This rhythm, evermore, establishes its beat, our positive-thinking tempo. The Epistle we have studied dances out for us, on its own stage through Peter, this throbbing, recurring pulsation. The Apostle's whole life demonstrates the steps.

Simon Peter is the patron saint of depressives. His old Bar-Jona family-of-origin neuroses show us our two shared temperament risks: (1) haste, or impetuosity; and (2) withdrawal, or giving up.

When Peter denied Christ, fitting in with the crowd the night our Lord was betrayed, he made clear once and for all his natural weakness—his mercurial impulsiveness, his fast spur-of-the-moment rashness, his fearful, loud and proud self-will.

Then, realizing what he had done and couldn't undo, and even after the resurrection overcome by his failure, he slunk away to make his calling-it-quits exit: "I'm going fishing."[24] He didn't mean a weekend's recreation. He meant back to the *old* life, the *old* days, the *old* futility. Back as if Jesus had never come, had never given him a new name. Back as if Peter the Rock had never existed. He meant *back*, back to hopeless transference, back to Simon *Bar-Jona*.

But say this for Peter: He was (in today's psychological jargon) *getting in touch with his feelings*. We must acknowledge our griefs to produce our growth. Denying our sorrows we defraud ourselves, and more important, defraud Christ who died to make *all* human suffering spiritually productive.

That denying-Christ failure, and its resulting sorrow, prepared Peter for his preaching at Pentecost role. Reading "the greatest story ever told" convinces me over and over again that the saga had been preplanned.

Even in our sinfulness we are in Christ. The protective envelope of God's love surrounds the cosmos itself: No suffering penetrates our lives without having penetrated Christ first. Long before he allows it to come to us, God plans resurrection from our pain. Never, never, never does God allow bad things to come into our lives without knowing, ahead of time, the good that can come out of them—the original, unique, and creative victories that could have come no other way.

His growth foreordained before Pentecost, then, Peter continued across the years to grow: "Rocky" finally became really rocklike. So the kingdom in us slowly produces our steadfastness and stand-firmness. And also, concurrently, lithesome agreeability. For this combination of sturdiness and flexibility, remember, Peter coined the term "living stones." Its relational suppleness shook loose

Rome's arthritic rigidity and started that stiff-necked circle dancing.

Some authorities argue that the Apostle dashed off this First Epistle hurriedly. I don't buy that. He planned its structure and he chose its words too carefully. Its logic persuades us; its coherence commands us; its upbeat practicality will not let us go. It braces us to face our ordeals unafraid: You don't run from your distresses; you overcome them.

No, this Letter writing could not, conceivably, have been hasty or rushed. The joy of putting down these words came only through the pain of hard work.

This Letter sparkles because, like a diamond from coal, it grew out of prolonged heat—and pressure. From a lifetime's accepted turmoil, it emerged in the persistent growth of Christlike character. Before they finished polishing their positive-thinking textbook, I'm convinced, Peter and Silvanus found their writing task delightful. If the input wasn't fun, how could the output be so terrific? Later, before Peter died, imagine his exhilaration at hearing how it helped people. In heaven today, I suspect, Peter celebrates with special jubilance over our profiting so much from his growing pains.

Resurrection Is a Way to Think

In the first paragraph on the first page of this book, I said that our troubles produce our growth. That premise, on which everything I've said has rested, in turn rests on this closing note about our being *scattered:* If we will only believe it, our suffering is always and only, "the sprinkling of *the blood of Jesus Christ."* That blood includes, inherently, forgiveness, hope, resurrection, consummation, victory, our everlasting joy.

Resurrection is a way to think. Resurrection itself is confidence that God is good, that Jesus—as he said—has conquered evil, and that by his word death itself will die. Jesus thinks as the ultimate practicalist. By his blood he convinces us that God's love—despite every evidence to the contrary—really is victorious. Resurrection thinking turns problems into opportunities, bad news into unfolding benefits, and setbacks into progress. Troubles sprinkled across our lives translate themselves into scattered growth.

Jesus goes *through* the cross, but he *is* the resurrection. He endured the cross "for the joy set before him:"[25] His pain always *thinks resurrection* to come—and so can ours. That's why, whatever problem you face personally just now, whatever despair you feel about America politically, no matter what fears you harbor about the future of the world—*don't unpack in the tomb.*[26] Instead, think resurrection, and dance forward steadily into joy.

The Steady Dance of Democracy: A Question of Character

If Jesus "learned obedience by the things which he suffered,"[27] so will we. Enduring democracy depends upon it: When we sign on to share the vote, whether we know it or not, we sign on to share the pain. I closed my book on leadership years ago by saying, "To lead is to suffer." Democracy's shared power means shared pain, or else there will be no democracy—or its cherished freedoms.

Democracy's dance flows forward only by pastoral flex: The people *obey* the government; the people *change* the government. *In rhythm*. Democracy functions by pastoral flex or it does not function. If it does not dance, it dies.

Democracy does not require, obviously—indeed by its nature of freedom, it *cannot* require—that everyone be Christian: Religious liberty constitutes its very soul. It does require, however, a leavening remnant, a preserving saltiness. It cannot be separated, therefore, from the acceptance of pain, because *character* cannot be separated from the acceptance of pain.

The burden of democracy is moral: The character of the governed ("we, the people") produces the character of our governors. In democratic government, we get what we deserve: Rule by "the consent of the governed" demands of itself *character* in both the governors *and* the governed. Reality offers us no shortcuts: No pain, no *character*.

The resurrection of Christ brings the sure promise of spiritual growth—*character*—out of our pain.

That fact surely explains G. K. Chesterton's comment, closing his study of world history, its religions, Christ, and his Resurrection:

> I have not minimized the scale of the miracle, as some of our
> milder theologians think it wise to do. Rather I have deliberately

dwelt on that incredible interruption, as a blow that broke the very backbone of history. I have great sympathy with the mono- theists, the Moslems, or the Jews, to whom it seems a blasphemy that might shake the world. But it did not shake the world; it *steadied* the world.[28]

Short Pain, Long Joy

Heaven's gyroscope dances forward by one inviolate movement: aching initially, succeeded by solace; griefs to begin, rejoicing to finish. Eternally it fits: The agony evaporates, but the elation keeps building up—and lasts.

So, in your disappointments, be gentle with yourself; later, you will find it easier to be gentle with others. The Maestro of spiritual music composes one never-copied pulsation: Short pain, followed by long joy.

The happiness outlives the hurt. The *length* of the two source words drums the steady beat: Short *cross*, long *resurrection*. Count the syllables and glory in the difference: One to four. Compare the pulse, the phonics: each word has a first vowel, but only one word, between the two, has three more vowels left over. You hear it, don't you? *Cross. Re-sur-rec-tion.* Life's Maestro gives you, past the pain beat of your cross, one more resurrection beat. But with it he gives you *three more* waltzing pulsations of joy. Extra, to spare. In those three additional beats, orchestrated, your eternity sings.

Just so, in the daily sandpaper of marriage, family, and work, *wise obedience*, giving thanks ahead of time for relational healing to come, accepts the hurt of accommodating others. Or instead, standing up and talking back first, *rational courage* refuses, or ceases, disobedient accommodation to them. Refusing or ceasing, on one hand, or taking the bruises, on the other, composes pastoral flex. Rhythm between them both is two sides of the same maturity, the heavenly dance. One or the other, your directing or else your accepting directions, leading or following either one, contains iden- tical, rhythmic, cross-resurrection choreography.

You swing and sway to the unseen Drummer, fit as a high-strung fiddle or loose as a limbered double bass. The Father gives *rational courage;* the Son brings *wise obedience;* in the Holy Spirit they come to us as one. Your best feelings about yourself, even when it hurts, constitute the Triune Drummer's different beat, as you sensibly, boldly, trip the light fantastic.

So whatever your discouragement may be, whatever your troubles, whatever your relational suffering—keep on moving! Through your obedient suffering, the dancing, singing, secular church loosens up the stiff, one-dimensioned, legalistic world and makes all heaven break loose.

Centering in: A Call to Courage

The modern age confirms "Sevareid's Law: 'The chief cause of problems is solutions.'"[29] The *real* solution is long and painful: Spiritual growth. There is no other way: "Joy is a fruit Americans eat green."[30] Don't fall for easy answers to hard problems—and miss the joy that comes with the struggle to grow.

Since this book hinges on the idea of a threefold, relational God, let me close with a series of "miniature trinities" that sum up my argument and point beyond it to our own personal centering-in. First, three presuppositions have undergirded all my thinking: (1) Christ was neither deranged nor a fraud, but in toto who he claimed to be; (2) His description of Scripture as pointing to his true identity is accurate; and (3) The Personal Intelligence behind Scripture is to all human solutions, through the ages up to and including the present, as nuclear war is to the slingshot, as interplanetary space exploration is to a horse-drawn buggy.

Spiritual growth makes sense: It alone provides the courage we need to triumph over our troubles. So my final description of Christ—and my final exhortation to you—is *courage*.

Isaiah foresaw Christ's persevering endurance eight centuries before his earthly arrival: "He shall not fail nor be discouraged."[31] Throughout history Christians have recognized that we need that kind of courage—Christ's courage—for our individual journeys forward.

John Bunyan confessed, "Oh, it is hard continuing believing, continuing loving, continuing resisting all that opposeth."[32] Jonathan Edwards warned, "The degree of religion . . . is to be judged by the fixedness and strength of habit that is exercised in affection."[33] At one desperate time years ago, healing strength came to me simply from the title of Paul Tillich's book: *The Courage to Be.*[34]

Discouragement is always of the Devil; its steady antidote in Christ comes, not only from His reliability, but also from our strength of habit, our spiritual fixedness. And three perennial resources, three sources of fixedness, offer us constancy and courage:

(1) *Scripture.* To soak in the Scriptures is modern humanity's greatest need. "Faith comes by hearing, and hearing by the word of God."[35] Pursuing spiritual growth without biblical study and reflection is like wanting to gain weight but refusing to eat.

(2) *Prayer and Meditation.* Prayer tunes us to the Triune, opening our lives to the wisdom of the Holy Spirit. The primacy of spiritual values shapes our lives through our customary daily agendas. Common flexibility in our timetables will be required; constant overcrowding of our calendars will not. Some appointments outrank others; it takes *time* to get centered.

(3) *The Church.* For the soul's development nothing takes the place of the worshiping Church. If private prayer and meditation offer us individual nourishment and growth, then the Church offers us communal health. Institutional churches, even with their fallibilities and faults, are crucial. But remember, beyond its walls, the Church is also found in faithful relationships: family, business, professional, social . . . Christian friendships scattered. Faith's congenialities, nurturing associations, trustworthy spiritual networks: All these companionships develop Triune connectedness.

Rightly understood, all three of these indispensable resources communicate the vitality of Christ to us. Only God keeps us from understanding them wrongly; appropriated wisely, *they have no substitutes.* To find and nourish their sustenance, these signposts help:

- Watch for lay-awakening churches.
- Watch for spiritual secularity.
- Watch for relational peace around and within you.

Markers like these keep us alert for the Triune God's unexpected appearances. They develop depth for our present citizenship in that coming-tomorrow age. They encourage our courage.

Winston Churchill once said, "Success is never final; defeat seldom fatal. In the end it's only courage that counts."[36] Courage is hope's walking shoes, the protection we need for taking that next stout-hearted unfaltering step, the next ordinary secular step.

The Center Holds: A Valedictory

Finally, in a world that sometimes seems to be coming apart, let us fix our concentration on Christ. We aren't expected to come up with our courage alone. Our spiritual bravery roots itself in Christ's triumphant blood: His overcoming blood *sprinkled* through our day-to-day lives becomes relational steadfastness *scattered* for each other.

Remember that, of the gyroscope's three axes—the vertical axis, the horizontal axis, and the spinning axis—only one point is fixed: the *intersection* of the three axes. Its constant freedom for its full rotation pivots strategically on that fixed center. In the widening gyre, it does not fall apart.

Only this, His spiritual indomitability in us, produces sustained human oneness in our marriages, families, and work, or in the expanding circles of healthy democratic growth around the world. We all long for this oneness.

We still run away from estrangements close at hand. Our ordinary, common, broken relational circles, their pain crying out to turn therapeutic, reveal our egocentric despair. Our lonely conceit then reaches out for the spasmodic society of other lonely runaways—unparented and unchildrened—who flit momentarily by. In them—all of us unaware—we continue searching for God's internal undividedness. We yearn for social human wholeness. Our self-important isolation grasps consecutive, temporary, fake unities in vain; in sex, work, reputation, government, even religion, we clutch for fleeting, artificial, manipulative coalitions. We fall for quick fixes: All of them evaporate.

We fear the abandoned aloneness of death. Unity's absence leaves us terrified. It should: We were created for society. The original party giver is Jesus; he got started at a wedding-reception bash; he winds up the whole human story at a huge wedding celebration. Triune Love's diverse but concentrated singleness is so intense it distills joy out of pain. Triunity makes all other community look pale. Christ's resurrection tells you that social-psychological unity thrives at the center and circumference of the universe.

So coming of age, but still beginners, we *never* have it all together. Yet *for us* it's all together the very moment we start.

I said that Yeats and his falconer sketched our twentieth-century political despair—the hopeless polarized terrors that assault us from the right and the left—the lurking fear that all our out-of-control circles of togetherness will fling themselves asunder.

Not surprisingly, speaking for Triunity and womanhood, Dorothy Sayers painted the alternative—through her secular detective-hero, Lord Peter Wimsey. In Sayers's greatest Wimsey novel, *Gaudy Night*, she closes a very long-running subplot of romance. Ultimately this love story within a detective story eclipses everything else in her classic drama, becoming its conclusion and climax. Sayers's own thinly disguised counterpart in the narrative, the "mystery fiction writer," Harriet Vane, finally agrees to marry Lord Peter—after years of her rejecting his dashing elegance, his faithful attentions, and his tireless pursuit.

The change in Harriet's recalcitrance comes when she encounters—in the investigative papers for the *Gaudy Night* case (which they are handling jointly)—Lord Peter's metaphysical love poem, written obviously for her.

The poem carries Wimsey's heart cry for Harriet to settle down with him in wedded oneness, as "in close perfume lies the rose-leaf curled." He prays for her assent, in faith that the breached isolation of their separate lives will be tied together in dynamic tranquillity. His poetry wins her. As the story closes, she yields.

From Lord Peter's rhythmic words of human love, Sayers calls us—not just the riven sexes, but the whole torn-family world—to our intended home, home to the man on the middle Cross, home to the bliss of Divine Triunity:

> *(W)e have come, last and best,*
> *From the wide zone in dizzying circles hurled*
> *To that still center where the spinning world*
> *Sleeps on its axis, to the heart of rest.*[37]

To which beauty I add only one comment, bidding you good-bye.
Never fear, my friends.
The Center holds.
Whether we are centered or not, the Center holds.

A Closing Word

On March 12, 1991, my father died, just before his ninety-sixth birthday. He was a great man, a wonderful father, and a business genius. Starting with nothing, he built a remarkable Texas food retailing organization. The company was—and is, through my brother Charles's leadership today—permeated by the qualities of his character. I am eternally proud to be his son. At his funeral our former pastor, Dr. Warren Hultgren, spoke of Dad's faith, his goodness, and his generosities: "He was a giver before he had anything to give."

Dad gave more than his money; he gave himself. He bestowed on his heritage a legacy of giving. He gave Mother the inspiration, resources, and support she needed for her social service; she gave him absolute, lifelong devotion. I had parents who functioned as a team. His self-giving made that possible.

Later, in the funeral service, Warren Hultgren repeated a poem by Will Allen Dromgoole. He said it described Dad. The Pastor had heard my Dad recite its verses on the March 1952 evening when he and I, father and son, had been ordained as deacons together. To me, my sister, Eleanor Crook, Charles, the grandchildren and thousands of others he touched as employer, Good Samaritan, citizen, and friend, Dad *incarnated* its words.

The Bridge Builder

An old man going a lone highway
Came in the evening cold and gray
To a chasm vast and deep and wide.
The old man crossed in the twilight dim,

The sullen stream had no fears for him,
But he stopped when safe on the other side
And built a bridge to span the tide.

"Old Man," said a fellow pilgrim near,
"You are wasting your strength with building here;
Your journey will end with the ending day,
You never again will pass this way,
You've crossed the chasm deep and wide,
Why build you this bridge at evening tide?"

The builder lifted his old gray head,
"Good friend, in the path I have come," he said,
"There followeth after me today
A youth whose feet must pass this way.
This chasm which has been as naught to me
To that fair-haired youth might a pitfall be,
He too must cross in the twilight dim,
Good Friend, I am building the bridge for him."[1]

· · ·

Rob Harrill's October 7, 1993, front page *Corpus Christi Caller Times* story began, "Mary Elizabeth Holdsworth Butt, whose husband built the H.E.B. grocery chain and whose philanthropy earned her statewide acclaim as a champion of children, the disabled and the poor, died early Wednesday.

"She was 90."

Mother had begun her life of social service in the early 1930s in the Rio Grande Valley, an area where today's array of governmental agencies was then nonexistent. Her dining room became an area office for the State Crippled Children's Program. She served as the first chairman of the Cameron County Child Welfare Board. She worked for the expansion of inadequate library services. She began an ambitious program of tuberculosis diagnosis and treatment throughout the Valley. She bought the first equipment for testing the hearing and vision of the area's elementary school children.

In Corpus Christi, the YWCA, County Home for the Aged, and District American Cancer Society were all organized in the Butt home. Troubled by the lack of day care for African-American children, she worked to establish the Mary Bethune Day Nursery. She served on the Community Chest Board for years, and was the prime mover toward the separate Nueces County Juvenile Center, removing young offenders from the jails. She helped set up a local tuberculosis hospital, serving five years as its board chairman.

As Dad's business interests and influence grew, her activities took on a statewide scope. She testified often before legislative committees on the budgetary needs of agencies with which she worked. In 1955 Governor Shivers appointed Mother to the Board of the Texas Department of State Hospitals and Special Schools (now the Department of Mental Health and Mental Retardation, MHMR); she served actively on this body for over thirty years, having been reappointed by five governors, and was in 1981 named a member emeritus, an honor never before granted to a member of any state board in Texas.

The *Caller Times* October 9, 1993, follow-up story, by Eleanor Mortensen, on the memorial service for Mother after her death, described the message there by our friend, the Reverend Clifford S. Waller, of San Antonio's St. Philip's Episcopal Church. The story quoted him about her State Hospital Board work.

"Waller said she 'went and stood her ground as the only woman member of the board' and effected profound changes. 'She challenged the status quo and would not allow people [MHMR clients] to be warehoused away from home,' Waller said. 'Today we have people treated close to their homes because Mary was there and responded to the need.'

" . . . [Waller] likened her service to the Biblical story [of Simon Peter] about feeding Jesus' sheep, adding that 'Mary loved to feed people [her sheep], and she had a lot of sheep to feed.'"

Notes

Introduction

1. The "bandaged, but battling" phrase came from my Houston, Texas, friend, Jack Modesett.

2. Oswald Chambers, *My Utmost for His Highest* (New York: Dodd, Mead, 1935), 131.

3. Alexis de Tocqueville, quoted by Robert N. Bellah, Richard Madsen, et al., *Habits of the Heart: Individualism and Commitment in American Life* (Berkeley: University of California Press, 1985), viii.

4. Charles Williams, *Descent of the Dove* (New York: Oxford University Press, 1939), 106.

5. Ernest Jones, *The Life and Work of Sigmund Freud* (New York: Basic Books, 1953), Volume 1, 241.

6. Ibid., 19.

7. Ibid., 1, 19, 241–42, 322–27.

8. Chambers, *My Utmost for His Highest*, 210.

9. The "my-life-for-yours" phrase is from my friend Tom Howard, the distinguished author.

Chapter 1

1. C. H. Spurgeon, "Address to the British and Foreign Bible Society, May 5, 1875," published in C. H. Spurgeon, *Speeches at Home and Abroad* (London: Passmore and Alabaster, 1878), 17.

2. Matt. 16:13–25, RSV.

3. Matt. 23:9, RSV.

4. John 1:18, author's paraphrase.

5. John 10:30, NKJV.

6. From the Nicene Creed, Rite One version, in *Book of Common Prayer* (New York: The Episcopal Church, Church Hymnal Corporation, and Seabury Press, 1977), 328.

7. Cullen Murphy, "Who Do Men Say That I Am?" *The Atlantic*, 258 (no. 6, December 1986), 53.

8. Eph. 3:15, my punctuation of Phillips.

9. Matt. 16:15–17, RSV.

10. James S. Stewart, *The Life and Teaching of Jesus Christ* (Nashville: Abingdon, n.d.), 16–17.

11. See Eph. 4:15, 26; Gal. 2:14–21.

12. Mark 2:17, Phillips.

13. Leo Rosten, *Leo Rosten's Treasury of Jewish Quotations* (New York: McGraw Hill, 1972), 648.

14. Ernest Jones, *The Life and Work of Sigmund Freud* (New York: Basic Books, 1957), Volume 3, 426.

15. John 10:30, KJV.

16. Anthony Lewis, *New York Times*, May 24, 1994, p. A-11.

17. Matt. 5:21–22, NEB.

18. 1 John 3:15.

19. Matt. 25:40, KJV.

20. 2 Cor. 5:21, RSV.

21. 2 Cor. 5:19, RSV.

22. John Donne, "The Litanie" in *The Complete English Poems of John Donne*, ed. C. A. Patrides (London: Everyman's Library, 1985), 456.

23. Matt. 16:22.

24. Matt. 7:1, RSV.

25. Matt. 7:3–5, RSV.

26. The "worship our brains" phrase came from Keith Miller.

27. Prov. 9:1–6.

28. Georg Christoph Lichtenberg, quoted in John Gross, ed., *The Oxford Book of Aphorisms* (Oxford: Oxford University Press, 1983), 78.

29. The "mystery of Godness" phrase came from my acclaimed preacher friend, John Claypool, at Laity Lodge.

30. Oswald Chambers, *My Utmost for His Highest* (New York: Dodd, Mead, 1935), 19.

31. See the Genesis 17:1 footnote in *The Scofield Reference Bible* (New York: Oxford University Press, 1945). See also Scripture references under "Breast (Hebrew) *shad*" in Robert Young, *Analytical Concordance of the Bible* (Grand Rapids: Eerdmans, 1970), 113. Likewise, W. F. Albright, "The Names 'Shaddai' and 'Abram,'" *Journal of Biblical Literature*, 54 (1935):183–93, and David Biale, "The God with Breasts: El Shaddai in the Bible," *History of Religions* (Chicago: University of Chicago Press, 1982), 21:240–56.

32. See Matt. 16:19.

33. Matt. 25:35–36, Phillips.

Chapter 2

1. John Peers, comp., *1,001 Logical Laws, Accurate Axioms, Profound Principles, Trusty Truisms, Homey Homilies, Colorful Corollaries, Quotable Quotes, and Rambunctious Ruminations for All Walks of Life*, ed. Gordon Bennett (Garden City, New York: Doubleday, 1979), 65.

2. 1 Pet. 1:3, 4, 14, 17–18, 22–23; 2:2.

3. 1 Pet. 1:3, 23; 2:2, NIV.

4. 2 Cor. 12:9, author's paraphrase.

5. Rom. 2:1, Phillips.

6. From personal correspondence with Ruth Bell Graham dated January 6, 1988.

7. Quoted from conversation with Coach Henry Parish, Laity Lodge tennis professional.

8. Ernest Jones, *The Life and Work of Sigmund Freud* (New York: Basic Books, 1953), Volume 1, 252.

9. John 3:7, KJV.

10. Mark 12:30–31, author's paraphrase.

11. Luke 10:29–37.

12. Luke 14:26–27, Phillips.

13. Daniel Goleman, *Vital Lies, Simple Truths* (New York: Touchstone, Simon and Schuster, 1985), 16–19, 165–79, 237–51.

14. 1 Pet. 1:14, NIV.

15. Archibald Thomas Robertson, *Word Pictures in the New Testament* (New York: Harper, 1933), 6:87.

16. From *ana,* "upwards," and *zonnumi,* "to put on one's girdle": Joseph Henry Thayer, *A Greek-English Lexicon of the New Testament* (New York: Harper, 1889), 34–35, 37, 274; *Analytical Greek Lexicon* (New York: Harper, 1852), 19, 22, 183.

17. From *tas osphuas,* "the loins, the body's reproductive zone, the sex organs." See Thayer, 457–58. And from *dianoias,* "the mind as the faculty of understanding, feeling, desiring," Thayer, 140.

18. *Analytical Greek Lexicon,* 353; Thayer, 70, 1, 551, 370; Robertson, 4:89.

19. 1 Pet. 1:18, Berkeley. In the Greek, *patroparadotou* comes from *pater,* "father," *para,* "of" or "from," and *didomai,* "to give." (Robertson, 6:90; *Analytical Greek Lexicon,* 312, 300, 98). The graphic concept "futile," comes from *mataias,* "vain, devoid of force, truth, success, result, to no purpose, leading away from salvation" (Thayer, 393); *"fruitlessly, without profit;* from the Heb., *erroneous* in principle, *corrupt, perverted" (Analytical Greek Lexicon,* 259).

20. From *humon,* "your," and *anastrophes,* "conduct" (from *ana,* "upwards, back, or again," and *strepho,* "to twist, turn," therefore together, "turning up and down, back and forth:" manner of life, way, or behavior). See *Analytical Greek Lexicon,* 19, 378, 25–26; Thayer, *Greek-English Lexicon,* 42.

21. Matt. 26:69–75; Mark 14:66–72; Luke 22:54–75.

22. Gen. 1:17, NEB; John 1:12–13, NEB; Matt. 6:14–15, Phillips; Matt. 18:21–22, Phillips; Eph. 4:32, Phillips; Gal. 4:26, NIV; Matt. 5:24, RSV; 1 Pet. 1:22–23, NIV.

23. Heb. 9:12, 26, 10:11.

24. *Oikodomeo,* "to build a house," is found in verses 5 and 7. *Eklecton,* "chosen," occurs in verses 4, 6, and 9. *Laos,* "laity" or "people of God," shows up once in verse 9 and twice in verse 10. *The New International Version Interlinear Greek-English New Testament* (Grand Rapids: Zondervan, 1976), 912–13.

25. 1 Pet. 2:9.

26. Oswald Chambers, *My Utmost for His Highest* (New York: Dodd, Mead, 1935), 15, 114. Keith Miller sent me this Chambers book, which became pivotal in my spiritual growth. A conversation with Keith also helped prepare me, at one particular point, for Chambers. Keith visited us to see Laity Lodge while it was under construction; his trip made him aware that Chambers would be helpful to me. He came back to Laity Lodge later that year (summer 1961) to share his personal Christian story during our first week of retreats. (See ch. 8) Those first retreats featured the distinguished Quaker philosopher and apostle of lay ministry, Elton Trueblood, who so impressed Keith that he left the oil business to go to Earlham College to study with Dr. Trueblood. After his time there, he returned to Laity Lodge as our first full-time director. During his tenure at Laity Lodge, Keith wrote his now classic *The Taste of New Wine* (Waco, Tex.: Word, 1965).

27. Chambers, *My Utmost,* 76, emphasis added.

Chapter 3

1. Matt. 16:23, RSV.
2. John Peers, comp., *1,001 Logical Laws*, 53.
3. An attributed quotation at Laity Lodge, summer 1987.
4. See Acts 1:13, NKJV.
5. Carol Gilligan, *In a Different Voice: Psychological Theory and Women's Development* (Cambridge, Mass.: Harvard Univ. Press, 1982).
6. Moffatt. Sources used in this paragraph are Alfred Marshall, *The New International Version Interlinear Greek-English New Testament* (Grand Rapids: Zondervan, 1976), 915–16; *Analytical Greek Lexicon*, 79–81, 384–85, 233; Robert Young, *Analytical Concordance of the Bible* (Grand Rapids: Eerdmans, 1970), 489–90.
7. William Wordsworth, "The Excursion," *The Poetical Works of Wordsworth*, Cambridge Edition, rev. and with a new introduction by Paul D. Sheats (Boston: Houghton Mifflin, 1982), 463.
8. Isa. 54:5, RSV.
9. Isaiah 62:5.
10. Margaret Mead, *Blackberry Winter: My Earlier Years* (New York: William Morrow, 1972), 189, emphasis added.
11. 1 Pet. 2:11–12, 15; 3:1–2, 7–8, 15–17; 4:3–6, 17–19.
12. 1 Pet. 2:12, NIV.
13. 1 Pet. 3:15–16, Beck.
14. Dr. George Schweitzer, University of Tennessee physicist, at the Layman's Leadership Institute, Houston, Texas, 1963.
15. See John 19:25–27; 7:1–31.
16. Oswald Chambers, *My Utmost for His Highest* (New York: Dodd, Mead, 1935), 76.
17. 2 Cor. 5:17–19.
18. Herbert Marcuse, *Reason and Revolution* (Boston: Beacon, 1960), vii.
19. Luke 2:46–51, NIV; Marshall, *NIV Greek-English New Testament*, 228, 232.
20. Phil. 2:8, NIV.
21. Adapted from Francis of Assisi's "Letter to the Rulers of the People," circa 1220.
22. Rom. 8:36, KJV.
23. Matt. 10:39, KJV.
24. Matt. 22:39, RSV.
25. 1 Pet. 2:18–25; 3:13–22; 4:1–19.
26. 1 Pet. 2:21, NIV; 3:17–18, NIV; 4:1–2, NIV Interlinear.
27. Rom. 9:13, Mal. 1:2–3, NIV.
28. 1 John 4:8.
29. Gen. 26:34–35; 28:6–9, Moffatt.
30. Gen. 25:25–27, Moffatt.
31. Myron Madden, speaking at Laity Lodge, July 1987.
32. Heb. 12:2, NIV.
33. Paul Tournier, *To Resist or to Surrender* (Richmond, Va.: John Knox, 1964), 45.
34. Charlotte Elliott (1789–1871) "Just as I Am."
35. Chambers, *My Utmost*, 165.
36. 1 Pet. 3:14; 4:14, RSV.
37. 1 Pet. 4:19.
38. 1 Pet. 4:15–16, author's paraphrase.
39. 1 Pet. 2:21–25.
40. Matt. 27:46; Mark 15:34; Luke 23:46, NIV.

41. 1 Pet. 3:10, NIV.
42. 1 Pet. 3:13, NIV.
43. 1 Pet. 4:15, KJV.
44. Chambers, *My Utmost*, 342.
45. Bruce Larson, quoted in *Southwestern News*, April 1983, 7.
46. Myron Madden, at Laity Lodge.
47. See Max DePree, *Leadership is an Art* (New York: Doubleday, 1989).
48. Peers, *1,001 Logical Laws*, 105.
49. Joel Dreyfuss, "Handing Down the Old Hands' Wisdom," *Fortune* (June 13, 1983), 97, 98, 100, 104.
50. 1 Pet. 2:7, NEB.

Chapter 4

1. Andre Bernard, *Now All We Need Is a Title* (New York: W. W. Norton, 1995), 120.
2. Leo Rosten, *Leo Rosten's Treasury of Jewish Quotations* (New York: McGraw Hill, 1972), 52.
3. T. S. Eliot, 1888–1965, "The Family Reunion," 1939.
4. 1 Peter 4:17.
5. Rom. 8:29, author's paraphrase.
6. C. S. Lewis, *The Joyful Christian* (New York: Macmillan Publishing Co., Inc., 1977), 228.
7. 2 Cor. 5:18, Phillips.
8. Col. 2:10, NKJV.
9. 1 Cor. 13:1, KJV.
10. Numbers 22:22–34.
11. Matt. 18:1–3, Phillips.
12. Matt. 5:13–16; Luke 13:21.
13. Howard Butt, *The Velvet Covered Brick* (New York: Harper, 1973), 112, 136.
14. Centuries of ecclesiastical preconception have gone into the ways this 1 Peter 5:1–7 scripture has been translated and—too often—interpreted. I believe my interpretation is faithful, both to the original Greek, and to the context of the entire epistle.

The Greek word Peter uses for "elder" here is *presbuteros*, from the preposition *pro*, "before, in front of, in advance of" and the noun *bous*, "an ox, bull, or cow" (therefore, "the leader of the herd"), referring to those in leadership. *Analytical Greek Lexicon* (New York: Harper, 1852), 341, 73; *Webster's Third New International Dictionary of the English Language, Unabridged* (1967), s.v. "priest."

Another New Testament word, apparently used interchangeably with *presbuteros*, is *episkopos*, from *epi*, "upon, over, of authority" and *skopos*, "to look around, survey a watcher" (together, "inspector, supervisor, watcher over, guardian"). This parallel word, usually translated as "bishop," is the root for our English word *Episcopalian*, just as *presbuteros* is the root of *Presbyterian*. (Both these denominations took their names from their leadership.) *Analytical Greek Lexicon*, 153. *Analytical Greek Lexicon*, 369. George Ricker Berry, *A New Greek-English Lexicon to the New Testament* (Chicago: Wilcox and Follett, 1944), 83.

H. M. Gwatkin, Professor of Ecclesiastical History at Cambridge University, says, "For the last two hundred years it has been generally agreed that bishops and elders in the New Testament and for some time later are *substantially identical.* . . . The general equivalence of the two offices in the Apostolic age seems undeniable. . . . The only serious doubt is whether bishops and deacons originally denoted offices at all. *The words rather describe functions.* Thus Philippians 1:1 "to bishops and deacons" (no article) will mean, such as oversee and such as serve—that is, the higher and lower officials, whatever titles they may bear." James Hastings, ed., *Dictionary of the Bible* (New York: Scribner's, 1947), 99, emphasis added.

Diakoneo, from which we get "deacon," means originally, "to serve or wait upon." Berry, *New Greek-English Lexicon,* 25. Therefore "bishop" and "deacon" convey the same psychological realities as Peter's "elders" and "youngers" here. Titles of "church officials" convey a reality—and a potential—far beyond the institutional church.

15. Literal translation, with author's editing, sequencing and punctuation from the Nestle Greek-English text; Reverend Alfred Marshall, *NIV Interlinear,* 920.

16. John 21:15–17, Phillips. In this passage, I have substituted the "Jona" form of Peter's father's name; the Phillips translation renders it "John."

17. Marcuse, *Reason and Revolution,* 116, from Hegel's *Phenomenology of Mind,* transl. J. J. B. Baillie, 2 vols., Swan Sonnenschein (The Macmillan Co., New York), London 1910, 182.

18. John 1:29, RSV; John 10:11, Beck; punctuation changed.

19. See 1 Pet. 5:1–4; the words translated "shepherd" and "flock" both stem from *poimén.*

20. My primary resource for this and the following transliteration and interpretation of 1 Pet. 5:1–5 is Alfred Marshall, *The New International Version Interlinear Greek-English New Testament* (Grand Rapids: Zondervan, 1976), 291–92. For this understanding of *poimén,* I also referred to Robert Young, *Analytical Concordance of the Bible* (Grand Rapids: Eerdmans, 1970), 357, "Flock," 5.

21. 1 Cor. 11:1, author's paraphrase.

22. Hyginus was a Bishop of Rome (A.D. 141–44?), who, according to the *Liber Pontificalis,* reorganized his clergy. Milton concluded that, ecclesiastically, Hyginus prepared the way for the priesthood of *only* the clergy. We can see Hyginus as something of an ecclesiastic forerunner for the union of church and state which took place under Rome's Emperor Constantine (A.D. 324).

John Milton, "The Reason of Church Government Urged Against Prelaty, 1642," found in Merrit Y. Hughes, ed., *Complete Poems and Major Prose* (New York: Odyssey Press, 1957), 678. See also Edward S. LeComte, ed., *A Milton Dictionary* (New York: Philosophical Library, 1961), 146.

23. Eberhard Bethge, *Dietrich Bonhoeffer* (New York and Evanston, Harper & Row, Publishers, 1970), 767–68.

24. Robertson, *Word Pictures,* 6:132, referring to John 13:4–17.

25. This is not an original quip.

26. Hastings, *Dictionary of the Bible,* 702.

27. John 14:9, RSV.

28. H. R. Macintosh, in Hastings, *Dictionary of the Bible,* 703.

29. Ps. 101:5, KJV; 75:4, LB.

30. Peter Berger, "Moral Judgment and Political Action," *This World* (Spring 1988), 13.

31. Prov. 16:5, LB.

32. Gertrude Behanna, from an address given at the Layman's Leadership Institute, Palm Springs, California, November 21, 1968.

33. Chambers, *My Utmost for His Highest* (New York: Dodd, Mead, 1935), 112.

34. Richard Niebuhr, *Christ and Culture* (New York: Harper, 1951), 190.

35. Ibid., 81.

36. Ibid., 190–229, *passim.*

37. Thomas Carlyle literally: "'Genius' (which means transcendent capacity of taking trouble, first of all)." *History of Frederick the Great* (1958–65) bk. 4, ch. 3; *The Oxford Dictionary of Quotations* (Oxford University Press, Oxford, New York, 1992), 180:18.

38. Eugene Peterson, *Psalms* (Colorado Springs, NavPress, 1994), 5.

39. Psalm 139.

40. Dietrich Bonhoeffer, *Life Together* (San Francisco: Harper, 1954), 23.

41. Proverbs 11:14, 15:22, 24:62

42. Colossians 3:15.

43. Alexander Chase, *Perspectives* (1966), quoted in *The International Thesaurus of Quotations*, comp. Rhoda Thomas Tripp (New York: Crowell, 1970), 240.

44. 1 Pet. 4:17, NEB.

45. Exod. 19:6, RSV.

46. George MacDonald, *Thomas Wingfold, Curate,* (London: Hurst and Blackett, 1876), Vol. II, 79–87, excerpted, edited, and repunctuated from the original by author. Text courtesy Harry Ransom Humanities Research Center, University of Texas, Austin. Currently available as *The Curate's Awakening*, Michael R. Phillips, Editor (Minneapolis: Bethany, 1985).

47. Ibid., 81.

Chapter 5

1. See Rom. 3:23.

2. Prov. 20:24, LB.

3. Rom. 16:19, Phillips.

4. C. G. Jung, *The Archetypes and the Collective Unconscious*, translated by R. F. C. Hull (Princeton, New Jersey: Princeton University Press; 1968), Second edition, Volume 9, Part 1, 103–4.

5. Ibid., Volume 9, Part 1, 104.

6. Ibid., Volume 9, Part 1, 104–5.

7. Allan Bloom, *The Closing of the American Mind* (New York: Simon & Schuster, 1987), 67.

8. 1 Pet. 5:8–9, NIV.

9. Robert Young, *Analytical Concordance of the Bible* (Grand Rapids: Eerdmans, 1970), 836; Rev. 9:11 footnote, NIV; John 8:44, NIV.

10. R. W. Moss in Hastings, *Dictionary of the Bible*, 190.

11. 2 Cor. 1:17–20.

12. Eph. 6:11–13, Phillips.

13. Wolfgang Borchert, "Die Drei Dunklen Könige," in *German Stories/Deutsche Novellen: A Bantam Dual-Language Book*, ed. and tr. Harry Steinhauer (New York: Bantam, 1961), 313.

14. 1 Cor. 15:26, KJV.

15. Heb. 2:10–15, Phillips.

16. See Mark 2:17.

17. A. J. Russell, *For Sinners Only* (New York: Harper, 1922).

18. 1 John 1:8 and John 8:44, author's paraphrase.

19. John Peers, *1,001 Logical Laws*, 140.

20. See Gen. 3:12.

21. Peers, *1,001 Logical Laws*, 178.

22. James Orr, gen. ed., *The International Standard Bible Encyclopedia* (Grand Rapids: Eerdmans, 1957) 4:2361.

23. James Cooper Gray and George M. Adams, *Gray and Adams Bible Commentary* (Grand Rapids: Zondervan, 1956) 4:222.

24. Mark 7:5, NIV.

25. Gray and Adams, *Gray and Adams Commentary*, 4:222.

26. Rom. 2:1, NIV.

27. Mark 7:10, from Exod. 10:12 and 21:17.

28. From my friend, the Dallas-based management consultant, Fred Smith.

29. C. S. Lewis, *The Screwtape Letters*, rev. ed. (New York: Collier/Macmillan, 1961, 1982), xii–xiii.

30. Ibid., xi.

31. Ibid., x–xi.

32. 1 Pet. 5:8.

33. Ps. 22:1, 13, LB.

34. Ps. 14:1b-4, RSV, author's arrangement; see also Ps. 53.

35. John 6:27–35, RSV.

36. Luke 24:13–35, KJV.

37. Luke 24:29–31, Phillips.

38. Luke 24:35–36, NEB.

39. Luke 22:19, Phillips; Matt. 26:27–28, Phillips.

40. Oswald Chambers, *My Utmost for His Highest* (New York: Dodd, Mead, 1935), 40, 41, 46, 56.

41. 1 Cor. 10:31, author's paraphrase.

42. Matt. 5:6, Phillips.

43. Gen. 3:1–13, RSV.

44. See Genesis 2:9, 2:17, and 3:3. The first of these scriptures describes Eden's two strategic trees: (1) The tree of life in the *midst* of the garden, and, (2) The tree of the knowledge of good and evil. The second of these scriptures, Genesis 2:17, makes clear that God's *only* command *not* to eat, was of the fruit from the second tree, "the tree of the knowledge of good and evil." The third passage, Genesis 3:3, quotes Eve talking to the serpent, and misquoting God's command. She said they could not eat of "the fruit of the tree which is in the *midst* of the garden." Nope. Wrong tree.

   P.S. That much is clear, but I cannot resist a further speculation: Since the chapter 2 commands, (2:9 and 2:17) describe God's words, and warning, to Adam *before* the chapter 2 account of Eve's creation, the story does not tell us whether or not Adam made *clear* to Eve—before the temptation of the serpent—the difference between the two trees. Could we be dealing here with the *primordial* failure in marital communications? If so, Adam set the stage for the whole tragedy by *not talking to his wife.*

45. See Gen. 4:9, RSV.

46. John 19:41, RSV; Rev. 22:2, Moffatt.

47. Matt. 12:38–40, author's paraphrase.

48. Young, *Analytical Concordance*, 548.

49. John. 1:15–2:10, Moffatt.

50. John. 3:10–4:11.

51. Young, *Analytical Concordance*, 549.

52. 1 Pet. 2:5, author's paraphrase.

Chapter 6

1. 1 Pet. 5:10, RSV.

2. C. S. Lewis, *The Weight of Glory*, (New York: Macmillan Publishing Co., 1980), 19.

3. Gen. 2:25 (quoted); 3:7, NEB.

4. DePree, *Leadership is an Art,* 9.

5. Matt. 11:30, RSV.

6. Matt. 11:27–30, RSV.

7. George A. Buttrick, ed., *The Interpreter's Bible* (Nashville: Abingdon, 1951), 7:391.

8. John Patton, *Is Human Forgiveness Possible?* (Nashville: Abingdon, 1985), 16.

9. M. Scott Peck, *The Road Less Traveled* (New York: Simon & Schuster, 1978), 17, quoting *Collected Works of C. A. Jung,* 2d ed., vol. 2, *Psychology and Religion: West and East,* tr. R. F. C. Hull (Princeton, N.J.: Princeton Univ. Press, 1973), 75.

10. 1 Cor. 15:19, KJV; Rom. 8:29–30, KJV. "The glorification is stated as already consummated." Archibald Thomas Robertson, *Word Pictures in the New Testament* (New York: Harper, 1933), 4:378.

11. Rom. 15:5, KJV.

12. Jean Cocteau, "Cock and Harlequin," in *A Call to Order* (New York: Haskell House, 1974), 36.

13. Rev. 13:8, KJV; 1 Pet. 1:20, NEB.

14. C. S. Lewis, *The Joyful Christian* (New York: Macmillan Publishing Co., Inc. 1977), 195.

15. 1 Peter 5:11.

16. Joseph Henry Thayer, *Greek-English Lexicon of the New Testament* (New York: Harper, 1889), 157.

17. Gerard Manley Hopkins, "Pied Beauty," *The Poems of Gerard Manley Hopkins,* 4th ed., ed. W. H. Gardner and N. H. MacKenzie (London: Oxford Univ. Press, 1967), 69.

18. Fran Tarkenton, quoted in William Safire and Leonard Safire, *Leadership* (New York: Simon & Schuster, 1990), 187, emphasis added.

19. Leo Furtad, "Can Ethics Be Taught?" *Alcalde* (November/December 1987), 21.

20. Thomas a Kempis, *The Imitation of Christ* (Westwood, N.J.: The Christian Library, 1984), 273.

21. 1 Pet. 5:12, RSV.

22. See Acts 15:22–18:5.

23. Acts 16:37–38, RSV.

24. 1 Pet. 5:13, NKJV.

25. Col. 4:10; 2 Tim. 4:11.

26. 1 Pet. 5:12, Phillips.

27. John 17:11,21–22, RSV.

28. John 12:50, Phillips. See also John 8:26–28; 14:10.

29. Matt. 16:21. See also Matt. 17:23, 20:19; Mark 9:31, Mark 10:34; Luke 9:22, 18:33, 24:7, 24:46.

30. 1 Pet. 5:13, NIV.

31. James Hastings, ed., *Dictionary of the Bible* (New York: Scribner's, 1947), 78.

32. Genesis 11:1–9.

33. Rev. 14:8, 18:2, NEB.

34. John 17:13–18, KJV.

35. George A. Buttrick, ed., *The Interpreter's Bible* (Nashville: Abingdon-Cokesbury, 1951), 2:560.

36. Gen. 10:8, Moffatt. See also Leon R. Kass, "What's Wrong with Babel?" *The American Scholar,* Winter 1989, 45.

37. Gen. 10:9, NKJV.

38. Rom. 1:18–32, NEB.

39. Isa. 40:31, Ps. 25:5, and other scriptures.

40. 1 Cor. 15:10, author's paraphrase.
41. Hastings, *Dictionary of the Bible*, 578.

Chapter 7

1. Harry Emerson Fosdick, *Great Voices of The Reformation* (New York: Random House, 1952), 7.

2. Harry Emerson Fosdick, *Great Voices of the Reformation* (New York: Random House, 1952), 7–8. For research assistance on this paragraph, I am also indebted to Thomas G. Oey. The unpublished adaptation of his 1991 Vanderbilt University Ph.D. dissertation is entitled *Wyclif's Life and Thought.*J

3. Lincoln's law partner, Thomas Herndon, was enthusiastic about the Transcendentalist-Unitarian Boston minister, Theodore Parker, who used the phrase often. Garry Wills, *Lincoln at Gettysburg* (New York: Simon and Schuster, Touchstone, 1992), 105 ff. See also Elton Trueblood, *Abraham Lincoln, Theologian of American Anguish* (New York: Harper and Row, 1973).

4. Exod. 19:6; Rev. 5:10.

5. History sobers us many ways. Consider the following, in light of the current climate of American political discourse and our need for pastoral flex: Thucydides, the famous Greek historian, said that Greek democracy's final collapse, ten years after "faction had already broken out," came through its heightened internal wrangling. Of Athenian democracy's ultimate defeat at the hands of Sparta's oligarchy, he wrote, "Nor did they give in until they destroyed themselves by falling upon one another because of private quarrels" (quoted in Donald Kagan, *The Fall of the Athenian Empire* [Ithaca, New York: Cornell University Press, 1987], vii–viii). Also note, in addition to this "internal" reason for the collapse of Athens' democracy, one of the "external" reasons: "The Athenians exercised more and more control over their allies without giving them any participation in the great decisions" (Kagan, ed., *Botsford and Robinson's Hellenic History*, 5th ed. [New York: Macmillan, 1969], 200). Both internally and externally, therefore, the collapse of Greek democracy can be traced to its lack of Trinitarian relational principles. Greek democracy's lack of pastoral flex dooms it ultimately to failure.

6. Edmund Burke, *Reflections on the Revolution in France* (New York: Arlington House), 61.

7. Plato, *The Dialogues of Plato, The Seventh Letter*, vol. 7, Great Books of the Western World, ed. Robert Maynard Hutchins (Chicago: Encyclopaedia Britannica, 1952), 412.

8. Plato, *Dialogues*, 401.

9. Does the thesis I present here characterize, in fact, the New Testament accounts of church government? I believe it does.

Some New Testament texts on church government emphasize "spiritual authority." See Acts 15:1–21. See also Acts 8:14–17, 14:21–25, 20:28; 1 Cor. 3:1–7; Gal. 2:1–10, 1 Tim. 3, Titus 1:5–9; Heb. 13:17. These "spiritual authority" texts speak of deference to, and servanthood within, *a self-confident pastoral leadership.*

Other New Testament texts on church government emphasize "participation and consensus." See Acts 15:22–41. See also Acts 1:23–26, 2:42–47, 4:32–37; Rom. 12:1–8; 1 Cor. 1:10–17, 12:12–30; 2 Cor. 2:5–8; Eph. 4:11–16; Phil. 2:3–4; Heb. 8:1. These "participation and consensus" texts speak of servanthood's protection of the minority and *the equal priesthood of all believers.*

These contrasting (but complementary) emphases illustrate the statement of Yale church historian Kenneth Scott Latourette, on the organization of the early church: "For the first two or three generations, the Christian community exhibited great variety"(*A History of Christianity* [New York: Harper, 1975], 1:115).

This "great variety," between the principles described in these two sets of texts, denotes in itself *great flexibility*. Such flexibility accomplishes two purposes for us today: (1) It reconciles the polarized conflict between partial truths which—seen as opposites—have so tragically split the church across the centuries. (2) It reflects a democratic ideal that is not a rigid, self-destructive "pure democracy" but rather one that is spiritually alive and relationally realistic. This flexible bond implements the Triune mystery—and democratic ideal—of servant-leadership and authority from the bottom up.

10. James S. Stewart, *The Gates of New Life* (New York: Scribner's, 1964), 42–43, 46, 49.

11. Gal. 5:22–23, RSV.

12. 2 Cor. 4:17.

13. John Peers, *1,001 Logical Laws*, 107.

14. Adolf Eichmann, "Eichmann's Own Story: Part II," *Life*, December 5, 1960, 161.

15. Gen. 22:18, RSV, emphasis added.

16. Frederick Dale Bruner, *The Christbook* (Waco, Tex.: Word, 1987), 3, 6, 12–13.

17. Mark 1:22, RSV.

18. Mark 7:26, RSV.

19. John 4:4–42, 12:20–23, RSV.

20. Luke 10:25–37.

21. Luke 4:14–21, NIV, with interpretation from Alexander Maclaren, *Expositions of Holy Scripture* (Grand Rapids: Eerdmans, 1952), 6:90–92.

22. Luke 4:22, NIV.

23. Luke 4:25–27, RSV.

24. Luke 4:29, RSV.

25. Matt. 16:26, KJV.

26. Alfred Marshall, *The New International Version Interlinear Greek-English New Testament* (Grand Rapids: Zondervan, 1976), 908.

27. "Down from," with the genitive (*Analytical Greek Lexicon*, 213). Both *theou*, God (*Analytical Greek Lexicon*, 3:193), and *patros*, "Father" (7:312), are in the genitive.

28. Gal. 2:1–21; 2 Pet. 3:15–16.

29. Gal. 1:15.

30. 1 Pet. 1:3, 23, Phillips.

31. Matt. 20:20; Mark 15:40; John 19:25.

32. John 5:18, Phillips.

33. John 14–16, particularly 14:15–27, 15:26, 16:7–15.

34. John 15:16, KJV (adapted).

35. James Orr, gen. ed., *The International Standard Bible Encyclopedia* (Grand Rapids: Eerdmans, 1957) 3:1707; J. D. Douglas and Merrill C. Tenney, eds., *New International Dictionary of the Bible* (Grand Rapids: Regency-Zondervan, 1987), 532 ff; James Hastings, ed., *Dictionary of the Bible* (New York: Scribner's, 1947), 475 ff.

36. *Encyclopaedia Britannica Macropaedia*, 1:1167; *Encyclopaedia Britannica Micropaedia*, 6:302; Hastings, *Dictionary of the Bible*, 549–51; J. O. Thorne and T. C. Collocott, eds., *Chambers Biographical Dictionary* (Cambridge: Cambridge University Press, 1989), 83, 660, 1064–65, 1452.

37. John 21:20–23.

38. See Acts 3–4; 8:14–25.

39. Earl Palmer, former pastor of First Presbyterian Church, Berkeley, California, now pastor, University Presbyterian, Seattle, Washington, speaking at Laity Lodge.

40. W. F. Albright, "The Names *Shaddai* and *Abram*," *Journal of Biblical Literature*, Volume 54, 194.

41. Douglas and Tenney, eds., *New International Dictionary of the Bible*, 475. See also Albert Hourani, *A History of the Arab Peoples* (Cambridge, Mass.: Belknap Press, div. of Harvard University Press, 1991), 13–19, 150.

42. *Encyclopaedia Britannica Macropaedia*, 9:928, 12:606–7.

43. Ibid., 12:606 and Hourani, *History of Arab Peoples*, 16.

44. This précis is a summation of material found primarily in two sources: Jane S. Gerber, "Anti-Semitism and the Muslim World," in *History and Hate Dimensions of Anti-Semitism*, ed. David Berger (Philadelphia: The Jewish Publication Society, 1986), 76, and Bernard Lewis, *Semites and Anti-Semites: An Inquiry into Conflict and Prejudice* (New York: Norton, 1986), 127–28.

45. Gen. 17:1. See also chapter 1, note 30.

46. "A Collect for Peace," *The Book of Common Prayer* (New York: The Episcopal Church, Church Hymnal Corporation, and Seabury Press, 1977), 57.

47. Peter Howard, *Ideas Have Legs* (New York: Coward-McCann, 1946).

48. Jean Paul Sartre, *Being and Nothingness*, tr. Hazel E. Barnes (New York: Philosophical Library, 1956), 439.

49. Matt. 10:34–39, RSV.

50. John 8:36 NIV.

51. Quotation from Dr. Richard Spencer, Austin, Texas.

52. John 10:9, RSV.

Chapter 8

1. Jim Morrison, "People Are Strange" [from *The Best of the Doors*, Electra Entertainment, 75 Rockefeller Plaza, New York, NY 10019].

2. Thomas Wolfe, *Look Homeward, Angel: The Story of a Buried Life* (New York: Scribners, 1929), 2.

3. From a television interview conducted during the crusade.

4. Fictitious narrative adaptation; last Twain quotation from our Trinity Baptist Church, San Antonio, Texas, pastor, Buckner Fanning.

5. Eph. 2:19–20.

6. Or however your Bible translates it: "sojourners, pilgrims, transients, visitors, refugees, exiles, aliens, foreigners." Archibald Thomas Robertson, *Word Pictures in the New Testament* (New York: Harper, 1933), 6:79.

7. Joseph Henry Thayer, *Greek-English Lexicon of the New Testament* (New York: Harper, 1889), 478.

8. Thayer, *Greek-English Lexicon*, 231–36; George Ricker Berry, *A New Greek-English Lexicon to the New Testament* (Chicago: Wilcox and Follett, 1944), 38.

9. John 17:6–19, RSV.

10. Eph. 2:19, author's paraphrase.

11. Thayer, *Greek-English Lexicon*, 488.

12. *Analytical Greek Lexicon* (New York: Harper, 1852), 3.

13. Matt. 27:51, RSV.

14. See 1 Cor. 3:16–17, 6:19.

15. Eph. 5:32, KJV.

16. Nat Tracy, chairman of the department of philosophy, Howard Payne College, Brownwood, Texas, speaking at Laity Lodge, during the late 1960s or early 1970s.

17. Gen. 2:4–15, RSV.

18. Harold Bloom, quoted in Peter Steinfels, "Beliefs," *New York Times*, March 3, 1991, 10. See also David Stern's review, "The Supreme Fictionalist," *New Republic*, February 4, 1991, 34–40.

19. Matt. 9:15; Mar 2:19–20; Luke 5:34–35; John 3:29; II Cor. 11:2; Eph. 5:25–28; Rev. 18:23, 21:2, 9 22:17, KJV.

20. Hos. 1:2–3:5, KJV.

21. Rev. 19:7–9, KJV.

22. G. K. Chesterton, quoted in W. H. Auden and Louis Kronenberger, eds., *The Viking Book of Aphorisms* (New York: Viking, 1962), 169.

23. Robert L. Wilken, *First Things*, June/July 1991, 13.

24. Unable to locate this source.

25. Leonard Hodgson, *The Doctrine of the Trinity* (London: Nisbet and Co., 1943), 10.

26. Ibid., 175. Emphasis added.

27. Ibid., 105.

28. Ibid., 93–96 ff.

29. Ibid., 93. Emphasis added.

30. Ibid., 129. Emphasis added.

31. Ibid., 138.

32. Matt. 7:16–19, author's paraphrase.

33. John 8:36.

34. John 1:1–2, 14, RSV.

35. Luke 1:38, RSV.

36. Luke 1:49–50, RSV.

37. Matt. 5:3, RSV.

38. Luke 18:9–14, RSV.

39. *Webster's New World Dictionary of American English*, 3d college edition, s.v. "elite."

40. Fernand Braudel, *A History of Civilizations*, translated by Richard Mayne (New York: Penguin, 1995), 333–34.

41. Ralph Ketcham, *James Madison: A Biography* (New York: Macmillan, 1971), 25–50, 51–67.

42. Edwin S. Gaustad, *A Religious History of America* (New York: Harper, 1966, rev. 1974), 120–31.

43. Edwin S. Gaustad, *Faith of Our Fathers: Religion and the New Nation* (San Francisco: Harper, 1987), 7.

44. Alfred Lord Tennyson, "The Grandmother," stanza 8.

45. Stanislaw J. Lec, *Unkempt Thoughts*, tr. Jack Galazka (New York: St. Martin's Press, 1962), 105.

46. Diogenes Allen, "Liberation from Illusion," *Christian Century*, 107 (August 22–29, 1990): 772, reviewing Gabrielle Fiori, *Simone Weil: An Intellectual Biography*, tr. Joseph R. Berrigan (Athens, Ga.: Univ. of Georgia Press, 1981).

47. Prov. 1:7–15, LB.

48. George Birkbeck Hill, ed., *Boswell's Life of Johnson*, 6 vols. (Oxford: Clarendon, 1934, rev. 1971), 1:444.

49. Ralph Waldo Emerson, quoted in Auden and Kronenberger, *Viking Book of Aphorisms*, 332.

50. From *Les Miserables*, tr. Charles W. Wilbour, quoted in Rhoda Thomas Tripp, comp., *The International Thesaurus of Quotations* (New York: Crowell, 1970), 816. Emphasis added.
51. Matt. 22:21; Mark 12:17; Luke 20:25.
52. The opening phrase (only) in this sentence comes from a book title: Harry Golden, *Only in America* (Cleveland, Ohio: World Publishing, 1958).
53. Charles Williams, *The Descent of the Dove* (New York: Meridian, 1956), 86. Emphasis added.

Chapter 9

1. John 8:58.
2. Acts 8:4, RSV.
3. Acts 8:1, RSV.
4. *The Oxford English Dictionary*, compact edition (1971), s.v "scatter."
5. Karl August Menninger, *Man against Himself* (New York: Harcourt, Brace, and World, 1966).
6. 1 Pet. 2:18, RSV.
7. Extracted and paraphrased from *Webster's Third New International Dictionary of the English Language, Unabridged* (1967); *Webster's New World Dictionary of American English*, 3d college edition, and *The Oxford English Dictionary*, s.v. "froward."
8. James Hastings, ed., *Dictionary of the Bible* (New York: Scribner's, 1947), 942; J. D. Douglas and Merrill C. Tenney, eds., *New International Dictionary of the Bible* (Grand Rapids: Regency-Zondervan, 1987), 1022.
9. Reprinted with adaptions, Alcoholics Anonymous World Services, Inc.
10. Adapted from *Alcoholics Anonymous Comes of Age* (New York: Alcoholics Anonymous World Services, 1957), 196.
11. Col. 1:24.
12. *Encyclopaedia Britannica Macropaedia*, 15th edition, s.v. "dance, art of."
13. W. B. Yeats, "The Second Coming," in *Later Poems* (New York: Macmillan, 1924), 346.
14. Col. 1:17, NIV.
15. Words and music by Ray Stevens, *Everything Is Beautiful* (1970 Ahab Music Company, Inc.).
16. 1 Pet. 1:3–8, RSV, emphasis added.
17. John Peers, *1,001 Logical Laws*, 108.
18. John 9:2–3, RSV. (Punctuation altered).
19. Matt. 24:44, author's adaption from the KJV.
20. Rev. 22:20, author's paraphrase.
21. Rev. 3:11, 22:7, 22:12, KJV.
22. Heb. 12:2, RSV.
23. This phrase from Keith Miller.
24. John 21:3, LB.
25. Heb. 12:2, KJV.
26. This phrase from my friend, the actress and playwright, Jeannette Clift George, of Houston's AD Players, in personal conversation, Laity Lodge.
27. Heb. 5:8, KJV.
28. G. K. Chesterton, *The Everlasting Man* (New York: Dodd, Mead, 1952), 338, emphasis added.

29. Peers, *1,001 Logical Laws*, 64.

30. From our friend, Dee Redding, Columbus, Ohio.

31. Isa. 42:4, KJV.

32. John Bunyan, "Christian Behavior," in *Practical Works of John Bunyan* (Aberdeen: George King, 1842), 193, quoted in George A. Buttrick, ed., *The Interpreters Bible* (Nashville: Abingdon-Cokesbury, 1951), 5:466.

33. Jonathan Edwards, *A Treatise Concerning Religious Affections*, quoted in Buttrick, *Interpreters Bible*, 5:466.

34. Paul Tillich, *The Courage to Be* (New Haven, Conn.: Yale Univ. Press, 1952).

35. Rom. 10:17, NKJV.

36. Unable to locate the original source; this quotation came verbally from my friend Tom Phillips, former Raytheon CEO.

37. Dorothy L. Sayers, *Gaudy Night* (New York: Harper, 1936), 370. Emphasis added.

A Closing Word

1. Will Allen Dromgoole, "The Bridge Builder," in *1000 Quotable Poems*, comp. Thomas Curtis Clark and Esther A. Gillespie (New York, Harper, 1937), 2: 157–58.